Principles of
Transport

Principles
of
Transport

•

R. W. Faulks FCIT, AM INST TA

LONDON

IAN ALLAN LTD

First published 1973

This book is for use in your own office on permanent loan, but the Group Information Unit may request you to make the book available to meet routine library requests.

If you are leaving head office, please return the book to the Group Information Unit to be put into the library stock or to be registered if you wish the book to be handed over to someone else.

CS 1678

Contents

Foreword

As President of the Chartered Institute of Transport, I am pleased to have the opportunity to write this Foreword. In the study of any subject, the young student needs to be able, at the beginning of his or her studies, to go to a basic book which sets out to describe, classify and provide a framework upon which can be built a firm base for future studies. In the complex and vital subject of Transport this is essential, and Mr. Faulks has in the compass of fourteen chapters provided all future young transport students with an indispensible tool.

The book will be compulsory reading for all those young persons embarking on a professional course of transport studies for the first time. In broad terms the content of the book adequately covers the subject "Transport" which is to be found in the Chartered Institute of Transport's recently revised professional Intermediate examination, and in the subject with the same title in the Ordinary National Diploma or Certificate in Business Studies and Public Administration, as well as the Scottish National Certificate in Business Studies. It will be relevant equally to the students of transport in Europe, as well as many other parts of the world.

The book provides the basic knowledge about transport from which students may be able to proceed by a combination of studies and practical experience towards professional membership of the Institute. Such training should lead to a sound understanding of transport management and its problems; the professional qualification of MCIT; and the stimulus to look to the future with keenness, and be able to accept the responsibility to change, in a rapidly changing world.

David McKenna CBE, MA, FCIT   *London/January 1973*

Introduction

Principles of Transport is the successor book to *Elements of Transport* which was first published in 1964. Although "Elements of Transport" ran successfully through two editions, not only much of the detail but also the academic approach to the subject has now changed and the original work is no longer entirely suited to present day concepts. It is partly for this reason that the Chartered Institute of Transport has seen fit to revise its syllabuses and one of the new papers, which is designated "Transport", identifies its subject as a separate discipline with unique principles and characteristics. In preparing this work, the needs of students studying for this new subject have been kept very much in mind and in so doing only a little more than fifty per cent of the original "Elements of Transport" text has been retained. Even this is presented in an updated and modified form. The remainder of the work is completely new.

Whilst this book is designed primarily for people preparing for the Intermediate examination of the Chartered Institute of Transport, certain of the chapters also have relevance to the subject "Control and Organisation of Transport" which is a part of the final examination of the same Institute. Furthermore, it covers much of the ground that has to be explored when preparing for the examinations of the Institute of Traffic Administration.

In order to give a better understanding of the subject, the practice was adopted in "Elements of Transport" of relating academic principles to practical application. Theory was thereby put into proper perspective. As treatment of the subject in this way has been well received by past readers, this method of approach has been retained and once again considerable help has been afforded by the managements of a number of undertakings connected both directly and indirectly with transport. Information has been supplied and in some cases drafts have been read and valuable advice given although the views expressed are nevertheless those of the author and are not necessarily also those of the undertakings to which reference is made. The author gratefully acknowledges such help so willingly given by the following organisations:

Associated Society of Locomotive Engineers and Firemen
Association of Public Passenger Transport Operators
Baltic Mercantile and Shipping Exchange
Birmingham and Midland Motor Omnibus Company
Blackpool Corporation Transport
Boeing Company
British Aircraft Corporation
British Airports Authority
British European Airways
British Hovercraft Corporation
British Overseas Airways Corporation
British Petroleum Company

British Railways
British Road Federation
British Shipping Federation
British Transport Docks Board
Central Office of Information
Civil Air Transport Employers' Secretariat
Civil Aviation Authority
Department of Employment
Department of the Environment
Department of Trade and Industry
Eastern National Omnibus Company
Freight Transport Association
French National Railways (SNCF)
General Motors Corporation
Goodyear Tyre and Rubber Company
Hawker Siddeley Group
Inter-Governmental Maritime Consultative Organisation
International Air Transport Association
International Civil Aviation Organization
International Road Federation
International Road Transport Union
International Union of Public Transport
International Union of Railways
Israel Transport Co-operative Society (EGGED)
Lloyd's Register of Shipping
Ministry of Posts and Telecommunications
Ministry of Transportation and Communications (Ontario)
National Aeronautics and Space Administration (USA)
National Dock Labour Board
National Freight Corporation
National Ports Council
Northern Ireland Railways Company
Passenger Vehicle Operators Association
P & O Group
Public Road Transport Association
Road Haulage Association
San Francisco Municipal Railway
Schiphol Airport Authority, Amsterdam
Wuppertal Municipal Transport

Thanks are also due to Mr. D. McKenna, CBE, MA, FCIT, Member of the British Railways Board and 1972/73 President of the Chartered Institute of Transport and to Mr. A.F. Beckenham, FCIT, Director of Education and Training of the same Institute, for their support and encouragement.

Additionally, a number of undertakings has supplied photographs and other material. Specific acknowledgements where appropriate accompany the illustrations and diagrams.

When the second edition of "Elements of Transport" was produced a new

Transport Act had recently come into being and a Post Office Bill was about to become law. These two enactments have now firmly become a part of British legislation and unlike the period that preceeded the publication of the second edition, there has been a surprising lull in political activity, at least in the transport world, which is even more surprising in view of the fact that there has been a change in government in the intervening period. Apart from a possible change in the licensing machinery for bus and coach services (and the chances can be rated no higher than that) there seems to be little on the horizon that is likely to be of any serious consequence to the transport student. Whilst on the subject of statutory control, however, it must again be stressed that all legal references in this book are based on British law. As far as this particular aspect is concerned, the same conditions do not necessarily apply in territories overseas. Although a similar position might pertain elsewhere, this feature must be remembered by students resident outside the United Kingdom.

As was the case with "Elements of Transport", it is hoped that in presenting this book, its pages will offer guidance and interest. Every effort has been made to check points of detail and it is sincerely hoped that inaccuracy or misrepresentation has not arisen. If some advantage is felt in the possession of general information in a summarised form which can be accepted as a pointer to further study, then its purpose will have been achieved.

RWF

1973

1 · The Role of Transport

Introduction
A proper understanding of the function of transport is not possible without some elementary grasp of certain basic economic principles, economics being that branch of social science which studies the activities of man and how he provides for his needs. It is the economic laws which relate to production and the satisfaction of human wants that have particular relevance to the study of transport.

Production
Modern society is dependent upon a multitude of skills. Everyday life demands warmth, clothing, food and shelter and seeks many kinds of amusements. These are our wants and anything that is able to satisfy a want possesses what is known as utility. The creation of these utilities is production, but production in the economic sense has a much wider application than the generally accepted definition as the bringing into being of something tangible. Production in the economic sense embraces any activity which adds utility and hence yields value. It is not confined to a change of form when, for example, seasoned timber is made up into tables and chairs although this change of form is certainly a part of the overall process of production. Other stages in the conversion of the raw material, in this instance the trunk of a living tree into a state suitable for the carpenter to transform into a table or a chair, also add value. The timber is worth more, that is, it has a greater value in exchange, when it is in the form of lumber in the hands of the merchant than when it is growing in the forest. It has still greater value after a period of time when it has seasoned and become ready for manufacturing purposes. The process continues through the hands of the carpenter and wholesaler and hence to the shop ready for ultimate purchase. Production in the form of manufacture is but a part of the many stages of overall production within the economic framework which converts the tree in the plantation to the table in the kitchen and this table is, of course, only one very small part of our many wants. The material needs of mankind are met by a blend of raw materials, specialised labour and personal services drawn from all parts of the world.

Value in Exchange
The worth or value in exchange of any commodity or manufactured article cannot be set without reference to a number of different factors. To quote again the example from the previous paragraph, the worth of timber as such could not be assessed unless its state, its form and its place were known. The state of a commodity may be changed by time, by chemical reaction or by some artificial means, but regardless of the method, the material in its new state, i.e., green, wood to seasoned wood, fermentation of sugar into alcohol, iron ore into steel, all add value to that particular commodity. Similarly, form can be changed.

15

A length of wood seldom has a use in its own right (although it has a greater use than when in the form of a trunk of a tree) but there is a demand for tables. Although, therefore, the wood in its seasoned but otherwise untouched form will have a value, the finished table made from that same piece of wood will have a greater value. Even then, the value of the table cannot be assessed without reference to location. What might have value in one place could be useless in another. A householder who purchased a table would require delivery to his door. He would assess its value under that condition and the table has a greater value in his kitchen than it has in the place of manufacture. It is with these thoughts in mind that it is possible to examine the primary function of transport.

The Primary Function

The function of transport is to move passengers or goods from where they are to where they would prefer to be or to where their relative value is greater. In the case of people this may be for a variety of reasons of an economic or personal nature and in the case of goods it may be dictated by the needs of further manufacture or processing or of ultimate consumption or use. In the development of industry, transport plays a vital part by linking the sources of raw material, the manufacturing or processing centres and the markets and it is also essential to enable people to travel between their homes and places of employment.

It has been shown that production is, in effect the creation of utilities. There are utilities of state, of form and of place and in a study of transport it is important to note in particular that production is not complete when an article appears in its finished form in the factory because a utility of place has still to be supplied. It is the primary function of transport to supply the utility of place and transport, therefore, as well as manufacture, has an important place in the overall production process.

The Demand

The demand for transport arises from the uneven distribution of raw materials, skill and labour. It has been seen that man has many wants and the sources of their satisfaction are world-wide. To meet his material needs, manufacturers require the movement of raw materials from their place of origin to the processing plant or factory and the finished product from where it is produced to where it is consumed. Consumer demand must be backed by requisite purchasing power and the recipient must, therefore, in turn be able to disseminate his own product. The circle is then complete and in the process transport is in demand by trade and industry. But there is also a personal demand. Goods are moved from place to place and their value becomes correspondingly greater but transport is by no means confined to the carriage of raw material or merchandise. Passenger requirements are also catered for. A man may travel from his home to a place where the value of his services and consequently his salary are greater than would be the case had he remained in his own immediate neighbourhood, which more than compensates for the time and cost of travel. The demand could also be purely for pleasure such as for visiting or recreational purposes, in which case the measure of pleasure derived as a result of travel is greater than what would have been enjoyed had those concerned stayed at home.

It may be noted at this juncture that transport is a service activity which usually stems from a derived demand. There is seldom a demand even for passenger transport in its own right; it is at best an adjunct necessary to fulfil some other desire. The best example today of travel for travel's own sake is perhaps a sea cruise where the very nature of the voyage is a relaxation in itself. Those participating are content to return to the port at which they embarked having done no more than experience a short spell of life at sea interspersed by a few brief hours ashore at selected places. Transport does not generally meet such a direct demand. It is a service which more often bridges the gap between dormitory areas and places of work or recreation and between producers and consumers. People must be transported to and from their homes and offices or factories and raw material must be taken from its source to the processing plant or factory. From the factory, finished products must pass through the wholesaler to the retailer and thence to the customer. For our amusement and pleasure we must travel to the cinema or the seaside or to visit friends. All of these activities necessitate the use of transport in one form or another. Without transport these needs could not be satisfied.

Everything that has been said so far relates to the economic demand for transport. The services provided by transport are vital to the sustenance of the economic life of a nation. Along with all other types of utility, the utility of place must be satisfied and it is this need that is fulfilled by transport. But unlike physics or mathematics, economics is not an exact science and its laws are not inviolable. If economic laws were allowed always to work themselves out without interference, much suffering could result and legislation is often introduced to mitigate what would otherwise be dire effects. A ready example was the introduction of rationing and price control in time of war when otherwise scarcity would have been balanced by exceptionally high prices beyond the reach of the majority. An example more appropriate to the present study is the provision of transport in rural areas where the demand is insufficient to justify cost of operation but where hardship to the few would arise if it were not provided. It follows, therefore, that as well as an economic need, there are also social needs. Rural bus transport is really providing nothing more than a social service as are lightly used railway branch lines and air services to such places as the highlands and islands in the north of Scotland. The retention of such services could be a political expedient. In some countries, shipping is subsidised for political or military reasons; tonnage in excess of what can be commercially justified or ships with greater power than is required for normal purposes being retained ready for quick conversion in case of a possible war emergency. Certain national airlines are maintained only for prestige reasons. The Roman Empire could not have developed as it did without its system of communication and in this case the roads met political and military needs.

Development of Civilisation

To appreciate the part played by transport in the development of civilisation, it is necessary to imagine life before the advent of the way and the wheel or, in other words, before the gap between the producer and the consumer had been bridged. Man was entirely dependent upon his own exertions and those of his immediate neighbours. He produced his own weapons with which to hunt to provide food and clothing in the form of meat and skins. He tilled his land, again for food, and built his dwelling places with material immediately available and with the simple tools which he manufactured himself. Man lived at that time either on his own resources or on the combined resources of a small self-contained community. The development of the road and the wheeled vehicle, although not mechanically propelled, permitted a limited mixing of the peoples and in consequence, an exchange of ideas and commodities. Communities of people became larger and individuals began to specialise in certain crafts. So evolved the division of labour. Specialists worked in a single trade in which they became skilled and thus stimulated a demand for their products. Not only were men by this time no longer dependent entirely upon themselves, but collectively upon each other; specialisation improved workmanship in the form of better clothes, better habitations, better food and hence an improved standard of living. Such development is synonymous with the development of communications and it is necessary only to reflect on our present day economic system to realise the part played by transport in the fulfilment of our now accepted standard of living. Without transport we would inevitably revert to the living of primitive man.

It is clear, therefore, that transport and development are very closely linked, but it is for consideration whether society at large still continues to rely on transport to open up new territory. Certainly, the introduction of scheduled air services has played no small part in the development of hitherto remote areas in, for example, Central and East Africa. When the London underground railway extended its tentacles into the green fields surrounding the metropolis the rural countryside quickly became a dormitory area which is now an integral part of Greater London. There are countless other similar examples and perhaps the greatest effect of all will come from inter-planetary flight. But to come back to present day reality, now that the feasibility of transport has become accepted it is sometimes overtaken by events and required to meet new demands. Industry and population may now spread into new areas in anticipation that its transport needs will be met. To quote again from the London area, Golders Green may well owe its birth to a speculative railway management; the railway came first and the people followed; but Harlow New Town, for example, did not come into being through the encouragement of any existing transport facilities. In this case a large urban area arose on what was formerly arable land. On this occasion the transport needs of the immigrant population have followed to meet the new demand. The developers did not consider the quality of any existing facilities but relied on the fact that adequate communication was a physical possibility and that the new demand would therefore be met.

The Objective

It was said earlier in this chapter that the function of transport is to move people from where they are to where they would prefer to be or to move goods to where their relative value is greater. It follows, therefore, that the objective or the end product of any transport system is the arrival. Clearly this must be a safe achieved owing to competition, first from coastal shipping and canals and more recently from road and air. Nevertheless, railway monopoly of the carriage of certain types of goods and passengers and even of all types of traffic in areas remote from other forms of transport, was almost complete between the end of the canal era and the dawn of the internal combustion engine.

Although in the past there have been fears of monopoly, history does not show that free competition in the provision of transport facilities is necessarily the ideal solution. The thinking that competition encourages enterprise and is a spur to improvement of quality and lowering of charges cannot be applied to transport to the extent that it might be applied to, say, the production of tinned foods. Circumstances are not the same. A competitive market in any industry is likely to result in a temporary excess of provision. Goods of one brand might sell faster than that of another and in the absence of an improvement in the quality or a lowering of the price, production of the inferior brand would in the longer term be adjusted to match a smaller demand. Transport, being a service industry, is highly perishable. It is, in fact, so perishable that unless the service is used the moment that it is produced, it is immediately destroyed. If a bus departs with empty seats, then the availability and hence the opportunity to "sell" those seats has gone for ever. Subsequent passengers can do no other than travel on a subsequent journey. Unlike the tinned foods, the empty seats cannot be stored until they are sold. It follows, therefore, that an excess of provision of transport services will result in waste far beyond what might be the case in other industries. To-day some passenger services are experiencing a severe economic depression caused largely by abstraction of traffic by the private car coupled with ever increasing costs. If services are to be maintained at all it is important that resources are not wasted and it is doubtful whether the availability of choice between operators or between modes can continue to be justified. It is reasonable for customers to expect to have the opportunity to select a higher standard of service on supplementary payment but this does not necessarily call for the selection of a particular mode. For merchandise, the standard of service is determined by speed of delivery if it is accepted that all modes produce a "satisfactory arrival". It has long been assumed by the majority that the Post Office will arrange for the carriage of its mail by the most expeditious means. We pay extra for next day delivery but we do not enquire as to the mode of conveyance. The current trend of transport legislation is towards limiting the availability of choice. To encroach again on Chapter 8, the National Freight Corporation is required to ensure that its traffic is carried by rail whenever it is efficient and economic to do so (although one is not, of course, obliged to utilise the services of the National Freight Corporation; there are alternatives). Also, Passenger Transport Executives are required to secure or promote the provision of properly integrated systems of public passenger transport within their areas which could well result in the exploitation of rail transport to the full wherever it is available and the reduction or withdrawal of parallel bus facilities.

It will be seen from Chapter 6 that different forms of transport have different characteristics. If a safe and satisfactory arrival is to be achieved at minimum cost, wasteful duplication must be eliminated and the features of each of the modes exploited to the full. In these circumstances, road, rail, inland waterway, sea and air cannot be accepted in isolation. Each is part of a complete system. In these conditions, the most appropriate service would be made available for the need that it is best fitted to fulfil but the availability of choice, which is not, in any case, sought for the conveyance of mail, would be lost. This subject is further considered in Chapters 6 and 7.

2 · The Way

Introduction

The way, the terminal, the carrying unit and the motive power constitute the physical components of a transport system. The characteristics of these different components vary between modes and each must be considered. This chapter is devoted to the way, which may be either natural, natural artificially improved or artificial. Natural ways, being the sea and air, are available for use without any cost in the form of either provision or maintenance. Both natural ways artificially improved such as a river made suitable for navigation or a purely artificial way such as a railway or road, are provided only at cost and the cost to the user is influenced by whether he shares the use of a common way or whether he is sole user of a specialised way.

These differences are fundamental. They have a very material effect on the type of vehicles and other conveyances and on the terminals and hence on methods and costs of operation. Another distinction is that on roads and inland waterways, vehicles and vessels are driven on sight. On railways and in the air, the movements of trains and aircraft are subject to independent control through a system of signals or navigational aids. Similar circumstances may apply to shipping, particularly in congested waters. The nature of the way influences the extent to which such services must be provided and for the purpose of this chapter, the special aids must be considered a part of the way and will be dealt with as such.

Artificial Ways

THE ROAD

Although use of the term "road transport" leaves little doubt in the mind of the reader regarding the actual mode of transport to which reference is being made, the definition of a road is either a track or way specially prepared for the movement of people, vehicles, etc., or a stretch of water near to the shore where ships may ride at anchor. This gives it a rather more general application. The word appears quite correctly in railway nomenclature, hence the expression "railroad" which is sometimes used and which has popular acceptance in North America. Perhaps the best description of a road in relation to road transport as we know it is a specially surfaced highway for the passage of wheeled vehicles, each being subject to individual and independent control and guidance. In what follows, therefore, the road and road transport is interpreted accordingly.

The road thus identified is something that has often but not necessarily grown out of a one-time footpath or bridle way (a way along which horses may be led) into a properly surfaced but at first narrow lane and thence through various stages of development into what in some instances has become a major traffic artery. The track or bridle path often took a devious route in order to skirt private property with the result that development in this way has produced in Great Britain a road system that is in many cases tortuous with sharp bends and unnecessarily severe gradients. With the significant increase in vehicular traffic over recent years, many of these roads are no longer appropriate for current needs. There is, therefore, a continual process of widening and re-alignment, even on secondary roads, within the financial constraints that are determined from time to time. Of particular interest is the fact that in the United Kingdom, the standard headroom is 16' 6", which has facilitated the use of double-deck buses as are discussed in Chapter 4. In Europe generally and in America, clearances are often very much less and in these areas double-deck vehicles are the exception rather than the rule.

According to its amount of use, a road may be narrow to the extent that oncoming vehicles cannot pass or wide enough to permit a centre reservation with three or more traffic lanes in each direction (i.e., a dual-carriageway). Beyond that, there is a specialised form of highway known in Great Britain as a motorway, which is a purpose-built dual-carriageway avoiding all towns and villages, with limited access and on which there are no frontages, stopping is prohibited except in emergencies, special traffic regulations apply and, most important of all, there are no conflicting traffic movements at intersections. The principle of the motorway and any other special purpose roads reserved exclusively for particular classes of traffic was recognised in Great Britain by the passing of the Special Roads Act, 1949, which gave the necessary powers for their construction. The first stretch of British motorway, the Preston By-pass, was opened in 1958 and the 1949 Act is now consolidated in the Highways Act, 1959.

In Great Britain, the more important roads are classified as either trunk roads or principal roads which together (including motorways) form some fourteen per cent of the national highway network and which collectively amounts to over 207 thousand miles. Costs of construction and maintenance of roads are met from either central or local government sources according to their classification. Central government maintains complete financial responsibility for trunk roads. Section 7 of the Highways Act, 1959, authorises the Minister of Transport (now the Secretary of State for the Environment) to keep under review the national system of routes used by through traffic and resulting from his considerations, he may designate highways as trunk roads as he considers appropriate. Some 75 per cent of expenditure on improvements of principal roads is also covered by Department of Environment grant but the remaining expenditure on principal roads together with that incurred on all other roads of a lower category is borne by local authorities although subject again to rate support grants from central funds. Local authorities may be employed as agents of the Department of the Environment to undertake roadworks but six Road Construction Units comprising technical staff from the Department and from County Councils have been established to design and supervise construction of most of the motorway and inter-urban trunk road schemes.

It will be seen that in Great Britain the cost of highway construction and maintenance is covered by either national taxation or local rates. Certain of the taxes, however, such as vehicle licences, fuel tax and purchase (or value added) tax on private cars are borne exclusively by road users. In 1970, revenue from these three sources totalled nearly £1,800 million, which compared with a road expenditure of £609 million. Only about a third, therefore, of the revenue derived from motor taxation actually found its way back into the roads. Nevertheless, the costs of the way are shared and even though the road transport industry together with the private motorist is making a sizeable contribution to the National Exchequer, the amount paid by the individual to gain his right to use a common way is relatively small.

Another alternative is the imposition of tolls. A toll is a charge levied at the time a particular stretch of highway is used and the system has the advantage that the expense incurred in the provision of particular facilities which perhaps involve abnormal cost is borne in full or in part by those that use them with corresponding relief to society at large. In Great Britain this method is sometimes applied to bridges or tunnels but elsewhere it may be extended to include long stretches of highway, as, for example, the autostrada in Italy or the turnpikes in the United States of America.

It has been shown that the costs of the road are shared by the users, with the result that the charge on the individual is relatively small. However, because of this collective use by a multitude of people, it is inevitable that vehicular movement will not be evenly spread. Peak traffic flows will arise and with it, congestion. The ever increasing ownership of private cars can only aggravate that congestion and create delay. This is of particular significance to bus operators who are unable to maintain their schedules. This not only increases journey times and with it costs of operation but also reduces the attractiveness of the service. Passengers are thereby tempted to desert the bus for the car, thereby creating still more congestion. There is, in any case, a physical limit to the number of cars that can be accommodated on a stretch of road and a limit to the number of roads that can be built. This limit is now being approached in many of the larger towns throughout the world and palliatives short of actual restraints on the use of the car are being sought. In terms of sheer numbers, if benefits to people rather than to vehicles are to be attained, then the high carrying capacity of the bus in relation to the road space that it occupies must be fully exploited in those areas where congestion is particularly acute. Maximum use of available highway space can be achieved by traffic management schemes, which include measures such as the introduction of one-way streets, the banning of right-turns and other conflicting traffic movements and restrictions on waiting. If such arrangements cannot be contained within the existing road layout, traffic engineering techniques are employed which involve road reconstruction and other special work such as the re-alignment of junctions, the provision of barrier rails to segregate traffic, etc. If the advantages of public transport are to be realised, bus priorities must be built into these traffic management and traffic engineering schemes. Special bus lanes with or against the traffic flow, perhaps with light signals geared to effect an advantage to the bus over other users, roads reserved for the exclusive use of buses and special movements for buses such as right hand turns that are denied to other vehicles and which could, thereby, avoid what might otherwise entail use of a one-way circulatory system, are all measures which are for consideration in this respect.

The construction of new motorways provides the possibility of incorporating

purpose built lanes for the use of buses. Such lanes could be in the median strip
with special provision made for occasional stopping points. It would be prudent
to allow sufficient space for subsequent conversion of these lanes into a railway
if and when sufficient traffic is built up. The former bus stopping points would
then become railway stations. This has, in fact, been done, for example, on the
Dan Ryan Expressway in Chicago, U.S.A. to considerable advantage with the
lines concerned now being part of the rail rapid transit system of the Chicago
Transit Authority.

The way in the form of a public road is available for all to use. But not only is
there a physical limitation on the number of vehicles that can use that road,
there is also a limit on the width and number of roads that can be built. Even if
financial considerations are disregarded, the land availability and geography of
the area will in the end dictate when no more roads can be provided. This is why
there must be thoughts on methods of maximising the use of the capacity that is
or that can be made available and beyond that, further exploitation of the railway in urban areas. The subject is further considered in Chapter 14.

Street Tramways
As the street tramway shares the use of the public highway with other users it is
appropriate that it should be considered with this study of the road. It is a "way
within a way" and pedestrians have free access to its tracks. For this reason, the
use of exposed live third and fourth rails for traction purposes would be a source
of danger and all rails must in any case be flush with the surface of the road. For
one reason or another, therefore, normal conductor rails are impracticable. It
follows that the electric street tramway has the alternatives of either overhead
catenary or an underground conduit in which a power line may be laid, current
being fed to the vehicle through a slot in the roadway. The latter method has
never been widely adopted on account of higher construction costs, although the
greater part of the tramway system constructed by the former London County
Council and later absorbed by London Transport worked on this principle up to
the time of final abandonment of trams in London in 1952. The features of the
street tramway, being a private specialised way set in a public thoroughfare, are
partly rail and partly road. Because the tramway is the sole user of its specialised
way, the operator is responsible for its provision and upkeep, but more than
that, because the lines are part of a public way, he is responsible also for the
provision of an adequate road surface both between the rails and, at least in
Great Britain, beyond the edge of the outer rails. The operator of the street
tramway is therefore in an invidious position, possessing the virtues of neither
rail nor road transport. He must bear the full cost of his "private" specialised
way, but in contrast to the railway, because his track is laid in a public road, he
cannot enjoy the advantages of a private way as ordinary road vehicles must
impinge upon his tracks. In other words he must suffer the effects of traffic
congestion — much of which he is helping to create — and must obey such traffic
signals as apply to other road users.

arrival. Passengers and goods must be taken to their destination in safety and without damage. The safe arrival is the product of the transport industry just as the product of a tailor is a well fitting suit. It is important that this primary objective is not confused with the profit motive. Certainly, people work to make a living. They work for the reward which they receive and businesses are built up with a view to securing a profit. This applies to the manufacturer, to the transport operator (unless political considerations override economic considerations and the profit motive is set aside) and to any other commercial enterprise. Profit may be the ultimate purpose of the individual or of the board of directors but the objective of industry is its ultimate product. In transport this is certainly a safe arrival but also, rather more than that, a satisfactory arrival. Arrivals or deliveries should be effected not only without injury or damage but punctually in accordance with the advertised timetable. This does not necessarily imply maximum comfort or speed. These qualities may vary according to the mode of transport or class of service that is selected and different standards are likely to be reflected in the rates that are charged. Different forms of transport have different characteristics in respect of speed, reliability and costs. This aspect is considered in Chapter 6. However, what has been said so far does indicate the possibility of choice, which must now be examined.

Availability of Choice

Public transport facilities were pioneered by private enterprise and it was not until comparatively recent times that many of the hitherto privately owned undertakings passed into public ownership — a matter which is considered in greater detail in Chapter 10. All branches of transport were developed in this way and competitive conditions applied where two or more services (of the same form or different forms) set themselves out to cater for similar traffics. Customers have, therefore, over the years, become accustomed to the availability of choice, particularly with regard to the mode of conveyance and this applies to the movement of both passengers and goods. As the industry expanded and competition between undertakings within each form of transport grew stronger, some units became large and powerful and a process of absorption led to something approaching monopoly conditions in certain fields, although the availability of choice between the modes remained.

A true monopoly means that control of supply is unified and the supplier, no longer restricted by the force of competition can, disregarding any legal requirements, either charge what price he likes for his product and let demand decide the number of units to be produced or control the number of units produced and let demand decide the price level. The effect on the purchaser is the same as on this reasoning he has to pay the price which the producer considers will yield maximum profits. Past governments have been mindful of these economic effects. The Tramways Act, 1870, for example and referred to in Chapter 8, resulted from a fear of the consequences of a private monopoly in the tramway industry, hence the powers of compulsory purchase conferred upon local authorities. The legislation affecting railway rates also discussed in Chapter 8 reflects the one-time fear of a railway monopoly of inland transport, although in the event a complete railway monopoly in Great Britain was never really

THE RAILWAY

Standard Duo-Rail

A railway is a specialised form of way. To put it simply, the track in its conventional form consists of two parallel and continuous strips of steel which give a smooth hard surface. Resistance to rolling is thereby reduced to the extent that on level ground a power of only 6½lb is required to pull a load of 1 ton. In the case of a rubber-tyred road vehicle, for example, the corresponding resistance to rolling is 44lb per ton.

The distance between these two parallel rails is called the gauge and for no reason except that it was the gauge of an old local colliery track, was set at 4ft 8½in by George Stephenson when he laid his first railway in 1814. This width is now recognised as standard throughout Great Britain, the Continent of Europe (except Spain, Portugal, Finland and Russia), Egypt, Turkey, North America, Australia and China. Other gauges in general use range from up to 5ft 6in in India, Pakistan, Spain, Portugal, Ireland, South America, Russia, etc, down to 3ft 6in in, for example, South Africa and Japan. Lines of metre gauge and even narrower can be found scattered throughout the world. This width of track is influenced quite considerably by the type of country through which the railway passes. For reasons to be explained, the line must be kept as level as possible which in mountainous or hilly regions, is likely to necessitate sharp bends. In these circumstances a narrower gauge must be adopted as wide track calls for more gentle curvature.

The width between the rails must not be confused with the loading gauge, which is the maximum permitted width and height of the rolling stock. A narrow gauge does not necessarily mean smaller vehicles. Because of raised platforms, low bridges, narrow tunnels, etc, the maximum permitted width of rolling stock in Great Britain on standard gauge track is generally only about 9ft. In North America, track of the same gauge may carry trains up to a width of 10ft 9in, whilst trains of 10ft width run in South Africa on a gauge of only 3ft 6in. Similar limitations apply to height. It is therefore the loading gauge perhaps more than the width between the rails which influences the size and design of rolling stock. Note in passing that whereas in Great Britain the headroom on the highway system is usually rather more generous than world standards, which enables double-deck buses to be widely used, on the railways, the reverse is the case. The loading gauge of British Railways is such that it has a very limiting effect on the size of rolling stock. Elsewhere, larger dimensions are permitting the development of double-deck trains as is mentioned in Chapter 4.

Track so formed by these two parallel strips of rail presents two problems: the fastening of the rail to the sleeper and the joining of the rails. The purpose of sleepers is to maintain the correct spacing of the rails between the inside edges (the gauge), and to even out the vertical stresses on the ground. They are embedded in ballast which helps to spread the load and prevent sliding as, for example, when braking. Ballast is made up of broken stone.

One solution adopted to fasten the rail to the sleeper is to utilise a chair in which the rail, essentially symmetrical in profile, is secured by means of wedges. The inevitable battering of the rail on the chair when trains are passing, however, tends to produce a noisy track, whilst the cost of this system is fairly high. Thus the chaired track is giving way more and more to a rail having a foot or base which is anchored to the sleepers with pads and springs held in position by large screws. Both types of rail are still used in Great Britain, being known respectively as the bullhead and flat-bottomed varieties.

The second problem, that of joining successive lengths, arises firstly because of the need for careful alignment and secondly because the resultant joint represents a weak point in the track. The normal method is to connect consecutive lengths of rail by means of fishplates and bolts. The resultant joints however cause the traditional and monotonous beat of the wheels and increase resistance to rolling. To alleviate this difficulty and to give a smoother ride, the modern tendency is to eliminate many of the joints by welding individual strips into continuous lengths. At the extremity of each long length of rail there may be a feathered joint which enables the end of the rail to expand in hot weather whilst at the same time maintaining continuity of the rolling surface.

If the railway is to follow contour it must climb and descend gradients and it is here that the advantage of low resistance to rolling becomes a serious handicap. On a 1 in 100 up-gradient, resistance to forward motion for a road vehicle goes up by approximately 40 per cent, but for a railway locomotive the effort required for the haulage of a train increases by some 250 per cent. Gradients of 1 in 12 or less which are found on the roads are quite prohibitive for express railway working. This factor, together with the need for curves of imposing proportions dependent upon the gauge of the track and the speed at which it is intended to run the trains, makes it easy to understand why the railway cannot adhere to the contour of the ground as well as can roads. This has led to magnificent feats of engineering in building bridges, viaducts, and tunnels, but such necessity adds materially to the cost of construction and upkeep of the way.

With regard to the siting of the line; in built-up areas the construction of a railway can seriously impede road traffic by the necessity of level crossings which, apart from the delay factor, are not in the best interests of road safety. This feature can be avoided if the railway is built at a different level, i.e., either above or below the surface — elevated or in a cutting. Certain local suburban systems are sometimes constructed entirely at a different level in relation to the surface, as, for example, the Hamburg Elevated Railway and the sub-surface Circle Line of London Transport which is in effect an underground railway built on the cut and cover principle. A development of this is the tube, built by burrowing through the soil and lining the tunnel with steel or concrete. The construction of this type of railway is extremely costly, so much so that its provision would never be considered outside highly congested areas where space on the surface is not available.

The constructional requirements of railways in Great Britain are detailed in the "Railway Construction and Operation Requirements for Passenger Lines and Recommendations for Goods Lines" issued by the Secretary of State for the Environment. The minimum requirements of the track, signalling, stations, bridges gradients, etc, may, however, be relaxed in certain instances having regard to any restrictions on the gauge, volume of traffic, axle-loads and speed limits. Each case is considered on its merits and lines which, constructionally and operationally, have these limitations and have been granted exemption from some or all of the minimum standards are known as light railways.

It has been seen that the railway functions on the movement of smooth steel wheels along a smooth steel surface. The power of the locomotive (as on any wheeled vehicle) is restricted by the friction between these two surfaces, but as, in the case of the railway, the surface is smooth and hard, resistance is reduced to a minimum. Even so, power is limited by the ability of the wheels to grip the rail or, in other words, the adhesion. The power of the locomotive, irrespective of its source, is taken up at the point where the driving wheels come into contact with the rail, as it is from this point that the wheels move. If the force is too great, the wheels will no longer grip but will slip and revolve without moving forward. The force transmitted from the driving wheels to the track is called the tractive effort, the technicalities of which do not concern us here. The point being made is that movement is dependent upon the wheel gripping (or adhering to) the rail and the railway's basic problem is to transport heavy loads with as low a tractive effort as possible.

Rack Railway
The rack railway is a specialised type of railway which enables purpose built locomotives to climb gradients that could not be negotiated by normal adhesion. Steel cogged rail is in this case laid between the running rails in which pinions on the train engage and so control movement. This type of railway is able to negotiate steep gradients and is used in mountainous regions, particularly in Switzerland. It is not limited to any one source of power. The first rack railway to be constructed in Europe, the Vitznam Rigi Bahn, which climbs the Rigi from Vitznam in Switzerland was built in 1871. Originally steam propulsion was used, but in 1937 the line was electrified, current being collected from an overhead wire. The only example of a rack railway in Great Britain is the steam-operated Snowdon Mountain Railway running from Llanberis in North Wales to the summit of Snowdon.

Cable Lines
For gradients which it would be impracticable to negotiate, even by a rack railway, cables may be used. These cables are set either between or beneath the tracks and are able to haul railed vehicles up a very steep incline. The funicular railway is, in effect, a cable railway. In this instance, two vehicles of similar weight are linked by cable, one being at the base and the other at the summit of the line. The cars balance each other as they ascend and descend respectively and if only a single track is provided, a passing loop must be installed at the centre point. However, as movement results from the car gripping the cable, the cable is not only a part of the way, it is also a means of propulsion and in consequence, is closely allied to motive power. Further reference to movement by cable is, therefore, made in Chapter 5.

A quite different form of cable way is that used in hilly regions either to ascend mountains or to cross valleys. In this case, cars are suspended from aerial cables. For this type of cable car, therefore, cables are not only power lines, they also constitute the way in their own right.

Monorail

An alternative to the duorail is the monorail. The monorail is in effect a continuous beam carrying a single running rail. The trains can straddle the beam and rail as in the case of the Alweg type or, as the monorail is usually elevated, be suspended from it, which is the principle of the Safege type. If the track is elevated, it must be supported on columns or suitable frames which, if the cars are suspended, must be sufficiently high to permit satisfactory clearance when crossing or running parallel with roads or other railways. The overhead railway does not occupy valuable space to the same extent as a surface railway as the land beneath can still be put to limited use and the cost of construction is substantially below that of a tube railway. But its capacity is less than the tube and the supports are unsightly. Furthermore, difficulty in switching is a disadvantage. This may be necessary on an extensive system both at junctions and at terminals and the switching gear (or points) tends to be cumbrous. Suspended trains are liable to sway in high winds, and some form of control may therefore be necessary, particularly at stations. Should a new and specific demand arise with a traffic potential insufficient to justify the cost of construction of an underground railway but too great to be absorbed by existing surface transport, it is then possible that a case for a monorail might be proved.

Numerous overhead lines have been constructed over the years mainly as pleasure attractions at exhibitions, etc, but a noteworthy commercially established successful line is the municipally-owned Schwebebahn at Wuppertal in Germany. The route follows a narrow river gorge from Vohwinkel to Oberbarmen. Inaugurated in 1901, it is 8¼ miles long and follows the course of the River Wupper throughout except for a short distance at the western extremity where it is suspended over Kaiserstrasse, a heavily-trafficked road passing through a residential and shopping area. The service is confined to a single route without bifurcations or short workings. A circle at the terminals eliminates the need to reverse. Switching is therefore confined to the depot and maintenance area situated at Vohwinkel. Some 50 cars provide a frequent service and the line, which is pictured at Plate 12, makes a valuable contribution to the local transport requirements of the area.

A more recent example is the line of the Hitachi Express and Tokyo Monorail Company, Japan, which provides a frequent service between Haneda Airport and Hamamatsu-cho, a distance of some eight miles. This line is of the straddle type in which the cars travel astride a single prestressed concrete beam. The greater part of the line is supported by reinforced concrete T-shaped pylons (as opposed to the A-shaped structures of the Wuppertal line) partly over land and partly over water, but because of special conditions applying at Haneda Airport and at the Ebitori River, part of the track runs either underground or underwater at these points. Trains are electrically operated and the signalling system is of particular interest. All signal indications are given inside the coaches and no wayside signals are used as the system whereby steel rails are short circuited by the wheels as described later in this chapter is not possible with concrete rail. Further reference to this aspect of the monorail is contained in a subsequent paragraph which is devoted to railway signalling.

Pneumatic Tyred Trains

A further variant to the specialised types of way required by fixed tracked vehicles is that prepared for the pneumatic tyred train. The track will vary according to the design of the vehicles that use it but it is likely to consist of two parallel strips of concrete or other material that gives a satisfactory running surface, with suitable guide rails, possibly supplemented by standard steel rails laid within the concrete tracks for use in an emergency together with electrical conductor rails. This type of way is illustrated in Plates 13 and 14. The pneumatic tyred train has its advantages in that it is quiet and gives a smooth ride. The important feature, however, lies in its resistance to rolling which is more akin to that of a road vehicle. Its ability to negotiate gradients does, therefore, compare favourably with the railway train of the standard adhesion type (steel wheel on steel rail) which was discussed in a previous paragraph. Although this feature may be both an advantage and a disadvantage, it can facilitate the construction of urban rapid transit type railways to the extent that varying levels of track and depths of tunnel can be joined by shorter albeit steeper connecting links. The three major systems which use pneumatic tyres, i.e., at Paris, Montreal and Mexico City are, in fact, basically underground railways of this type. Capital costs, however, are heavy and as far as the way is concerned, particular difficulty arises with switching. It is a similar difficulty to that which is experienced with monorails and the equipment necessary to allow a bifurcation is again cumbrous as the illustration at Plate 16 shows.

Signalling

When high speeds are to be maintained by trains on lines of high traffic density with many conflicting movements, regulation is essential. Control through a system of signalling is therefore necessary and in this context, fixed signals must be regarded as part of the specialised way.

The system of signalling is based on the block principle, with the line being divided into sections (blocks), the lengths of which vary from about a quarter of a mile to up to several miles, being determined by such factors as traffic density and speed. Each section, the entrance to which is controlled by a signalbox, is considered blocked until the signalman (or blockman) there has first obtained permission from the signalman at the far end for a train to proceed through it. Such permission is normally sought sufficiently early to ensure that the speed of trains is not unnecessarily retarded, subject to the section being clear as shown by the block indicators. Communications are in code and are exchanged by means of single stroke bells often incorporated in the block indicator unit.

Signals themselves may be conveniently divided into two groups — caution and stop. As it is difficult for a heavy train running at speed to pull up, especially on falling gradients, the signals are arranged so that the driver first comes to the caution (or distant or repeater) signal. If the caution signal shows clear, he knows that the next signal, which may be towards a mile further on, will also be clear and he can maintain his speed. To be fully effective the distant signal is sited at a braking distance suitable for all classes of trains from the stop signal ahead of it. The distance between these two signals is, therefore, governed by the train which requires the greatest length of line in which it can be brought to a halt. If the distant signal is at caution the driver may pass it but he must be prepared to stop at the next stop signal. Mechanism in the signalbox lever frame prevents the distant signal from being set at clear until the stop signal has also been set at clear, making it impossible except in emergency for a driver to be suddenly confronted with a stop signal.

The lever frame mechanism is interlocking. Before the signal relating to a particular line can be placed in the clear position, the points must first be set up for that route. At a large junction with many crossings and routes, the interlocking becomes more complex. If a train is to cross through several sets of points, they all have to be in position, tightly fitting and so locked, before any signal relating to that route can be released. On the system being described, this interlocking is usually obtained by mechanical means but in modern installations electrical devices are used as will be discussed later in this sub-section.

The general pattern of signals as seen by the driver is distant, home and starting, but the number of stop signals is frequently amplified at places where heavy traffic has to be handled or to cover particular station layouts controlled from a signalbox. In all cases, however, the interlocking ensures that the distant signal will not come off until all the stop signals to which it applies have first been cleared.

The older type of signal with arm and two colour glass spectacle is known as a semaphore signal. In Great Britain the arms of the home and starting (stop) signals have squared blunt ends, painted red with a white stripe and with a red/green spectacle. The distant (caution) signal arm is cut away in the shape of a fish tail, painted yellow with a black chevron and with a yellow/green spectacle. Most semaphore signals are of the upper quadrant type, the arm being raised to an angle of 45 degrees for the clear position. The arms of semaphore signals are readily seen during daylight hours and the spectacle is illuminated by an oil lamp for indicating the position of the signal during darkness. An advantage of the upper quadrant type is that in case of failure of the operating mechanism it remains or falls to the danger or caution position more reliably.

Colour-light signals are commonplace in many areas. They are electrically lit with the light focussed through a large lens to produce a powerful beam of light which greatly assists visibility. Colour-light signals are usually of the multi-aspect type, capable of showing two, three or four aspects combining the functions of distant and stop signals. Thus, whilst the red aspect indicates stop and the green aspect clear, the yellow aspect indicates caution and carries the meaning of the distant signal that the line is clear up to the next signal only. The fourth, being a double yellow aspect, indicates preliminary caution and is followed in sequence by the yellow aspect.

A big advance in train signalling has been the extensive installation of track circuits. A track circuit is made by two individual rails of a section of track, insulated at their ends. Current is fed into the section at its front end and flows to a relay at its rear end. A single axle is sufficient to short-circuit the current supply and to de-energise the relay. The operation of the relay to the de-energised position can be used to prevent the movement of points, to lock a signal at the danger position or, in the case of automatic block sections, to maintain a red light in the signal aspect controlling the entrance to the section.

A feature of this system and which is in fact a function of all recent re-signalling installations is that it keeps trains moving rather than stopping them. Signals are kept in the clear position unless the section is occupied instead of deliberately clearing a signal to permit the passage of a particular train.

A feature introduced in France and subsequently adopted on some lines in other countries is that known as banalisation. This entails signalling lengths of line for two-way working, the signalling being electrically interlocked to prevent conflicting movements and supervised by one controller. The benefit of this arrangement is that peak traffic flows may be routed over the two-way signalled section, thereby increasing line capacity and providing greater flexibility for traffic movement.

In areas where main lines are of single track with passing loops, an arrangement known as ctc (centralised traffic control) has been introduced to make the most efficient use of line capacity and reduce signalling operating costs.

These are the fundamentals of railway signalling. However, as railways are being modernised, not only are the semaphores giving way to multi-aspect colour light signals but the numerous lineside signal boxes are being replaced by power boxes able to control over 100 route miles of track. This is the case, for example, on one of the main lines of British Railways which runs from London to Glasgow and which is already electrified as far as Preston. The signalling equipment of the new power boxes is operated from consoles which contain an illuminated track diagram showing all signals and points and the positions of trains throughout the particular areas that are under their control. Illuminated indications display continuously the state of the line and all the functions which are under the signalmen's control. A comprehensive system of monitoring advises them of the condition of the equipment. Included in the panel are the controlling push-buttons and switches which have replaced the old mechanical type of signalling which required the movement of levers to operate individual signals and points. Signalmen on the modernised lines can set the routes for trains merely by pressing the appropriate buttons. Providing conditions are safe for them to do so, all points along the route will move to the required positions and when other safety requirements have been met, the signals clear automatically. The design of all the signalling circuits is such that no error in working on the part of the signalmen will prejudice the safety of trains.

Another development is that of the automatic warning system, usually referred to as aws. Equipment is fitted to locomotives and also on the track approaching distant signals. When the locomotive approaches the signal the driver is given an audible indication that he is approaching it. If the signal is set at clear, a bell rings and no special action is required. But if the signal is at caution a horn sounds and unless the driver takes action within three seconds, the train brakes begin to be applied. A visual indicator is fitted to augment the caution horn and to remind the driver that he has taken action to control the train and that he has passed a signal showing caution.

An alternative method of signalling is one whereby indications are given inside the driver's cab instead of from wayside signals. Such a system has been adopted on the Tokyo monorail where a concrete way prohibits the use of track circuits. In this case signal indications are supplied to trains by means of induction cables installed continuously along both upper shoulders on top of the track beam. A development beyond this is the fully automated railway whereby trains do not require continuous physical action by the driver as is the case with, for example, the new Victoria Line of London Transport. On this line, trains progress in response to electrical impulses conveyed from the track through coils mounted on the train. Currents of varying frequencies control speeds and also braking, either for station stops or when the section of track ahead is not clear.

INLAND WATERWAYS

An inland waterway suitable for transport purposes may take the form of a natural river or an artificial canal. It is very probable, however, that a natural river will have been artificially improved by deepening, by the provision of landing stages and by the construction of locks to overcome differences in levels that in the natural form would have resulted in rapids and waterfalls. Furthermore, the path of a natural river is often very circuitous and a more direct route is sometimes made by the construction of a cut across the neck of a meandering loop. For this reason and for the sake of convenience all types of inland waterways are here grouped under the general heading of artificial ways.

Canal water is derived from various sources. In Great Britain the most important is reservoirs of water from natural sources which feed a great deal of the system by natural gravitational flow. Supplies of water also come from small streams flowing into the waterways, from drainage from the surrounding land and from supplies pumped up in some areas from mine workings or from wells. In addition, supplies come into the system from sewage disposal works (after treatment to standards prescribed by river boards) and there are surface water discharges from canalside factories and other sources. River navigations largely depend of course on the natural river flow.

Climate also has its effect. In very hot regions it is unlikely that a sufficient water supply would be maintained either because of a shortage or of loss by evaporation, whilst in colder areas, ice impedes movement. A further requirement is that the soil should not be too porous. Puddled clay has been widely used to prevent leakage.

The physical characteristics of Great Britain militate against a healthy growth of a comprehensive waterway system. It is by no means a flat country. In fact, by comparison with parts of Europe (and that is with those parts where there are waterways in abundance), the vertical rise per mile is far greater, which necessitates a multiplicity of locks. But sufficient water is not always available in Britain to permit the construction and use of the wider waterways and locks and for this reason many canals of smaller dimensions were built. There is, therefore, no uniform gauge in this country and the larger craft can proceed to only a few of the inland waterheads. In consequence British waterways fall into two groups — the wide navigations along which can pass the estuarial and seagoing vessels with a beam of 14ft or more and a capacity of up to about 400 tons, and the narrow canals allowing the passage of boats with a beam of only 7ft and a capacity up to about 25–30 tons.

Ship Canals

Certain canals have been constructed of a sufficient width and depth to accommodate the seagoing ships themselves. These waterways perform a different function. They cater for international traffic and their purpose is either

    (a)   to maintain deep water access to the sea for old ports,

    (b)   to convert inland towns into seaports, or

    (c)   to shorten a through journey by making possible a short cut across a narrow isthmus thereby avoiding what would otherwise be a circuitous routing by sea.

In the case of (a) and (b) the port served constitutes either the beginning or the end of a voyage (or an intermediate calling point), but in the case of (c) it is part of a through route and although the ship may stop for technical reasons the call may have no commercial significance. In fact there need not be a port as such within the canal zone.

An example of the first type of waterway is the Noord Zee Canal in Holland which gives Amsterdam an outlet to the North Sea. At one time Amsterdam was a port on the now inland Ijsselmeer, which is in the process of being drained. At home, the Manchester Ship Canal is a good example of (b). This canal has given port status to the inland town of Manchester whilst further afield the canals forming part of the St. Lawrence Seaway have opened up the Great Lakes to world shipping. The reader will not need to be reminded of such well-known canals as Suez, Panama, Kiel, etc, which fall within the (c) classification.

Locks and lifts

In order to overcome changes of height either when negotiating hilly country or when different water channels are linked, it is usual to construct locks which are in effect short sections of river or canal contained within sluiced gates. The operation of the lock involves filling the chamber with water from the upper level which is then slowly drained down to the lower level. This is the reason why the use of locks involves a wastage of water. The vessel or vessels rise or fall within the chamber according to the direction of travel.

A lesser-used alternative, but suitable when the difference in height is considerable, is the lift. By this means, the whole basin in which the vessel is floating is transferred from one level to the other. An example of the lift is at Anderton in Cheshire which raises and lowers canal boats vertically through a height of 50ft between the Trent and Mersey Canal and the River Weaver. It is also possible for the lift to be made through an inclined place, the principle being that either a tank full of water and large enough to float a barge, or alternatively the barge itself is drawn out of the canal and placed on a cradle supported on wheels and drawn up on an adjoining inclined railway track by some outside power. The inclined plane lift has little commercial significance, but neither this nor the vertical lift involves wastage of water as do locks. However, there is a size limitation to which this principle can be applied, they require expensive equipment and are costly to operate, whereas locks are of a more simple construction with lower running expenses.

At best, locks are time consuming and extravagant in the use of water. If an adequate water supply is not available, particularly at the highest points of the system, canal construction could quite easily be impracticable. Although therefore physically essential, locks impair the attractiveness of the waterway and should be kept to a minimum. However, it is unlikely that any territory is sufficiently flat to eliminate entirely the need for locks, quite apart from the influence of tides (the effects of which are annulled by the presence of a lock). Hence the need for fairly flat country and an adequate water supply to meet lock requirements and also to maintain a sufficient width and depth.

Use of the way

Inland water transport is akin to the road to the extent that the way (i.e. the river or the canal) is shared by different carriers. In Great Britain the canal navigating undertaking (that is, the authority which owns the way), is for the most part the British Waterways Board which is also one of many canal-carrying undertakings. But this is incidental. The functions of canal navigating and canal carrying undertakings are quite distinct as are the functions of a highway authority and those of a bus or road haulage operator. Unless it is also the navigating authority, the canal carrier (who may be either a public carrier or a trader carrying his own goods in his own vessels) uses the canal upon payment of tolls. However, unlike road vehicles, the owners of which pay a fixed annual tax in the form of a vehicle licence which permits unlimited use, tolls imposed on canal carriers are at present based on ton/miles which do therefore vary in proportion to use.

PIPELINES

The pipeline for transport purposes is unique inasmuch as it does not require a separate carrying unit, the commodity to be transported being conveyed within the "way" itself. This of course gives a financial advantage of considerable appeal compared with the more orthodox forms of way. There is a limited but not exorbitant cost in provision and maintenance and the pipeline may be reserved for the exclusive use of the products of one particular manufacturer or alternatively the owner may undertake to convey traffic for other people. In other words, the pipeline may be used for either public or private purposes depending largely on whether the owner is a manufacturer who requires his own private facilities for distribution, or whether his business is that of a public carrier. For a considerable time the tube or pipe has carried mankind's water supplies, and over the years the pipeline has also been the means of distributing domestic gas. But the pipeline is now developing as a multi-user. Its use is no longer confined to the supply of gas and fresh water and the removal of waste, or to private internal distribution. The pipeline has proved particularly suitable for the bulk transport of oil and it is also carrying semi-solids and solids.

Today hundreds of thousands of steel pipelines cover large distances crossing deserts, mountains and rivers, carrying oil and other commodities. Steel pipe may be seamless or welded. The seamless pipe consists of tube made from a solid blank which is rolled lengthwise over a mandrel to the required length and wall thickness. The welded tube is formed by welding together the edges of steel strip or plate that has been bent into the form of a cylinder. For the smaller welded pipe one strip may be used, but for the larger sizes it is a matter of welding together the four edges of wider strip of sheet. The most recent development is spirally welded pipe which is made from steel strips wound spirally to any desired diameter. By this means, large diameters of great length can be produced.

Most major pipelines are laid underground in a trench with about 3ft of earth cover. Before lowering into the trench the pipe is covered with a thick layer of bituminous enamel and wrapped with a protective covering. In certain desert countries oil pipelines have been laid above the ground, which is cheaper and reduces the problem of corrosion, but owing to the large variations in temperature, allowance has to be made for expansion and contraction. The physical obstruction caused by an overground pipeline however makes this method less attractive in cultivated or inhabited areas.

The Conveyance of Solids

For conveyance by pipeline, the commodity must be fluid, but a wide range of solid materials can be suitably adapted. The idea is not new. In 1850, solids were handled by pipelines in the Californian Gold Rush and the earliest patent is dated 1891. In 1914 there was a small pipeline conveying coal in water at Hammersmith Power Station in London and the pumping of gravel, slurries and sewage through pipes over relatively short distances has been common practice for years. Long lines, however, are now in use and in America there is a line over 100 miles long carrying coal in water, and another over 70 miles long, carrying gilsonite (a form of bitumen), also suspended in water. A problem is that in some cases the material conveyed, for example, in water, may have to be separated and dried at the far end before it can be used. In many chemical processes, however, this does not arise and in some cases a coal slurry can be burned in a wet state.

The design of pipelines for the conveyance of solids brings in several factors additional to those concerned with the flow of normal fluids. Although in long-distance pipelines solids are normally suspended in a liquid, pneumatic transport is also possible.

The following list shows the wide variety of solid materials which are or could possibly be conveyed along pipelines using liquid (usually water) to convey the solid material:

Fine pulverised coal
Irregular lump coal (pieces up to one-third of the pipe diameter)
Gravel
Granite chips
Stone dust and chips
Ashes
Fly ash
Limestone
Cement
Concrete
Dusts
Clays
Sand
Potash
Gilsonite
Bauxite

Various slurries and mixtures in chemical processing
Wood chips
Wood pulp
Bully-beef tins
Furniture parts
Sewage and rubbish disposal.

Probably the most important developments in this respect are pipelines for coal (both lump and pulverised), limestone for cement making, china clay and lines for the disposal of fly-ash from power stations.

Crude oil lines

A comparison of pipelines in various regions shows great diversity in detail; diameter of pipe varies from 6in to 48in, lines may be single or multiple, buried or laid on the surface and pumping stations may be as near as 25 miles or as far as 150 miles apart. This lack of uniformity results from the large number of factors which have to be taken into consideration. The pumping of a specified quantity of a given oil over a given distance may be achieved by using a large diameter pipe with a small pressure drop, or a smaller diameter pipe with a greater pressure drop. The first alternative will entail a higher capital cost with lower running costs, and the second a lower capital cost with higher running costs. It is necessary to strike an economic balance between these two. The choice is dictated by local circumstances and the economies of maintaining pumping stations. It would not, for example, be practicable to install pumping stations with their attendant labour requirements in the heart of desert country.

In designing a pipeline it is necessary to find the best balance of the following variables — diameter of the pipe, its thickness and quality which sets the maximum safe pumping pressure and the spacing and number of pumping stations. The limited number of pipe sizes available from manufacturers reduces the practical combinations.

Products lines

The design of pipelines for the transport of white oils, that is, products ranging from motor spirit to gas oils, differs very little from that of crude oil lines. Since, however, such lines are frequently used to transport several different products, steps must be taken to minimise contamination between succeeding batches of different products although it is not usual to use the same line to convey both white and black oils. In some cases rubber and/or metal plugs, known as "batching pigs" or "spheres" are used to separate out products in the line, but careful design and rigid adherence to a recognised operating cycle make these unnecessary in most cases.

Pumping Stations

Pumping stations are necessary to "propel" the commodity through the pipe and are, therefore, an integral part of the pipeline installation. At the same time they do, in a sense, constitute the motive power for this particular mode of transport. It follows that pumping stations do not fall easily into either the "way" or the "motive power" classifications. Whilst, therefore, brief mention of the need for pumping stations is made here, further reference in rather more detail is made in Chapter 5.

Natural Ways

With the exception of natural rivers, the various types of way mentioned in the preceding paragraphs are all artificial and constructed at a cost. The sea and the air are natural and free and the operators of ships and aircraft have no specialised way to provide or maintain. The way is available for all to use subject only to artificial restrictions such as territorial rights and rules of navigation. Nevertheless, the nature of these ways dictates the type of construction of the vessels and aircraft which, but for very short journeys, must be large and sufficiently robust to provide adequately for safety and comfort. The carrying unit is therefore expensive. Furthermore, specialised terminals are essential and costly and carriers must pay harbour and dock dues or landing fees to those who provide and maintain the terminal facilities. They may also be faced with payments for assistance such as the pilotage charges for ships. Navigational aids are also necessary but unlike the railway, which is the sole user of its private and specialised way and provides its own signalling, such aids are not provided by operators but by independent bodies. In the United Kingdom the provision of air navigation services is the responsibility of the Civil Aviation Authority to which reference is made in Chapters 8 and 10.

Air Traffic Control

In inclement weather ships can remain at rest in their own element, needing only guides to direct them to their terminal or to warn them of hazards. Aircraft cannot bide time by remaining stationary in the air and their fuel reserves are not sufficiently large to allow them to remain airborne in motion indefinitely. There must therefore be vast networks of navigational equipment to pinpoint their location and control their landing. With the ever-increasing speed and volume of air travel, these aids have become complex and costly. Subject to political considerations within territorial waters, shipping enjoys complete freedom of the seas. But it is not practicable similarly to route aircraft entirely over the sea. Unless on either a domestic service or an international service which joins two neighbouring states, it would be inconvenient or even impossible not to fly over territory of countries having no commercial interest in the flight and at which the plane will not call. In international civil aviation there is national control of airspace over certain nationally-owned territory, hence government interest in navigational services. Outside these areas there is freedom of movement and flight information regions exercise control by advice and not by law. The danger of collision on high density routes is however such that no regular airline operator is likely to act contrary to information received from a flight information centre.

The first consideration of air traffic control must be the safety of aircraft, their passengers and crews and on operational and technical grounds it is essential that the civil en route services be provided by a single agency covering the whole country. Also, the close interaction between en route services and aerodrome technical services at certain main aerodromes makes it highly desirable that the same agency should provide the technical services at those aerodromes. This is, in fact, the case as is described in Chapter 10.

The en route services provided for civil air traffic must also work in conjunction with the service which controls military air traffic and there is a common use of facilities. Moreover, the system must be compatible with those in operation in other countries and to ensure this, international collaboration at government level is necessary. This collaboration is already achieved through the International Civil Aviation Organization described in Chapter 9. Following the Eurocontrol Convention, air traffic control in the upper air space of member states (of which the United Kingdom is one) has become the responsibility of Eurocontrol. The services within the United Kingdom air space are carried out by NATS (see Chapter 10) as an agent of Eurocontrol.

Control of services to Heathrow Airport
By way of illustration, the method of control of services into Heathrow Airport is explained.

NATS has three main control centres for the purpose of the control of air traffic over Great Britain and it is the London Air Traffic Control Centre at West Drayton which directs and assists air movements over Southern England and adjoining sea areas. Radar scanners situated in the north-west corner of Heathrow Airport by the Bath Road and remoted radars in other parts of the country revolve continuously to supply information to the controllers watching the cathode ray tubes.

Airliners flying to Heathrow Airport are directed along specific air lanes, and they follow instructions from the London air traffic control centre until they reach a point where they are handed over to Heathrow airport approach control. There are four such hand-over points, one at Ockham and one at Biggin Hill in the south and one at Bovingdon and one at Ongar in the north and they are signposted by radio aids. London approach control is housed near the top of the control tower which dominates the buildings in the centre of the airport. Like the air traffic control centre, it relies on radar to see the movements of the airliners. The task of the approach and radar controllers is to maintain the flow of arriving aircraft in orderly sequence towards the runway or runways in use.

When low cloud or fog reduces visibility, the pilots of incoming airliners use radio aids to help them descend accurately to the threshold of the runway. One of these aids is ILS (Instrument Landing System) which gives the pilot information on height and direction through the medium of two pointers on an instrument on the flight deck. Another aid is PAR, the Precision Approach Radar talk-down system. The precision talk-down controller takes over from the radar approach controllers when the aircraft is about eight miles from the runway at an altitude of 2,000ft. While he watches the movements of the aircraft on his radar screens the talk-down controller issues instructions over the radio telephone (RT) which enable the pilot to bring down the aircraft at the correct rate of descent and on an accurate heading to an altitude of some 150ft at a point 400yds from the threshold of the runway. The landing is then completed visually. When an airliner is approaching with the aid of ILS its progress can be followed on the radar screens by the precision talk-down controller but he does not issue any instructions unless his help is needed. All aircraft approaching a busy airport must be able to communicate by radio telephone with Air Traffic Control

The final stages of the control of incoming airliners are exercised from the glass penthouse at the top of the tower. This houses the aerodrome control where the functions are divided between the air controller and the ground movement controller. From their vantage point they have an unobstructed view of the sky in all directions and of the runways and taxitracks. The air controller is concerned with the movement on the runways of aircraft actually landing or taking off. Unless aircraft are being talked down he takes over from Approach Control when the aircraft is established on final approach and is about six miles from touchdown. He hands on each aircraft to the ground movement controller when it has finished its landing run and is clear of the runway. The ground movement controller speaking on RT directs the aircraft along the system of taxitracks to its allotted parking bay on the apron. All motor vehicles that are permitted on the runways and taxiways must be fitted with radio so that they also may be directed by the ground movement controller.

Space
Yet a third medium in this classification of free and natural ways, at present on the threshold of development, is space and it is probable that interplanetary craft will at some time be commonplace. The essentials of space will be similar to those applicable to air today. The way will be free, but it seems reasonable to assume that the expense of this form of transport will lie in the high cost of the carrying unit, fuel, aids to navigation, etc, again as a result of the nature of the way.

3 · The Terminal

Introduction

A terminus may be described as the furthest point to which anything extends. A terminal assumes in this text a wider sense and covers any point where access is available on to a specialised form of way, or where interchange facilities are available between different ways. Hence intermediate railway stations and halts could for this purpose be regarded as terminals, but the station at the end of the line is also a terminus.

Terminals vary considerably in their design, extent and equipment between different forms of transport, within the same form of transport and between those designed for passengers and those for the handling of freight.

So far as passenger transport is concerned, amenities provided differ according to the extent of use, the size of the carrying unit, the length of journey, special considerations affecting the journey and the degree of comfort normally provided. For example, in road and air transport the unit is relatively small in each case, (although aircraft are rapidly becoming larger) and this affects the number of people that are involved in any one arrival or departure. Furthermore road transport operations are not generally seriously affected by adverse weather conditions and the timetable can be compiled and maintained to very fine limits. Road transport terminals (where they are provided) can therefore be quite small and compact without leading to congestion, and the size of waiting rooms, etc, need not be great. Air transport on the other hand is liable to heavy delays in bad weather with a number of planes grounded simultaneously. Moreover, distances covered are great and a high degree of comfort is expected. In these circumstances more elaborate amenities are necessary. Another feature of air transport is the length of runway required for take-off and landing. The area required for an airport is in consequence greater than for the terminals of other forms of transport catering for comparable numbers of passengers and it cannot be strategically sited near the centres of towns. Rail transport, like road, works to fine timetable limits, but the unit may be large and for this reason adequate facilities must be provided at the busier stations to cater for heavy surges of traffic. Sea transport would seem to possess all the qualities which require elaborate terminals — the journey is usually long, the timetable is subject to the vagaries of the weather and a high degree of comfort is usually required. In effect, although ocean terminals are provided for passenger traffic, lavish facilities are not vital as the ship itself is generally in a position to provide adequate accommodation. Equipment is, of course very necessary for the handling of merchandise.

The more important terminals for all forms of transport tend to be of a complex design and in most cases, apart from the provision of facilities necessary for the handling of passengers and goods including accommodation for H.M. Customs and Immigration officials at terminals which deal with international traffic, there must be means of servicing the vehicles, aircraft, or ships which use them. However, in the case of road and rail transport where terminals are generally strategically situated as near as possible to a town centre (and where the cost of ground is therefore at a premium and in any case difficult to obtain), these servicing facilities may be some distance from the terminal itself. Where this is so it is desirable that the distance should be kept to a minimum to avoid unnecessary empty workings.

Terminals may be owned either by the operator (if he is the sole user), one of the operators or jointly between various operators (if the use is shared), or by an independent authority. It is unusual (but not unknown) for sea and air carriers to provide their own terminals because the traffic of each individual operator is small in relation to the whole and costly equipment would not be fully utilised. It is only when the owner of the terminal is able to co-ordinate the demands of the various users that full use can be made of the elaborate facilities available and in these cases an authority independent of the providers of transport — in other words, an ancillary concern — is appropriate. Operators are thereby relieved of capital expenditure, maintenance and administration and they pay only to the extent of use. At the same time, in employing the services of another, they have less control over staff and of the movement of their vessels, etc., than they would if the terminal was a part of their own organisation. Whether or not full ownership can be justified is a question of economics and the extent of use.

So much for the generalisations. Whilst all terminals have a common purpose, there is much specialisation between the modes as the different characteristics call for particular requirements. These special needs will now be examined.

Road Transport

Bus Stations
The provision of a bus or coach station is not essential. Vehicles are able to set down and pick up passengers at the kerbside without the provision of any special facilities, although stop signs, perhaps with timetable displays, are often desirable with possibly barrier rails or queue shelters at busier points. Convenient places must, however, be found for vehicles to stand. In towns with a large number of terminating services it is sometimes difficult, in the absence of a bus station, to accommodate all such services in one place, in which case all routes cannot terminate at one point. This is inconvenient for supervision and passenger interchange, a feature which a central bus station does remedy.

Bus and coach stations provide a means of removing stationary vehicles from the highway where they are liable to cause obstruction. It is partly for this reason that local planning authorities are often keen to incorporate a bus station in new development plans. But if it is to be used by the public, a bus station must be conveniently sited for the town centre and main shopping area — in other words, where land is costly. There is a danger, therefore, that such a bus station might be expensive, particularly if additional mileage is incurred, bringing with it fuel cost and, if the extra running time could not be contained in the schedule, even extra vehicle and/or crew costs.

Goods terminals

Apart from garaging and maintenance purposes, a terminal is necessary for the transhipment of goods between local collection and delivery services and the main trunk haul. The need for convenient pedestrian access to a town centre as in the case of road passenger transport does not arise, but siting is nevertheless important. As with a bus station, there must be convenient vehicular access, but advantage can be taken of lower ground rentals outside the more heavily-congested central areas. The ideal location depends on individual circumstances largely revolving around the type of traffic carried and area served. Depots handling miscellaneous traffic could be conveniently located within an industrial area which would keep mileage run to and from local factories for collection and delivery purposes at a minimum. On the other hand, an undertaking which concentrates on traffic destined for a particular area could with advantage locate its depot on a directional basis. A haulier who caters for traffic say for example from London to South Wales might find that a depot placed on the western outskirts of Greater London would, by reducing the length of the main trunk haul, enable it to be worked on a single shift basis.

In addition to a loading bank and garage or parking facilities and maintenance area, the depot requires a general office together with staff facilities and possibly warehouse accommodation. There must also be an adequate circulating area.

The loading bank

The loading bank is a platform to which vehicles can reverse thereby affording convenient access. It is the focal point of the goods terminal and is the place where unloading, sorting and reloading is undertaken. It is, therefore, a necessary feature when goods are collected and delivered by different vehicles. The loading bank must have shelter from the weather, provide a sufficiently wide circulating area for sorting purposes and be adequately lit. The work of unloading and loading is assisted by a variety of aids according to the type of traffic handled and the degree of mechanisation at the particular depot, a selection of which follow:

Mobile handling aids

Simple two-wheeled and four-wheeled trucks; two-wheeled crowbars; fork-lift pallet trucks — hand operated or power controlled; tractors and trailers; gravity roller conveyors; power operated conveyor belts; mobile cranes; lifting platforms; etc.

Fixed and semi-fixed handling aids

Overhead pulley blocks and hoists; lifts; conveyor belts at floor level; spiral chutes; overhead travelling cranes; floor rollers, etc.

Railways

Passenger

The variation in size and activity of passenger stations is very marked. At one end of the scale is the bustle of the large main line terminus with its complicated track layouts and numerous train movements to and from a number of different platforms, whilst at the other is the small wayside station with perhaps only an island platform set between a double track or even an unstaffed halt on a single track. The larger railheads serve a dual function — operational and commercial. Their operational role consists of control of the movement of trains, i.e., receiving, marshalling and dispatching at the correct time. Their commercial role is to maintain liaison with the customer. Broadly speaking, the operational function is carried out on the track and the commercial function in the station buildings.

The tracks must enable train and shunting movements to be carried out with the minimum of crossing movements. The passenger buildings must incorporate essential services such as a booking office, parcels office, enquiry and seat reservation office, and suitable staff accommodation together with such amenities as a restaurant or buffet, bookstalls and shops for the sale of sweets, tobacco, etc, waiting rooms, cloakrooms, post and telegraph offices, etc, according to the size of the station. The approach to the station entrance should allow easy interchange with road transport — buses, taxis and private cars, together with an adequate car park.

Goods
Railway goods terminals are the medium for the reception of railborne traffic either for collection or for subsequent delivery by road, or inwards traffic destined for dispatch by rail. Such depots consist of a yard and a shed and warehouse. The yard is in effect a group of sidings usually laid out in pairs with a roadway between which is used for unloading and loading most station to station traffic — that is, consignments for which the rate paid does not include a collection or delivery service. Full wagon load collection and delivery traffic and other bulky loads regardless of classification are also usually dealt with in the yard. Consignments dispatched under the collection and delivery service are otherwise handled in the shed.

A railway goods shed may be either a through or dead-end type. In the first instance, sidings are carried right through the shed, whereas in the second alternative they usually terminate at right angles to the main distributing stage alongside which road vehicles can reverse on to the opposite side. Fixed stanchions in the loading areas are avoided when new terminals are constructed and mechanical appliances improve the means of transporting goods from wagon to road vehicle or vice versa. An example of this is the conveyor belt, where the centre of the main unloading platform consists of a continuously moving belt on to which goods from the wagons are unloaded. The belt conveys traffic to the cartage bench, where it is removed at the appropriate bay for loading on to road vehicles for conveyance to the ultimate destination.

Over recent years the trend has been to close the smaller goods terminals and to concentrate traffic into a fewer number of larger terminals serving a wider catchment area on a zonal basis. Although this increases the length of the road haul for individual consignments it has enabled substantial economies to be made in the cost of railway operation. As, however, is said in Chapter 6, the railway is by its nature a bulk carrier and current policy is to concentrate on complete train loads running to and from private sidings, suitably equipped to deal with specialised traffics. Much of the miscellaneous traffic is carried in containers on pre-scheduled liner trains which are packed and emptied at a point off the railway system. Special reference is made to container handling later in this chapter.

The Marshalling Yard

The conveyance of merchandise on a large railway system necessitates a network of sorting points. The goods shed is a sorting point for sundries traffic and the station platform for parcels, but for fully loaded wagons, en route, this need is met by the marshalling yard. It is not a terminal in the true sense of the word as it does not constitute a means of transfer between different modes of transport. It is, nevertheless, an essential part of railway operation and one which can most conveniently be contained within this review of terminals.

Unless traffic is sufficient to form a complete train load for direct conveyance between two points, a goods train must consist of wagons originating from and destined for a variety of places. Apart from a new concept which, if it ever reached fruition, would enable self-propelled, unmanned wagons to move individually, it is not economic to haul wagons in small numbers as self contained movements direct from starting point to destination. It is necessary therefore that the stock should be assembled into trains at strategically placed focal points on the railway system, a procedure which has been facilitated by the introduction of zonal goods terminals, as has already been mentioned.

Sorting at the marshalling yard is done by using appropriate switches to direct individual wagons to tracks according to their particular destinations. The modern marshalling yard consists of reception sidings converging on a focal point and fanning out to a large number of train formation and departure sidings. Incoming trains of wagons are brought into the reception sidings whence a locomotive pushes them towards the departure bays. On the way the wagons are separated (or "cut") individually or in small groups according to destination. In some yards the focal point includes a hump, which is an embankment or artificial hill. In this case, once over the hump the wagons run into their appropriate departure lines by gravitation. Operations are subject to direction from a hump room and a control tower, the former controlling the movement of the shunting locomotive and the work of the men who make the cuts. Once a cut has been pushed over the hump it is in the charge of the control tower staff who are responsible for setting the appropriate wagon paths and controlling the movement of the wagons.

Air Transport

Airports

The siting of an airport has already been mentioned. At this stage it must be accepted that the airport is unlikely to be placed in a position most suitable for passenger convenience but that it occupies an area which is flat, well-drained and easily accessible from the air (i.e. it is not in a steep valley and is not, as far as possible, surrounded by concentrated development). Operationally these latter requirements must be met (although there is still, nevertheless, an unfortunate tendency for airports to become hemmed in by other development even though situated outside congested areas) and commercially the site will be something of a compromise with the best possible direct service by surface transport to town. Provision must therefore be made not only for aircraft but for access by feeder

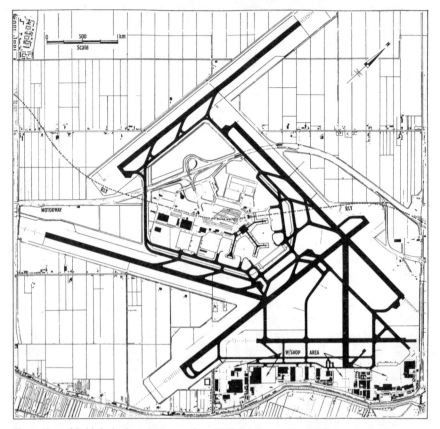

Fig 1. Plan of Schiphol Airport, Amsterdam, Holland. [*Reproduced by courtesy of Schiphol Airport Authority*

services, generally road, but sometimes rail as for example at Gatwick Airport.

Unlike land transport, it is the usual practice to provide maintenance facilities for aircraft at the terminals themselves, hence airport administration embraces three functions which between them produce the following essential services:

Engineering:	Maintenance facilities
	Hangarage facilities
	Provision for refuelling
Operating:	Air and Ground Traffic Control
Commercial:	Passenger reception
	Booking facilities
	Other passenger amenities.

The ancillary services are also important. As a high proportion of air traffic is international in character, customs facilities are necessary, fire-fighting, medical and security services must be available and it is usual at the larger airports for accommodation to be set aside for spectators.

A plan of Schiphol Airport, Amsterdam, appears at Figs 1 and 2. The four main runways, each 11,000ft long, can be seen in the smaller scale plan, while the layout of the airport's terminal area is illustrated at Fig 2. The more important of the various facilities which together form the make-up of an air terminal are numbered and should be studied. The traffic area of Schiphol Airport is established within the pentagon formed by the runways and taxitracks. This area contains a large size terminal building with a three-finger system and 34 Avio bridges for the embarkation and disembarkation of passengers, the control tower, a freight terminal, a freeport building, restaurants and a hotel, offices, shops, car parks, etc. The airport is situated some eight miles from Amsterdam, being linked with the capital by a six-lane state highway along which airport coaches complete the journey. A direct railway link between Amsterdam, Schiphol and The Hague is to be constructed, for which a tunnel under one of

 1 Terminal building
 2 Airport Authority building
 3 Air Traffic Control tower
 4 Crew centre
 5 Building of the Civil Aviation department
 6 Building of Martinair Holland
 7 Building of Transavia Holland (to be completed end 1970)
 8 Catering building, KLM
 9 Freight Terminal with office building
10 Public Bonded warehouse
11 Offices and workshops, oil companies
12 Freight building, Aero Groundservices Ltd
13 Workshops Avis and Hertz Rent-a-Car system
14 Police & Fire Fighting Services
15 Service station, Purfina
16 Aviodome (National Aeronautical Museum)
17 Central heating plant
18 Service stations, BP, Total
19 Road patrol post
20 Shipside (tax-free cars)
21 Bus terminal Maarse & Kroon
22 Technical services, Schiphol Airport Authority
23 National Highway No 4 (The Hague-Amsterdam)
24 Tunnel
A Main entrance
B Car park passengers, welcomers and escorts
C Car park personnel
D Car park airport visitors
E Railway, Amsterdam-The Hague-Rotterdam
F Traffic apron
G Freight apron

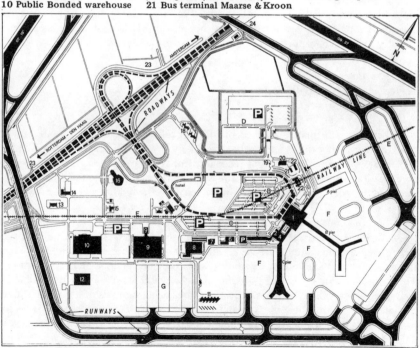

Fig 2. Plan of the traffic area at Schiphol Airport [*Reproduced by courtesy of Schiphol Airport Authority*]

the runways has already been built while another 300 feet tunnel and underground station in front of the terminal is now under construction. The terminal building itself will be more than doubled in size and a connecting fourth finger will be built for the jumbo jets. Construction started at the end of 1971 and will be completed by 1975.

The replacement of piston-engined aircraft by the heavier and faster jet airliners which gradually took place from about 1959/60 has produced particular problems for airports. The increased weight of the jets has brought with it the need for more heavily constructed runways. The larger dimensions of the aircraft and the blast from the engines require more spacious positions on the traffic apron and the very high fuel capacity of long-range jet aircraft calls for large fuel storage and high speed pumping facilities. As far as parking is concerned, nose-in parking has been introduced for bigger aircraft in order to save parking space. Aircraft refuelling at the new finger referred to above will be done by means of a hydrant system.

Such are the requirements of a modern airport and the cost of construction and maintenance is indeed heavy. Income is derived from landing and aircraft parking fees, rents for hangars and office accommodation and from concessions to firms providing facilities such as shops, restaurants, banks, etc. Landing fees vary according to the weight of the aircraft, the flight which it has made and the number of passengers on board. To give some idea of the amounts involved, a Boeing 707 arriving at Heathrow Airport with 140 passengers on an inter-continental service would pay a charge of £296.70. A further possible source of income is a passenger service charge, although this has been discontinued in this country at British Airports Authority and most other aerodromes.

Sea Transport

The Harbour

A seaport may be sub-divided into:

    (a)   the harbour, and

    (b)   the port.

A harbour is primarily a haven or place of refuge for shipping, situated on or near the coast. It can be natural but it is likely to be artificially improved. River estuaries, offshore islands, coral reefs and fjords for example can produce suitable natural conditions which, if the site is also satisfactory for the development of a port, are frequently improved by the addition of breakwaters, jetties, etc.

A harbour must give adequate protection against wind and waves, there must be sufficient space to permit manœuvring of ships, the water must be of a sufficient depth to accommodate vessels likely to require the use of the port but on the other hand it should not be so deep as to preclude anchorage in the harbour. There should be good holding ground and the water should as far as possible be free from strong tidal currents. These are the basic essentials of a good harbour. But the sea is constantly moving and even if suitable facilities are endowed by nature, they will not necessarily remain satisfactory for all time. The sea bed is liable to silting, particularly at river mouths, and constant dredging is necessary to preserve a satisfactory depth. This is one of the most important operations in keeping a port safe for ships. The term dredging means the removal of silt brought from inland and sand washed up by the tide so that a constant depth of water is maintained thereby assuring safe passages from the sea. Owing to the increasing size of modern vessels, dredging has become an onerous burden to all port authorities and it is necessary to keep special vessels equipped with machinery to dig out the channel bed. These may be bucket or grab dredgers or sand suckers according to the type of silt. The vessels can be either dumb or self-propelled and either discharge the spoil into other vessels or carry it away themselves to the open sea. In certain places it is pumped ashore to help reclaim marshy land. The work of the dredgers is often hindered by bad weather and rough seas and the cost of dredging is in most cases the heaviest single item of expenditure for port authorities.

It is incumbent upon the port authority to ensure as far as is possible that a ship is able to navigate the harbour approaches and through into the port itself in safety. The approach channels must therefore be kept free from obstruction. and navigational aids in the form of buoys, lighting, etc, are provided and maintained. Visual signals between ship and shore are now supplemented by vhf radio telephony thereby permitting speech communication which together with radar equipment gives the authority a complete picture of the movement of vessels. However, notwithstanding the provision of such aids to navigation, movement through very restricted channels calls for local specialised knowledge which the master of a ship may not have. A pilot must therefore guide the vessel through these waters and the harbour authority must ensure the availability of an adequate pilot service. Within the dock area it is seldom practicable for large vessels to proceed under their own power, in which case towage facilities must also be available. In Great Britain this service is often performed by privately-owned tugs.

The Port
Docks and quays
Docks or quays are constructed to meet the commercial requirements of shipping. Open berths are generally regarded as quays whilst those enclosed and approached through a lock are known as docks, although this interpretation is not rigid as witness Southampton Docks which are mostly open quays. But whatever their nomenclature — open or closed — docks and quays are man-made improvements to river estuaries or other havens. The harbour itself is usually unenclosed and hence tidal and it follows that the unloading and loading facilities at open quays and jetties, unless they are in a specially protected area, are also subject to tidal conditions. Because docks are normally enclosed and approached from the sea or river through a lock, the water inside the dock area is maintained at a constant level and it is sometimes necessary to pump water back into the dock basin to compensate for loss when ships enter or leave.

Siting
A port is the medium through which passengers and goods transfer between sea and land. Quite logically therefore, not only must the port have a good harbour and approaches for shipping, there must also be adequate land access by road and rail and perhaps also by inland waterway. Furthermore, every port, if it is to prosper, must have a good hinterland, which is the area on which it relies for its

traffic, both imports and exports. The depth of the hinterland is largely determined by the inland transport facilities which radiate from the port and the proximity of a neighbouring port. It is interesting to recall that for reasons of safety, and this means safety not only from storms but also from pirates, some ports were originally located a considerable distance up a river, Because of the increase in size of ocean-going ships serious physical difficulties subsequently arose and some of these inland ports cannot be adapted to deal with the larger boats. Their importance must therefore decline, but in some cases it has been possible to develop subsidiary ports nearer to the sea as for example Bremerhaven, Le Havre and Tilbury, which are more recent offshoots of Bremen, Rouen and London respectively.

Port requirements

A seagoing ship can carry cargo equivalent to the capacity of many railway wagons, road haulage vehicles or canal boats. Consequently one problem of a port authority is to ensure an easy flow of transport to and from the ship's berth. It frequently happens that each of the inland transport systems will be involved in the loading or discharge of the same ship and easy access must accordingly be arranged for road and rail vehicles from the landward side of the vessel and for barges on the offshore side. This calls for good initial planning and organisation by the various bodies concerned with the movement of cargo such as the shipowner's representatives and stevedores who attend to the unloading and loading. A ship is designed for movement of cargo and passengers on the sea, therefore time spent in dock is a loss to the owner. A quick turn-round is the hallmark of a well-run port. What then are the fundamental requirements of a modern seaport? A ship needs a safe berth in which to unload and reload, it needs a good approach with an adequate depth of water, navigational aids, and pilotage and towage facilities. But what of the port itself? If a ship is to have a quick turn-round there must firstly be an adequate labour force supplemented by mechanical aids, which are discussed below, but because of the large capacity of the ship, adequate storage space is also necessary. In addition, a number of ancillary services must be provided if the port is to function satisfactorily. Particular attention must be given to these features.

Storage space

To facilitate the movement of cargo and to reduce congestion on inland transport, storage accommodation of both the open and covered variety is provided according to the type of trade. In a big general port, single and double-storey transit sheds are available at each berth. Apart from goods which are held to facilitate inland movement, some merchants prefer to store their goods at the port, selling by sample. Where there is a demand for this service, multi-storeyed warehouses are provided and specialist labour trained to deal with valuable commodities. To reduce congestion, such warehouses are normally constructed away from the immediate vicinity of the berths. In many ports, bonded warehouses are also provided for the safe keeping of imported goods awaiting customs clearance or re-export. In some instances a "cage" is constructed inside a transit shed to serve a similar purpose, usually for exports awaiting shipment. Cages would not, however, be used for long-term storage.

Mechanical aids

With the complexity of modern ports and the increasing cost of manual labour, mechanical aids have been developed. The main purpose of all such appliances is to speed the turn-round of ships thereby reducing cargo-handling costs. Many millions of pounds have been spent on floating, quayside and mobile cranes, mechanical and magnetic grabs, pneumatic plant for handling grain, etc, conveyor belts, pumping equipment for bulk liquids and a host of smaller dockside equipment such as fork-lift trucks, portable stackers, mobile conveyor belts, shunting tractors and a variety of electric and petrol driven runabout trucks with or without trailers. Care must be taken to use this equipment to maximum advantage but its unloading capacity must be related to the shore reception facilities. Clearly cargo must not be discharged at a rate faster than it can be cleared into land vehicles or transit sheds and mechanisation does therefore influence the layout of the dock area. The width of quays, availability of roads, types of transit sheds and number of lines of railway track must be considered in relation to the speed of unloading and loading. However, owing to the great variety of general cargo it is difficult or impossible to adopt any form of standardisation, which means that in planning for such mixed classes of traffic there must be a compromise. In the process of unloading, therefore, available facilities are used to the greatest effect according to the nature of the merchandise being handled.

Most modern ports have developed gradually over a large number of years. Sea transport was one of the earliest means of communication and some ports have been in existence for centuries. With the passing of time, methods of working have grown up and come to be regarded as the "custom and practice" of the port. Such methods have been developed to meet local circumstances and have sometimes continued long after the original need has disappeared. Consequently, an operation may be performed in one way at a certain port whilst at others the system might be totally different. Because of these local customs in an industry which does not in any case lend itself to standardisation, comparison between the work performed at different ports is difficult. Even when operations are similarly named, differences may in fact exist.

Ancillary Services

Ship Repairs

Shipowners are required to put passenger vessels into dry dock approximately once per year and cargo vessels somewhat less for survey and inspection. Furthermore there is a periodic need for overhaul work and for major and minor running repairs arising either from the effects of heavy weather conditions or through normal wear. The demand for suitable facilities is therefore both regular and sporadic and it is important that there be specialised firms available to carry out such work at short notice. For the port authorities however this does present a problem of space. Shipping lines like to have their vessels overhauled during a short off season which in itself introduces a peak problem. But the dry dock is normally required only for a short period of the total time spent on overhaul which means that the owners seek a wet berth in which to complete the maintenance work. We have already seen that wet berths are generally equipped with cargo handling facilities and these are unemployed if the berth is occupied by a ship undergoing refit. At the same time, other boats waiting to discharge and reload could become subject to delay. Nevertheless, notwithstanding this problem, the organisation is such that it is seldom necessary for a shipping company to send ships away from their base port for maintenance purposes.

Bunkering

To the uninitiated, bunkering is the mariners' term for refuelling. At one time, most ships were coal burning when it was necessary for them to move to special coal tips to take on fuel. The prime mover is now oil and today bunkering is invariably taken care of by the major oil companies. To meet the ever growing demand for bunker oils, a chain of bunkering installations has grown up at ports throughout the world and there are now few ports of any consequence where at least one company has not oil bunkering facilities to offer shipowners. Ships may be bunkered either through pipelines or from barges and in many cases delivery can be made by pipeline while the ship is unloading or loading cargo.

Victualling

To victual a ship is to supply it with food and drink necessary for passengers and crew during the forthcoming voyage. Fresh water tanks must be cleaned and replenished and large quantities of foodstuffs supplied together with many other items required by ships in large quantities such as fresh linen, paint, etc. These needs are likely to be met by private contractors, but the port authority must ensure that facilities are available.

HM Customs

The effects of import tariffs, etc, on retail prices are well known and smuggling can be attractive while it lasts. But, lucrative as it may be to the individual, to the national economy it is damaging and cannot be tolerated. It is therefore the responsibility of HM Customs' officers to prevent the illegal entry of goods into the country. In the course of their duty, officers of the uniformed preventative section are empowered to search ships and the baggage of passengers and crews for contraband and to collect such tax or duty as may be chargeable on the articles declared. The ship's documents are also examined and spaces containing dutiable stores such as spirits, etc, sealed. Other officers regularly have opened and checked a percentage of all cargoes to ensure that goods comply with entry documents and that duty is paid where necessary.

It is a statutory requirement that suitable and adequate facilities be provided at ports for HM Customs.

Security

There are several aspects of security of direct or indirect concern to the port authority. Entry into the country of foreign nationals is subject to control and HM Immigration officials must be in attendance to examine the documents of all immigrant passengers. Facilities for the general examination of passports must also be provided. CID officials may well require to board vessels for the purpose of examining passenger lists for undesirable persons and also to investigate any crime which may have been committed on board during the voyage. But the security aspect with which a port authority has a more direct interest is the protection of property within the dock area itself. The value of goods in transit, either in warehouses, in open store, or on the ships, will probably amount to many thousands of pounds at any one time. Unauthorised entry on to the boats or even into the dock area must be prevented. There must be a check on all goods leaving the confines of the port and the premises made subject to frequent patrol. Policing of the docks is therefore essential and this service is provided either by a private force of the port authority or by the local watch committee.

Medical

Just as we must guard against smuggling and the illegal entry of undesirable people, so precautions must be taken to avoid the carriage of disease into the country by infected people, animals or merchandise. The port medical officer must satisfy himself in this respect before disembarkation is permitted.

Passenger facilities

Special facilities must be provided for passengers if their numbers are sufficiently large. Usually the accommodation consists of fixed or floating quays at which the largest liners can berth at any state of the tide, with special halls laid out for sorting and examination of baggage, checking of passports, etc. There should be covered access to boat trains, which calls for close co-operation between the port authority, the shipping companies and inland transport undertakings, and car parks are desirable. The usual services such as postal, banking and refreshment facilities must also be provided in passenger terminals. In addition space must be afforded to the motoring organisations which play no small part in vehicle documentation. This need is particularly apparent at the cross-channel ports.

Roll-on, Roll-off Terminals

The roll-on, roll-off ferry boat as is described in Chapter 4 calls for a specialised terminal as provision must be made for vehicles to drive from shore to ship and vice versa. It is essential that the connecting pontoons have a vertical play as the levels of the vessels will vary according to the state of the tide. This does mean that in waters where the difference in levels at high and low tide is considerable, the approach (or exit) will, on occasions, be relatively steep. However, as was mentioned in Chapter 2, rubber tyred vehicles are able to accept inclines of moderate severity. This is not so with rail-borne vehicles and when the roll-on, roll-off principle is used for railway trains, variable inclines must be avoided for this reason as well as to avoid the possibility of derailments. To achieve a constant level, therefore, terminals for railway ferries may have to be constructed in enclosed waters and approached through a lock.

Another feature insofar as roll-on, roll-off ferry terminals are concerned, and this applies particularly to the road ferries which are used by large numbers of miscellaneous cars and commercials is that vehicles must be properly assembled prior to embarkation. A large circulating area is, therefore, necessary for this purpose.

The Port of Goole

The foregoing gives a brief review of the salient features and requirements of a modern seaport. It is a useful exercise to examine the facilities available at a typical port to see how the principles outlined are developed in practice. For this reason, there follows a short account of a small but flourishing British port, the Port of Goole, selected not because of any outstanding features but (a) because it is not complicated by size and (b) because it provides a link between the sea and three different forms of inland transport. Its relative simplicity is advantageous to the student who at this stage need master only the fundamental principles of port operation.

The Port of Goole stands on the River Ouse near the confluence of the Rivers Trent and Ouse at the head of the Humber and offers geographical, commercial and economic advantages because of its close proximity to the highly industrialised areas of the North Midlands and the Yorkshire Coalfields. Hence the requirement of a good hinterland as indicated on page 49 is met.

The port can accommodate vessels of up to approximately 2,500 tons capacity with a draught of 17ft 6in at high water spring tides. There are three entrance locks, the largest being 368ft long by 80ft wide, and vessels can arrive and depart through the locks during a period of three hours before and up to high water. For the convenience of vessels using the port, berths are provided at Blacktoft Jetty midway between the docks and the Humber estuary for vessels unable to complete the Goole-sea journey, or vice-versa, on the tide.

Nine wet docks are all interconnected and are maintained at a constant depth whilst three miles of commercial quayage affords adequate berthing facilities. A port specially adapted to afford speedy and economic service to vessels engaged in coastwise and short-sea trades, Goole is provided with efficient appliances and equipment together with warehouse and transit shed accommodation designed to effect rapid handling of all classes of cargo. It has good communication with the large industrial hinterland extending over the whole of West and South Yorkshire, East Lancashire and the North Midlands. Road and rail services are supplemented by an extensive canal system operated by the British Waterways Board and by the navigational stretches of the Rivers Trent and Yorkshire Ouse. Thus it is a common feature of activity to observe vessels discharging simultaneously to rail, road and water transport as well as to shed and quay.

Goole has long been established as an important terminal port for general cargo liner services to and from the Continent and weekly and twice-weekly services are operated to numerous European ports.

Imports include bacon, butter, lager beer, cheese, farina, glucose products and confectionery, chemicals and chemical fertilisers, crude tar, sulphur, iron and other ores, iron and steel goods, sand for glassmaking and moulding, plate glass and earthenware, furniture, machinery, timber and wool. As far as exports are concerned, up to 800,000 tons of coal-class traffic passes each year, but this does not nevertheless represent the whole of the port's export trade. Iron and steel manufactures, machinery, agricultural implements, motor vehicles, electrical appliances of all kinds, textiles, bricks and building materials, potatoes, electrode pitch, refined tar and creosote, barley and many other commodities are regularly handled both on liner services carrying general cargo and charter vessels taking complete cargoes of a particular commodity.

The shipment of coal both foreign and coastwise is worthy of special mention. The Yorkshire and East Midlands coalfields have their outlet to the sea through the Humber, and Goole is the nearest and most convenient port. Both rail and canal-borne cargoes are dealt with, the latter method being unique to Goole and involving the use of the 40-ton capacity compartment boats which are towed from the collieries in trains of nineteen, each compartment being subsequently lifted bodily from the water by 52-ton boat hoists and the contents tipped direct into vessels. Appliances for the shipment of rail-borne traffic comprise two conventional wagon hoists tipping direct into vessels through a chute and two cranes, one 50-ton and one 40-ton, which lift the coal wagons over the ship's hold where the end door of the wagon is released and the coal tipped direct into the hold. The two coaling cranes are also used extensively for heavy lifts to and from ships so that lifts of up to 50 tons have come to be a normal everyday feature of the general cargo trade.

It is not without interest to comment on the character of the trade of the Port of Goole. Apart from the general cargo liners which cover France, Belgium, Holland, Germany, Spain, Sweden, Norway and Denmark, there is in addition a considerable trade by charter vessels to and from these countries as well as to Scandinavia and the Baltic. There is a considerable timber trade from Baltic and Russian White Sea ports which in itself accounted for some 130 inward cargoes in 1967. Regular shipments arrive at Goole direct from such widespread sources as Baltimore, USA, and Casablanca on the North African Atlantic seaboard and there is a certain amount of two way trade with Mediterranean ports in Italy, Greece and other Mediterranean countries. Due to the cargo liner connections a considerable volume of transhipment traffic to or from world sources is exchanged at Continental ports, including Australian and New Zealand wool, Far East textiles, United States steel and other products and occasional shipments to and from India. Groupage services enable traffic to be carried at competitive rates to or from central European areas. It is of some significance that coastwise coal shipments have decreased sharply over recent years, due partly to the use of natural gas, and a berth that was once used for coaling has now been converted to a container berth with a 32-ton scotch derrick. Furthermore, the import of Renault cars through Goole has now commenced. This trade is served by car carrying vessels (roll-on roll-off), the cars being driven ashore direct ex ship. Up to some 40,000 Renault cars are imported annually in this way.

A study of the plan at Fig 3 should complete the picture and give the reader a basic grasp of the general layout of a port.

Container Ports

Reference to container ports has been put deliberately at the end of this chapter on terminals as the container is not linked to any one form of transport. Remember, it is the container, not the vehicle, that follows the required path according to the destination of its contents. A journey may well, therefore, take it by road, by rail and by sea. Furthermore, although the goods that are being carried are likely to be of assorted shapes and sizes, the container itself is a standardised unit and the vehicles and vessels that carry them are suitably constructed for the purpose as will be seen in Chapter 4.

In view of this standardisation of the unit being carried, it follows that the requirements of a container terminal, which provides for their transhipment between one form of transport and another, are specialised but relatively simple.

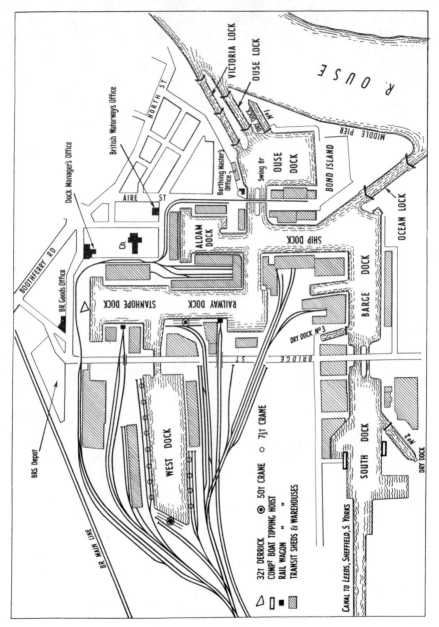

Fig 3. Plan of Goole Docks. [*British Transport Docks Board*]

Briefly, all that is required to effect the transfer is provision for the physical approach of the different modes, a large circulating and standing or stacking area and suitable equipment in the form of purpose built overhead cranes. An illustration appears at Plate No. 20.

A unique feature of the container terminal is the requirements for siting. As the container itself represents a "door-to-door" facility, the beginning and end of its journey is likely to be on the road. Although in the course of that journey it may well travel by other modes, that is of no particular interest to the customer and the siting of container terminals is, therefore, primarily a matter of operational and physical convenience in relation to major traffic flows without the same regard for the needs of the individual consignor as must be the case with other terminals. A conventional seaport, for example, requires a good hinterland and a railhead must be suitably placed commercially for approach by individual road hauliers.

Another feature of the container is that for international traffic, it could be convenient for Customs clearance to be effected at inland "container ports", after which they may be sealed and dispatched to their destinations overseas regardless of the various modes that they may encounter en route. Such an arrangement is not, however, exclusive to the container. It can also be adapted for traffic carried by T.I.R. vehicles (see Chapter 9) which use the roll-on, roll-off ferry services.

4 · The Carrying Unit

Introduction

The word "vehicle" is often loosely applied to represent the carrying unit whether it be by road, rail, sea or air. However, the dictionary states categorically that a vehicle is a carriage, cart or other *land* conveyance. If this interpretation is to be respected it is better to avoid the use of the word "vehicle" in connection with water or air transport, for which "vessel" and "aircraft" are in any case very suitable. Even then, railway vehicles are more commonly and quite correctly referred to as "rolling stock". The degree of flexibility of these different types of carrying units depends on both the type of way used and whether the unit has a specialised application. Considering first the way, aircraft, vessels and road vehicles are very flexible because apart from terminal or other space restrictions, the movement of one has no physical effect upon the movement of another. In contrast, railway trains and trams are tied to a fixed track. One cannot overtake another without the provision of special facilities and the movement of any one is dependent on the movement of the one preceding. In the event of a failure or the obstruction of the way, delay is inevitable. Secondly, some vehicles are more flexible than others inasmuch as they can be easily adapted to carry many types of traffic, whereas others have a specialised application which makes them inflexible. For example, vehicles constructed for particular purposes such as a milk tanker cannot be used for the conveyance of any other commodity and a railway sleeping car has not the same general use as has an ordinary second class passenger coach. A third consideration of flexibility is whether units can be easily diverted or switched from one area or route to another. This will depend on various physical factors, but the unit with maximum flexibility, i.e. the one that can be used anywhere, has a number of operating and economic advantages. The propelling power can be either incorporated within the carrying unit itself as in the case of a motor car or an aeroplane, or contained in a separate tractive unit as for example a railway locomotive or a river tug. Separate tractive units are designed to haul trains of non-powered carrying units in the form of railway wagons or passenger carriages, barges, or road trailers.

Because of the great contrasts in the characteristics of the various types of way, there must be similar marked differences in the fundamental designs of the carrying units, all of which are purpose built for use on their particular forms of specialised way. Again, therefore, each mode of transport must be considered separately.

Road Transport

Passenger

Public passenger services by road are provided by buses and coaches. The distinction between the two is arbitrary. Buses are generally regarded as catering for relatively short distance traffic and working on routes on which a large number of intermediate stops are observed, while coaches cater more for longer distance passengers on a limited stop basis or for private tours. For this reason, coaches are generally a more luxurious type of vehicle.

In the United Kingdom and also in certain territories overseas, particularly in areas which have been subject to British influence, the double-deck bus as pictured at Plate 1 is widely used. This is largely because of the availability of sufficient headroom as was explained in Chapter 2. The difference in operating costs between the double-decker and the larger types of single-decker is not great and the additional seating capacity afforded by the double-decker (the Daimler Fleetline pictured at Plate 1 seats 76) as opposed to standing space in a single deck "standee" type vehicle is attractive. The trend in vehicle design over the years has been to build larger units and statutory regulations which limit maximum overall dimensions of buses and coaches in the British Isles have been gradually relaxed. Even so, the limitations still do not necessarily apply overseas, hence the large Continental single-deck articulated units such as the vehicle pictured in the form of a trolleybus at Plate 5. At the other end of the scale, minibuses with bodies of the type pictured at Plate 2 and which can seat up to about 12 people are sometimes used in rural areas where the maximum load is never very great. The original transverse toastrack type seating as pictured at Plate 3 permitted absolute maximum seating capacity. The absence of a central gangway necessitated an entrance-exit at the end of each row of seats and was adopted by the old type charabancs in the early motor coaching period. The design was not suitable for local stage carriage work and longitudinal type seating with passengers facing inwards on to a wide gangway was used. Seating capacity was less than the toastrack layout, but there was room for standing passengers. Actual capacity was therefore greater. The standee type bus has perpetuated this design and is used on some short routes at home but more often abroad where the need for maximum capacity often has priority over personal comfort.

Goods

The road haulier has a variety of vehicles from which to choose, both in size and design, according to the type of traffic with which he deals. Basically there are two groups — rigid and articulated. Either type may be fitted with a variety of bodies for general or specialised traffic. The advantage of the articulated vehicle (in this sense a vehicle where the motive unit is separate and easily detachable from the body which is in the form of a semi-trailer), is that the driving unit (which is the most expensive part) can be put to more productive use. Only the semi-trailer need be left at the loading bank while the forward portion is available for use elsewhere (with another semi-trailer). Another advantage of the articulated vehicle is its small turning circle. This greater manoeuvrability is useful in narrow streets and in circulating areas of haulage terminals. Observe the fundamental difference in the design of the vehicle hitherto described and the articulated trolleybus pictured at Plate 5. In the latter the power unit remains an integral part of the forward portion of the main body. The former type could be and occasionally is adapted for passenger work but the same need does not arise as passenger vehicles are not held for extended periods for the purpose of loading and unloading.

The variety of bodies available for road haulage may be classified as follows:

Covered vans ranging from the small all-purpose vehicle, through the various sizes used for general parcels traffic up to the large pantechnicon for household removal, etc.

Open trucks for merchandise not subject to damage through exposure.

Platform vehicles (i.e. as open trucks but without sides) suitable for stacking boxes, crates, etc, possibly under a tarpaulin, or for the conveyance of containers.

Low loaders to facilitate loading and unloading of heavy and bulky consignments. Vehicles of this type can be constructed to take exceptional loads of anything up to 240 tons. Many low loaders have ancillary equipment such as winches, hydraulic hoists and ramps.

Tippers for the carriage and rapid discharge of sand, gravel, etc.

Two-tier car transporters capable of conveying six or more light vehicles.

Vehicles for the carriage of livestock.

Refrigerated vehicles for the conveyance of perishable foodstuffs, ice cream deliveries, etc.

Vehicles adapted for use as travelling shops, fish and chip bars, X-ray units, mobile dispensaries, etc.

Specialised vehicles used for public services such as fire engines, ambulances, street cleansing vehicles, tower wagons for the maintenance of street lighting, vehicles for refuse collection, etc.

Special vehicles for carrying long lengths such as steel girders, tree trunks, etc.

Hopper vehicles for the carriage of grain in bulk.

Tankers with capacities of up to about 6,000 gallons, or even more, suitable for the conveyance of practically every type of liquid or powder. Liquefied low-pressure gases can also be carried.

The very diverse types of traffic encountered in the haulage industry and the range of vehicles contrast with the comparatively standardised passenger units. This, of course, is the case in all forms of transport and the parallel of many of the specialised types of road vehicles mentioned above can also be found amongst the rolling stock of railway undertakings.

Railways

Passenger

Passenger rolling stock design is influenced by the conflicting requirements of capacity and comfort. Broadly speaking, traffic may be divided into three groups — long distance, local suburban and the very short distance "in-town" movement.

These three types of traffic call for three basic designs for passenger coaches.

(i) Long-distance trains.

Apart from a comfortable seat, access is required to toilets and when provided, to restaurant or buffet cars. Long-distance stock therefore has a corridor (at the expense of seating capacity) either through the centre or along one side of the coach. A flexible connection is generally available for communication between each coach of the train. As there is little or no intermediate boarding or alighting, doors can be confined to the vestibules at the ends of each coach. An outside door opening directly into a passenger compartment introduces an element of discomfort and inconvenience to seated passengers, particularly in inclement weather. There are two basic types of long-distance coaching stock, the centre gangway open type vehicle and the side corridor with separate compartments leading off. But there are countless variations in detail, determined by local requirements. Routes possessing high scenic value might justify provision of special observation cars and the climate often calls for heating or air-conditioning equipment. For exceptionally long journeys it might be convenient to install daytime seating capable of quick conversion into two-tier berths (sleeping cars as such are not suitable for both day and night use) and dining facilities must be considered. Although for reasons of economy space must not be wasted, on long distance trains emphasis must be on comfort rather than capacity if traffic is to be attracted and retained.

(ii) Suburban and other stopping trains.

The design of rolling stock suitable for use on suburban and other stopping trains must allow for the different pattern of traffic from that carried on long distance main line trunk routes. Suburban services are likely to meet heavy bursts of works and business traffic in the peaks. Time is the vital factor in the passenger's mind and punctual arrival at destination is bound to take precedence over a comfortable ride. Nevertheless, individual journeys are likely to be of sufficient length to justify demands for at least a secondary standard of seating. A heavy intermediate traffic means a continual process of boarding and alighting. Rolling stock used for traffic of this nature must therefore have (a) maximum seating capacity even at the expense of individual comfort and (b) maximum number of points at which passengers may board and alight.

Reference has been made to the "toastrack" vehicle typified by the old charabanc and which does, in effect, produce the maximum number of seats and entrances within the floor space available. The separate compartments of the older British style suburban railway coach are an advancement of the toastrack. There is no space allotted to a corridor and a door for each compartment speeds boarding and alighting of large numbers of people who could not all funnel through the end doors of a main line corridor coach in the limited time available at intermediate stations. Although the compartment type stock offers maximum seating accommodation, it may, even so, become inadequate in high density traffic areas and the design is not ideal for standing passengers. A popular and more recent alternative is again the open car with a centre gangway (but perhaps with a lesser number of wider sliding doors) which, at the expense of seats, allows better standing accommodation.

Of interest but so far, rather limited application is the double-deck train. This type of railway coach can be found, for example, on the Chinese Railways and on certain commuter lines in the United States of America, where both countries have a liberal loading gauge. A picture appears at Plate 24. Double-deck trains are also running or are being developed on other railways including the French SNCF where physical conditions permit.

(iii) Short-distance "in-town" trains.

Finally there is the train built to cater for the very short distance traffic such as is experienced on the Underground lines of London Transport. Here, emphasis must be on wide entrances and exits again with sliding doors and ample accommodation for standing passengers. Seating has now become a rather secondary consideration as was the case with the standee bus described in the previous chapter.

Goods

Goods wagons are required to move a very wide range of products and materials. Those used for general purposes are basically covered box wagons or open trucks, but certain traffic calls for specialised stock. We thus find an assortment of tankers, hoppers, refrigerated and specially ventilated wagons, horse boxes and other vehicles suitable for the carriage of livestock, flats for the conveyance of containers, etc, and a host of other types according to local commercial practices and hence the traffic likely to be moved. Another consideration is the flat car used for the carriage of road trailers. This principle, known as the "piggy-back" train, is really the railway counterpart of the "roll-on, roll-off" ferry described later in this chapter whereby the same vehicle (or trailer) passes from one medium to another, thus eliminating the need for unloading and re-loading.

In contrast to Continental practice, the bulk of the goods wagon fleet of British Railways was at one time equipped only with hand-operated brakes. The trains were loose coupled and power to stop was dependent on the brakes of the engine and guard's van. Much of British Railways goods stock has now been fitted with continuous brakes as are all passenger trains, the advantages and disadvantages of which are as under:

(a)   The very limited braking power of an unfitted train necessitates for safety reasons a speed restriction. As the movements of these trains conflict with faster passenger trains they must at times be shunted on to refuge sidings to avoid obstructing the line. Fitted trains can travel at speeds more comparable with passenger trains which, in addition to giving a more attractive service, eliminate the need for this shunting movement and at the same time permit more economical track occupation and scheduling.

(b)   Loose-coupled trains cannot produce the smooth stopping movement customary with fitted trains. Each successive wagon is inevitably brought to a halt in a jerky and noisy "snatch" as the buffers make contact with those of the surrounding vehicles. The smooth running quality of fitted trains reduces breakages which again gives a more attractive service.

(c)   Fitted wagons may be attached to passenger trains.

(d)   The fitment of wagons involves additional capital cost and maintenance. Although this may well be justified, the cost factor must not be overlooked.

(e)   The marshalling of goods wagons calls for easy coupling and uncoupling. Automatic couplings have been developed but this could nevertheless be a marginal advantage of the unfitted train.

The Tractive Unit

After having considered the different types of rolling stock, it must be noted that whilst goods trains are hauled by a spearate tractive unit in the form of a locomotive, passenger trains may, as an alternative, have their motive power incorporated within the train itself. In other words, they may be propelled by powered axles fitted sporadically throughout their length. The coaches, some of which therefore have motored bogies whilst some may be non-powered trailers are, in this instance, coupled together to form what is known as a multiple-unit train. Each power unit is linked by control cables and the entire train, which may be diesel or electric, is controlled by a single driver. The principle operating features of this type of train compared with separate locomotives are as under:

(a) As a number of axles have motors, it is possible to produce great power without the concentrated heavy weight of a locomotive. Very rapid acceleration is therefore possible.

(b) Multiple-unit trains have a constant power-weight ratio irrespective of the length of the train. Speeds, and hence punctuality, are not therefore affected by strengthening at peak periods.

(c) Multiple-unit trains may be driven from either end — a distinct advantage at a terminus when the need for a locomotive to run round the train does not arise. This advantage can, however, also be met with separate tractive units if used on the push and pull principle.

(d) Being propelled from a number of different points, the multiple-unit train tends to produce a swaying side to side movement compared with the steady haul of a locomotive.

(e) Multiple-unit trains require specially equipped coaches, either powered, or, if non-powered trailers, fitted with control cables. Unfitted stock is not therefore suitable for mixing with multiple-unit stock. For through services over electrified and non-electrified lines therefore, it is necessary to sue separate locomotives which are exchanged at the point of transfer between the different systems.

(f) The multiple-unit principle is not suitable for application to goods trains which are not kept permanently coupled into standard units. Conventional freight rolling stock is non-powered and the various wagons must be quite independent for frequent coupling and uncoupling. Separate locomotives must therefore be available for goods trains which, if not fully employed, could also be used for passenger work. Multiple-unit trains preclude this possibility.

(g) The composition of locomotive-hauled trains can be adjusted at short notice to meet traffic demands and individual goods wagons may be attached even to passenger trains. This is not usually so in the case of the multiple-unit train which is lengthened only by the addition of other suitably equipped sets of coaches.

It will be seen that the multiple-unit has both advantages and disadvantages and both systems are widely adopted according to the local requirements of the line.

Air

It is neither possible within the limited space available nor necessary within the terms of this book to describe each of the many different types of aircraft.

However, to give the reader some idea of the principal features of typical designs, brief details of selected types currently in use by either BOAC or BEA together with the supersonic *Concorde* follow:

The VC10 is manufactured by the British Aircraft Corporation Limited. It is 158ft 7in long with a wing span of 146ft 2in and is powered by four Rolls-Royce Conway R.Co.42 by-pass jet engines. Each engine has a take-off thrust rating of 20,370lb. The engines are mounted aft of the passenger cabin, leaving a clean wing and thus improving the aircraft's airfield performance. A second advantage of this engine arrangement is that all passengers sit forward of the engines and thus enjoy the advantage of the considerable reduction in the level of engine noise in the passenger cabin. The VC10 carries up to 126 passengers and has a speed of up to 600 mph. Fully laden, the aircraft weighs more than 314,000lb and its four engines together produce approximately 30,000 horsepower. There is also a Super VC10 with a length of 171ft 8in which together with higher powered engines can carry up to 157 passengers.

The Boeing 747 known colloquially as the jumbo jet is manufactured by the Boeing Company of Seattle, U.S.A. It is 231ft 10in long with a wing span of 195ft 8in and an all-up weight of 355 tons. Accommodation is provided for an average of 380 people but seating for up to 490 is possible. The four pod-mounted Pratt and Whitney JT9D—3A engines develop a total of some 174,000lb thrust at take-off. Thrust reversers are provided for both the engine tail-pipe and the fan exit of each engine. External noise suppression is provided by the cowling which incorporates acoustic lining. Cruising speeds range from about 550 mph to more than 600 mph at a cruising altitude of 29,000/45,000ft. The fuel capacity is more than 39,000 Imperial gallons.

The Trident series is manufactured by Hawker Siddeley Aviation Limited. The latest variant, the Trident 3B, is the high capacity shorthaul version. It is 131ft 2in long with a wing span of 98ft and is powered by three Rolls-Royce Spey 25-512 by-pass jet engines which are rear mounted, one on either side of the fuselage and one directly above, but all to the rear of the passenger compartments. The average cruising speed of the shorter variants of the family is 606 mph at an altitude of 30,000ft and they seat 80—139 passengers. The 3B seats up to 160 passengers. The Trident was the first civil aircraft to be designed and built from the start to carry the equipment necessary for fully automatic blind approaches and landings. In May, 1972 the British C.A.A. (see Chapter 8) gave approval for B.E.A. Trident operations in I.C.A.O. (see Chapter 9) Category 3A conditions.

The Sikorsky S.61N helicopter is a product of the American Sikorsky Company. As its name suggests, it is a member of the rotary-wing family of aircraft, the term "helicopter" being derived from the Greek words "helix" (spiral) and "pteron" (wing). The S.61N is one of the larger helicopters with seats for up to 28 people. It has twin GE T58 turbine engines giving a speed of some 140 mph. The vertical take-off and landing properties of the helicopter make it extremely versatile and this particular model is fully amphibious, which makes it very suitable for over-water operations. In addition to use on its scheduled service between Penzance and the Isles of Scilly, B.E.A. employs the S.61N on charter work, notably but not exclusively in serving the North Sea oil rigs.

The Concorde

On the threshold of becoming the first form of supersonic (faster than the speed of sound) transport to enter public service and is currently on order by BOAC and other airlines. It is a joint product of the British Aircraft Corporation of Great Britain and Aerospatiale of France. Concorde is a delta-winged aircraft and is basically of aluminium alloy construction; it cruises at Mach 2 (i.e. twice the speed of sound or about 1,350 mph) and is powered by four Rolls-Royce/ SNECMA Olympus 593 turbojets mounted in paired nacelles beneath the wing. Seating is available for up to 128 passengers depending upon the standard of accommodation required.

Concorde's entry into airline service will undoubtedly inaugurate a decisive stage in the development of air transport. Its great asset is, of course, speed, so much so that no two points on the surface of the earth will be more than about twelve hours apart. When used on appropriate services, its higher operating costs will be, to a great extent, offset by its high seat-mile productivity and as subsonic flight times for long distances could be cut by about half, the aircraft could command a higher fare. The manufacturers predict that the introduction of Concorde and its correct integration into airline operation will lead to improved overall profitability. It will act as a catalyst in the development of a new air transport philosophy in much the same way as it is fostering closer study of air traffic control techniques, international air transport regulations and meteorological conditions. Concorde will provide rapid long-haul transport and its main appeal will be to businessmen for whom time-saving and reduction in journey fatigue will justify a fare premium. It would then be logical to operate the large capacity subsonic aircraft (of the jumbo jet variety as already described) for the tourist mass-travel market for whom the cost of the fare is more important.

Airships

Having reached the age of supersonic transport, it is interesting as a contrast to recall the more leisurely way of travel by air — the slow but none the less colourful airship.

The principle of the airship is that it is a lighter-than-air craft. It floats in the air, but otherwise, movement is achieved in the same way as that of a conventional piston engined aircraft, by means of an engine linked to a propeller.

Although lighter-than-air flight in the form of balloons can be traced back into history, this form of conveyance really came of age during World War I when airships built by Count Ferdinand von Zeppelin enabled Germany to bomb targets in Britain. Between the wars they were used for civilian transport purposes but were virtually overtaken by events with the development of more promising heavier-than-air machines. Even so, it was not until 1962 that the U.S. Navy finally phased out its last airship. Airships had three types of classification, depending upon their construction, being rigid, semi-rigid and non-rigid. The German Zeppelins and the big British R100 and R101 had metal frameworks within their envelopes to maintain their shape. The lifting gas was contained in a series of separate cells carried within these frameworks. In semi-rigid construction, the airship had a rigid or jointed keel which ran the length of the envelope. This keel and the pressure of the lifting gas gave the envelope its shape. In non-rigid models, the envelope shape is maintained entirely by the internal pressure of the lifting gas aided by air cells or ballonets to compensate for pressure differences. There is no internal framework.

The airship has long since lost whatever commercial value it might have had but as a means of transport it has been kept alive by the Goodyear Tyre and Rubber Company, which operates them for publicity purposes and in the United States of America to display public service messages as well as for carrying passengers and as platforms for television or film cameras. These craft are of the non-rigid type, being the only class now in existence, inflated with helium (a non-flammable gas) and fitted with Twin Continental engines which give a cruising speed of 35 mph with a maximum of about 50 mph. Their 23ft long cabins have accommodation for six passengers plus the pilot.

Water Transport

General

The vehicles and aircraft described in the preceding paragraphs have a common feature not shared by ships — a high degree of standardisation. There are many hundreds, even thousands, of road and rail vehicles, each one identical to the other and similarly in the air, only a relatively few basic designs cover the larger types of aircraft. But the merchant ship is more individualistic. It is usually built to a particular specification and the owner is unlikely to have many vessels exactly alike. Sister ships are not twin sisters let alone identical twins. They could well be the same type with similar characteristics and serving the same purpose, but there are likely to be differences in design not found in the mass produced units of other forms of transport. This, of course, is a natural consequence bearing in mind the size of the seagoing vessel. The flow-line process which mass produces private cars, etc, does not lend itself in the same way to shipbuilding. But whilst in the main the merchant fleet does not contain large numbers of identical vessels, ships do fall into a relatively small number of distinct groups. Seagoing craft can firstly be classified into ocean-going vessels and those used on the shorter sea routes. Secondly, there are ships built for the liner trade, either for passengers, for goods, or for both where many different consignments are carried at one and the same time and on the other hand there are the bulk carriers and the tramp steamers which are chartered as a whole, usually for the conveyance of one particular commodity. Tankers as a specialised bulk carrier form a group on their own as do tankers that are capable also of carrying other commodities (oil/bulk/ore ships), roll-on, roll-off ferries and container ships which because of their special interest are discussed in greater detail below.

It is not proposed to elaborate on the many different types of cargo vessel, but a few words on the basic principles which influence the design of ships are necessary. A ship is a form of conveyance designed to carry passengers and goods between ports across the sea. It must provide adequate protection for its passengers and/or cargo from the effects of the sea and also from the effects of the weather and it must carry suitable appliances to permit the loading and unloading of cargo at ports, particularly where there are no suitable shore facilities. There must be machinery to propel the ship with adequate space for fuel, accommodation for the crew and for stores and it must be equipped with the necessary aids to navigation.

The size of a ship is expressed in tons. All British ships must have a tonnage measurement before registration and other ships trading with Britain might seek similar measurement upon arrival at a British port for the purpose of assessing payment of dock dues. There are different methods of assessing tonnage and it is the displacement tonnage and the deadweight tonnage which refer to the ton in terms of 2,240lb. The displacement tonnage is, as the name implies, the weight of the water the ship displaces, which, in accordance with Archimedes' Principle, equals the total weight of ship plus all that it contains. Deadweight tonnage is a measure of what the ship is designed to carry, that is, cargo, passengers, stores, fuel, water, etc, and represents the difference in displacement tonnage when the ship is light and when it is loaded. The gross registered tonnage (GRT) and net registered tonnage (NRT) are measurements of cubic capacity, the ton in this case being taken as 100 cubic feet. The gross registered tonnage is a measure of the total cubic capacity of all (with certain exceptions) enclosed space, that is, space under deck, 'tween decks and enclosed spaces above the upper deck, whilst net registered tonnage is a similar measurement but excluding all spaces necessary for working the ship, i.e., machinery spaces, crew's quarters, etc. NRT, therefore, represents carrying space and is a measure of the ship's earning capacity. It is the net register figure on which most harbour dues and other charges are based. Another consideration is speed. Speed is referred to in terms of knots which, as a measurement, represents nautical miles. A nautical mile is the equivalent of approximately 1.14 statute or land miles. A speed of 20 knots therefore amounts to nearly 23 mph. Fuel consumption rises steeply in proportion to increases in speed which, apart from the cost, means that more fuel must be carried. This can be done only at the expense of cargo space which reduces the payload. Speed therefore is expensive, but conversely the faster the ship, the greater is its earning power as it can perform more trips in a given period of time.

To keep down costs, time spent both at sea and in port must be kept at a minimum. Speed of operation is influenced by the technicalities of hull resistance and by improvements in marine engineering, details of which will not be considered here. A quick turnround calls for mechanisation in the ports and it is the general cargo which produces the greater problems in loading and unloading because of the different equipment needed for different types of goods. This accounts for the trend to specialisation and the development of the bulk carrier. On the passenger side, the additional refinements compared with a cargo boat are expensive which, together with the considerable extra costs of manning, result in much heavier overheads. For passenger ships, therefore, it is even more important that they should not be held in dock unnecessarily and to tie up this more expensive capital asset for the sole purpose of unloading and loading cargo is (other factors being equal) not sound economics. The resultant tendency is for ships to cater specifically for either passengers or goods and the cargo boats in turn to concentrate on the carriage of particular commodities thereby permitting the use of specialised gear for loading and unloading. There is nevertheless a limit to specialisation. In any case the liner trade must cater for miscellaneous traffic

1 Signal Mast
2 Radar Scanners
3 D/F Loop
4 Funnel
5 Standard Compass
6 Navigating Bridge
7 Officers Accommodation
8 Crew Accommodation
9 Lifeboat
10 Refrigerated Cargo Spaces
11 Main Engine
12 Alternators
13 Propeller Shaft
14 Propeller
15 Rudder
16 Double Bottom Tanks
17 Five ton Crane
18 Twin 11 ton Cranes
19 Bipod Mast for 100 ton Derrick
20 Hundred ton Derrick
21 Ten ton Derricks
22 Cargo Winches
23 Cargo Hatches.
    Dimensions No 1
    43ft 6in × 26ft 6in
    No 2 46ft 9in × 36ft 0in.

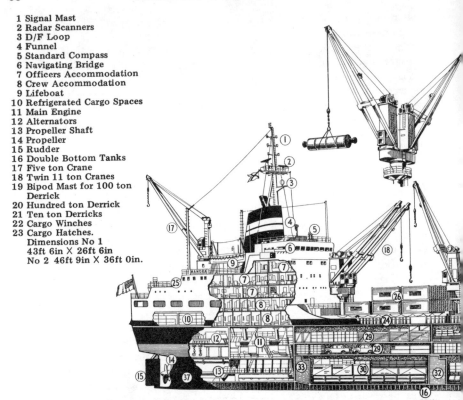

Fig 4. Cutaway drawing of the cargo ship *Manora*. [*Reproduced by permission of the International Relations Division P & O Steam Navigation Company*

consisting of many different commodities destined for many different people and boats designed for the carriage of general merchandise remain an essential part of the merchant fleet. The hulls of these vessels are usually divided by decks and bulkheads into many compartments and may include insulated and tank space to facilitate stowage. A cutaway illustration of the cargo vessel "Manora" of the P & O Steam Navigation Company which is designed to cater for a fully palletised/unitised operation is shown at Fig 4. Notwithstanding the advantage of segregating passengers and goods, on some routes, the demand is insufficient to support a separate ship for each class of traffic with the result that some liners built for passenger traffic do also convey considerable quantities of cargo. It is also quite usual for cargo liners to carry up to 12 passengers which they may do without the need to obtain a passenger certificate. The nature of the accommodation provided by a passenger liner depends upon the traffic potential of the service on which it operates as some routes support a higher proportion of superior class accommodation than others.

Except in the case of tankers and other special types of craft, it has in the past been usual to place the engine amidships, even though this calls for a long

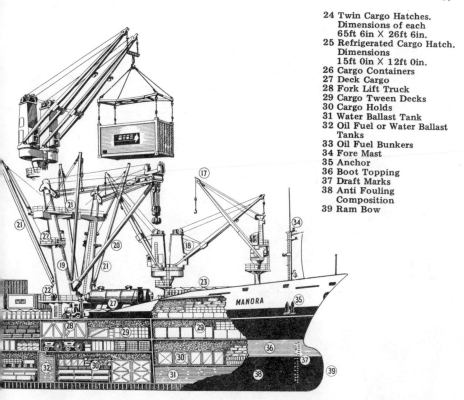

24 Twin Cargo Hatches.
   Dimensions of each
   65ft 6in × 26ft 6in.
25 Refrigerated Cargo Hatch.
   Dimensions
   15ft 0in × 12ft 0in.
26 Cargo Containers
27 Deck Cargo
28 Fork Lift Truck
29 Cargo Tween Decks
30 Cargo Holds
31 Water Ballast Tank
32 Oil Fuel or Water Ballast
   Tanks
33 Oil Fuel Bunkers
34 Fore Mast
35 Anchor
36 Boot Topping
37 Draft Marks
38 Anti Fouling
   Composition
39 Ram Bow

length of shaft to reach the screw at the stern. However, the propellers have not always been so placed. It was common in the early days of steam for ships to be propelled by paddles which were often fitted amidships on each side of the hull and the old paddle steamer is still to be seen. Even some paddle steamers however had their paddle aft. This type of ship is now outdated, having given way to the screw-driven vessel but, by and large and until recently, the engine has remained amidships. There is now a breakaway from this hitherto accepted practice by placing the engine aft. Not only does this reduce the length of the shaft to the propeller but it also permits better utilisation of space amidships.

The foregoing outlines the basic essentials in respect of the design of sea-going vessels. Specialised craft have, however, been developed for particular traffics and a selection of the more important of these groups will now be discussed in a little more detail.

Tankers

The modern oil tanker is basically designed to ensure stability when a large volume of liquid cargo is carried. To prevent excessive surging of the liquid when the ship rolls and pitches, its free surface is reduced by athwartship and longitudinal bulkheads to give some thirty or more separate oiltight compartments. There is an extra bulkhead at both the forward and aft ends of the cargo-carrying

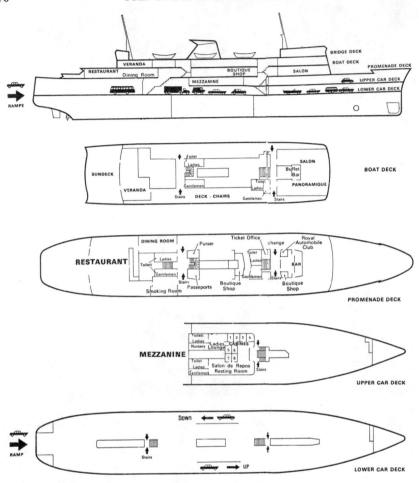

Fig 5. Cutaway drawing of the 'roll-on roll-off' car ferry *Valençay*. [*S.N.C.F.*

space, forming cofferdams, to isolate the cargo from the forehold and the engine room respectively. Tankers can handle a number of different grades of oil, although they do not normally carry "white" oils, i.e., motor spirit, kerosene, etc, and "black" oils, such as crude and fuel oil, at the same time.

The cargo is normally loaded by shore pumps, but the ship's pumps are used to discharge cargo through large flexible hoses connecting the deck pipelines to the shore lines. A tanker can load and discharge at rates up to 15,000 tons per hour and even more depending on the size of the ship, grade of oil, etc. When the oil has been discharged some of the cargo tanks are ballasted with sea water to give the vessel suitable sailing trim.

The engines of a tanker are placed aft instead of amidships for reasons of safety as well as of convenience and economy. This arrangement avoids having a tunnel for the propeller shaft running through the cargo tanks which would reduce cargo space and be difficult to keep oiltight. At the extreme ends of the ship are peak tanks used for trimming the vessel with sea water. Adjacent to these tanks are spaces for carrying the ship's own supply of fuel oil.

A feature of tanker operation is the relatively quick turnround and they do in consequence spend more time at sea than other cargo ships. It is partly for this reason that the standard of crew accommodation and victualling of a modern tanker is often very high. Because of the nature of the specialised cargo, the standard of maintenance must also be high which calls for qualified and experienced personnel.

Of particular interest is the size range of these vessels. Since the closure of the Suez Canal, regard has no longer been paid to the limitations of that particular waterway and the economies of scale are being fully exploited. From vessels of some 10–20,000 tons thirty years ago the 215,000 tons tanker "British Explorer" illustrated at Plate 35 is a typical very large crude carrier (V.L.C.C.) currently in service. Plans for vessels up to 1,000,000 tons are on the drawing board.

Ore/Bulk/Oil Vessels

Oil is essentially a one-way commodity. It moves from the areas of production to the areas of consumption and tankers which specialise in this particular traffic must, in consequence, undertake a large number of voyages in ballast. The ore/bulk/oil ship (known as the O.B.O.) is a multi-purpose bulk carrier designed not only for the conveyance of oil but also of ore and other commodities in bulk such as grain. These vessels, which are similar in appearance to conventional tankers with engines aft, are, of course, extremely versatile. They are able to take advantage of changing market conditions but have a proportionately higher initial cost.

Roll-on Roll-off Ferries

The roll-on, roll-off ferry is in principle a development of the floating bridge, which has for many years provided a facility for vehicles to cross rivers at places where normal bridges are not available. An example is the Woolwich Ferry in London where road vehicles drive straight on to the ferry boat. The roll-on, roll-off ferries are an extension of this principle applied to short sea routes where seagoing ships are specially constructed to allow all types of vehicles and mobile equipment to be loaded and discharged on their own wheels under their own power.

A cutaway drawing of the "Valencay" (3,460 tons) owned by S.N.C.F. (French National Railways) and which is used on the cross-Channel service between Newhaven and Dieppe appears at Fig 5 and an exterior view is shown at Plate 37. This particular vessel, which is powered by two diesel motors and has a cruising speed of 21 knots, can carry 1,200 passengers and 150 cars but other boats such as, for example, certain of those on the more heavily used services from Dover, can carry over 200 vehicles. The same principle has been applied to the carriage of railway wagons and passenger coaches and some ships of this type are specially constructed with railway tracks for this purpose.

Although the principle of the roll-on, roll-off ferry has certain economic advantages as it simplifies loading and unloading, the design and construction of these vessels is highly specialised. The naval architect is required to provide the maximum amount of unhindered space for the accommodation of an assortment of vehicles, the size, shape and weight of which will vary voyage by voyage whilst at the same time the ship must ride easily at sea to ensure that this cargo of vehicles does not shift. Large watertight doors for entry and exit are required and are generally placed at the stern although they are also sometimes provided in the bows also on ships destined to ply in more sheltered waters, which permits a drive through arrangement. Ships of this type must, of course, also operate in conjunction with specialised shore facilities, to which reference was made in Chapter 3.

Container Ships

The development of the "through" concept in the form of the container is described in Chapter 7 and it is sufficient here to consider only the vessel that is purpose built to carry that container.

These ships are built in a series of cells (i.e. the "cellular" ship) designed to house the standardised boxes which contain general cargo. A feature of these vessels is the absence of derricks as they are used in conjunction with specialised lifting gear on shore as was mentioned in Chapter 3. Engines and crew accommodation are placed aft to allow maximum space for stowage and the larger container ships have a capacity of upwards of 1,500 containers.

All the vessels described so far have one thing in common; they are conventional boats that float in water. This in itself is a barrier to fast movement with the result that speed is not a characteristic of water transport. If the hull of the vessel can be lifted above the surface of the water then the effects of certain frictional forces are reduced and greater speeds become possible. This is the common factor between the two otherwise totally different concepts that are now to be described.

Hovercraft

The word "hovercraft" describes the form of transport employing the principle of riding on a cushion of air generated beneath the craft and retained by an air curtain. In its most versatile form, the hovercraft is truly amphibious, being equally at home over land or water, and can transit from one to the other by way of unprepared beaches or simple ramps. This type of craft does not need to keep to deep-water channels or to avoid such hazards as sand or mud flats and it can therefore follow more direct routes. It is faster than a boat, the water speed in calm conditions being in the region of 60 knots, and it does not require complex and costly dock or terminal facilities. A small area of beach or hardstanding is all that is required for loading and unloading passengers and freight.

The most widely used hovercraft currently available is the British Hovercraft Corporation's "Winchester" (SRN6). The standard version of this hovercraft can carry up to 38 passengers or 3 tons of cargo and among other operations, is in use on the scheduled passenger services operated by British Railways and Hovertravel between the mainland of southern England and the Isle of Wight. Power for the cushion lift and propulsion is provided by a 900shp. Marine Gnome gas turbine situated behind the passenger cabin. The curtain air is supplied by a centrifugal lift fan situated in the lower structure, emerging from flexible duct extensions beneath the craft. Variable pitch propellers provide the propulsion which may be either in the air (as in the illustration) or immersed in the water. In the latter case, the craft does, of course, lose its amphibious qualities.

A buoyancy chamber is incorporated which enables the craft to float on water and proceed as a boat. The flexible, structure between the craft and the surface over which it travels, known as a skirt and made of a rubberised fabric, gives a significant increase in the hovercraft's capability to operate over solid obstacles, ditches and rough seas.

The latest development in hovercraft is the 200-ton *Mountbatten* (SRN4) Class passenger/car ferry as depicted at Plate 33, designed for operation on open-sea ferry routes. An all-passenger version of the *Mountbatten* accommodates over 600 people, whilst the car ferry version carries 30 cars with 254 passengers. A stretched version of the SRN4 capable of carrying 282 passengers and 37 cars is now being built and will enter service on the English Channel in 1973. Fitted with 8ft skirts, the SRN4 is capable of operating in 10ft seas, normally the most severe conditions experienced on open water routes such as the English Channel. In calm weather this craft cruises at speeds approaching 70 knots. The success of long skirts has in fact led to the thought that a hovercraft of the order of 200 tons could undertake ocean going duties.

Hydrofoil

Very simply, the principle of the hydrofoil is the same as that of the flight of an aeroplane except that one flies in water and the other in the air. Both make use of foils or wings which deflect some of the water (or air) downwards and so create a lift. The point might be better understood if the relationship between boats and airships is considered. The hull of a boat floats in water just as the airship floats in the air and as in the case of the airship, the function of the ship's engine is to overcome the drag and so propel the vessel. The aeroplane will not of course float in air hence the power from the engines must, through the agency of the wings (or foils), create a lift as well as a thrust. Similar principles apply to the hydrofoil boat and the boat can, when stationary, float quite naturally in its own "way". Nevertheless, when in motion, the action of the foils against the water (like the action of the wings of an aircraft against the air) creates a lift and so the hull rises. In so doing it reduces the drag which enables a corresponding increase in speed. At the same time it creates far less wash than an ordinary boat which makes it very suitable for rivers and lakes where heavy surges of water cause damage to banks and adjoining property. There are now a number of examples of this type of craft in operation.

River and Canal Craft

Like the railway, the width of the track or way has a considerable bearing on the design and size of canal carrying units and whilst the wider canals can pass different types of estuarial craft — indeed the major ship canals accommodate ocean-going liners — specially designed vessels are required to navigate the narrow British waterways.

Although rivers and canals have only a limited application to passenger transport, pleasure boats do ply in certain of the more attractive areas together with purpose built ferries as dictated by geographical conditions. The designs of these craft conform basically to the principles that have already been enunciated in respect of sea-going vessels but scaled down to accord with the width and depth of the waters that they are required to use. In the case of inland waterways, however, there is a third dimension that also exerts its influence in relation to overall size. Rivers and canals are frequently crossed by road and rail, with the result that bridges may impose a severe height restriction.

For the movement of freight, specialised vessels such as tankers may be used, subject again to the overall size limitations, including height, but for general traffic, the wider canals are worked by barges or lighters (a lighter has flat ends rather like a punt) often strung together and pulled (or sometimes pushed) by a tug.

The development of the hovercraft and hydrofoil as discussed in previous paragraphs must not be overlooked in this connection as these types of craft may also be used to advantage on inland waterways as well as on estuaries and the open sea.

The most common type of boat used on the British narrow canals as were described in Chapter 2 is the narrow boat (sometimes known as the monkey boat) built of wood or steel, about 70ft long but only 7ft wide. Because of their narrow width they cannot be classified as barges (which have at least 14ft in beam), and they often proceed in pairs, the powered boat (or the "motor") pulling another boat without any means of self-propulsion (the "butty").

Plate 1 Daimler Fleetline one-man operated double-deck bus of the West Midlands Passenger Transport Executive in service at Moseley, Birmingham. Note the single entrance/exit. Alternative designs are available which provide for separate entrances and exits but only at the expense of seating capacity. The vehicle illustrated accommodates 76 seated passengers.

Plate 2 Ford mini-buses of the Government of Ontario (GO Transit) seen at Pickering Station, Bay Ridges (near Toronto), Canada. These buses provide a door-to-door service between the GO Transit railhead at Pickering from which there is a train service into Toronto and the residential area of Bay Ridges. Each journey is routed in accordance with passenger requirements. The vehicles seat 11 people exclusive of the driver.

Plate 3 A low-powered mini-bus of a special type operating a sea front service at Sitges, Spain. Note the toastrack style seating of the trailer which provides maximum seating capacity in a given area but without a central gangway. Physical communication within the vehicle is not, therefore, possible.

Plate 4 A typical peak hour scene in suburban Birmingham. The cars in the foreground were together carrying under 20 people whilst the bus had over 70. The message is clear.

Plate 5 Articulated trolleybus pictured at Bologna, Italy. Vehicles of this type in the form of diesel buses, trams and trolleybuses are quite common on the continent of Europe and can accommodate, including standing, some 150 passengers.

Plate 6 Bus station, West Bromwich. Vehicles enter from the far end for lateral parking at their appropriate set-down/pick-up point and then proceed progressively to the exit in the foreground. Alternative designs provide for head-on or echelon parking, for passengers to reach any bus without crossing other bus lanes, which is necessary in the type illustrated; however, a bus reversing movement is involved.

Plate 7 PCC type trams of the Toronto Transit Commission in Toronto, Canada. Most of the trams that are now operating in North America are based on principles laid down in 1927 by the President's Conference Committee of the transit industry and were put into series production in 1935. A new design of tram has now been evolved by tramway operating interests in North America and this new type could eventually replace those pictured here. Although trams (or streetcars as they are known in North America) generally operate singly, this picture depicts cars coupled in a pair and up to three cars linked as a train operate on certain streets in Boston, Massachusetts.

Plate 8 A cable-car of the San Francisco Municipal Railway (known locally as the "Muni"). Dating back to 1886, this car is seen climbing a 21.3% gradient in Hyde Street, San Francisco, USA, against a background of Alcatraz Island, until recently a Federal penitentiary. Seating is provided for 30 people but as the picture suggests, cars often carry many more than that. The track gauge is 3 ft 6 in and the speed of the cable is 9 mph./*San Francisco Municipal Railway*

Plate 9 Milwaukee—Douglas rapid transit line of the Chicago Transit Authority seen in the median of the Kennedy Expressway in Chicago, USA. The freedom of the railway compared with road congestion on the expressway is very evident. This is Chicago's third application combining rail rapid transit and a multi-lane motorway in the same grade-separated right-of-way.

Plate 10 Approaching Dempster Station on the "Skokie Swift" rapid transit line of the Chicago Transit Authority. This line provides a high speed connecting service with trains which run to and from the centre of Chicago and is heavily used by commuters who park and ride. The station car park accommodates 555 cars and a local feeder bus service is also provided.

Plate 11 Danforth Station, Toronto, Canada, served by trains of the Government of Ontario's GO Transit and worked under contract by Canadian National Railways. This section of CNR main line between Toronto and Pickering (together with a similar section on the other side of Toronto) has been upgraded at minimum cost to accommodate a commuter train service in order to relieve acute pressure on parallel highways.

Plate 12 Wuppertal, Germany, has one of the few commercially successful monorail systems. It does not occupy road space as does a street tramway and it is not subject to delay through traffic congestion. Trains are seen here outside one of the 18 stations on the line./*Wuppertaler Stadtwerke AG*

Plate 13 A Metro train of Sistema de Transporte Colectivo seen reversing at Taxquena Station, Mexico City. The cars used are mounted on pneumatic tyres and the track is formed of three pairs of parallel steel sections. Two H-beams form the track which is used by the running wheels and two guide rails located at either side of the track receive the thrust of the horizontal wheels (also fitted with pneumatic tyres) which form part of the truck assembly and which guide the train. These guide rails are also conductors of the electric power (750 volts d.c.) which is taken up by metal shoes mounted on the trucks. Additionally, two 80lb steel rails are provided which constitute a second safety track to support conventional steel car wheels which are also mounted on the trucks and which only operate in case of a blow-out or loss of pressure in a load or guide tyre or when the train passes over a point. It is also these rails that complete the electrical circuit.

Plate 14 Close up of a bogie of a train of the Mexico City Metro. Note the main running wheels (with rubber tyres which are, incidentally, inflated with nitrogen to avoid arcing in the event of a collapse), the rubber tyred guide wheels and the current collector shoe.

Plate 15 The projected Westinghouse Skybus of the Port Authority of Allegheny County, referred to as TERL (Transit Expressway Revenue Line) seen on a test track in South Park, Pittsburgh, USA. Transit Expressway is a rapid transit system based on the use of lightweight automated vehicles operating singly or in trains on a frequent headway. The system is designed to provide a continuous service, round-the-clock, with a train every two minutes. To meet fluctuating passenger volume demands the train length will vary from one to ten vehicles whilst the headway remains constant. A feature of the system is that it is a rapid transit line on which both capital and operating costs are substantially below those of a conventional system.

Plate 16 A switch on Pittsburgh's projected guided Expressway. Note the cumbrous nature of the turnout which is a feature of all systems which rely on rubber tyres and also of monorails.

Plate 17 A Freightliner train hauled by an electric locomotive is seen moving at speed with its trunk haul of containers. On the road below, a lorry is moving a container on the local journey between customer and the Freightliner terminal./*British Railways Board*

Plate 18 A mobile conveyor unit of Canadian National Railways seen handling a container at a road/rail transhipment point at Montreal, Canada./*F.J. Lloyd*

Plate 19 A purpose-built crane transferring a container from road to rail./
National Freight Corporation

Plate 20 An elevated view of activities at a Birmingham Freightliner terminal. The overhead crane in the background is able to move along the length of the yard on its special track, one line of which can be seen passing through the centre of the picture./*NFC*

Plate 21 Road trailer vehicles being conveyed on flat railway wagons of the Atchison, Topeka and Santa Fe Railway Company (the Santa Fe line) of the USA. This is known as the piggyback system. An alternative method which allows the bogies of the road vehicles to stand in specially constructed wells in the railway trucks necessitates the use of purpose built railway vehicles which in this case are known as kangaroo wagons.

Plate 22 An electric locomotive of the Société Nationale de Chemins de Fer Français hauling the *Etoile de Nord* en route from Paris to Amsterdam via Brussels. Note the flat bottomed rail and also the lightweight catenary structures that are possible because of the high voltage system (50 cycles current at 25,000 volts a.c.) that is used./*Société Nationale de Chemins de Fer Français*

Plate 23 Steam as a form of motive power has disappeared from the standard gauge railways of Great Britain. Steam locomotives are extravagent users of coal and attention required by way of taking on water, cleaning, greasing, etc., is such that their daily average mileage compares most unfavourably with their electric and diesel counterparts. Here, one of the last of the remaining steam locomotives that is still in use by SNCF is seen hauling a goods train in the south of France./*SNCF*

Plate 24 In areas where the loading gauge is wider than British standards, double-deck railway passenger coaches are becoming more widely used. This illustration depicts one of the few remaining local passenger trains which continue to run in North America. A diesel hauled double-deck train is pictured on one of the Chicago suburban lines of the Chicago and North Western Railway.

Plate 25 In contrast to the wide loading gauge required by the double-deck train, this electric multiple unit set was built for the small bore tunnels of the London Transport system. It is now in the service of British Railways and is pictured at Ryde, St. Johns Road Station, Isle of Wight. Note the bullhead type rail and the third rail method of electrification.

Plate 26 Manchester, Piccadilly Station of British Railways. This is part of the modernised system with high voltage overhead catenary and colour light signalling. Being a terminus, train reversing facilities are necessary, hence the scissors crossover just beyond the platform which allows trains to cross on to their correct path before or after changing direction.

Plate 27 Coastal railway lines do tend to isolate the seafront from the township in the rear. At Calella in Spain the east coast main line of the Spanish National Railways does just that. Buildings of Calella can be seen to the left of the track and access to the beach is obtained in this instance by an under-bridge through which a horse and cart is about to pass. It is of interest that the track gauge of the Spanish and Portuguese railway systems is 5ft 6in, which is 9½in wider than standard.

Plate 28 British Railways three car diesel multiple unit approaching Solihull Station. It is evident from the illustration that this station offers park and ride and bus terminal facilities, a practice that it is planned to extend.

Plate 29 The Advanced Passenger Train of British Railways. The objectives of the APT projects are to reduce journey times by exploiting fully the potential of existing track and signalling equipment and to provide superlative comfort at 155 mph. This picture shows APT-E (experimental) on its first main line proving run prior to starting the most stringent test programme ever devised for a railway train. Information from APT-E will be used in designing two prototypes, APT-Ps, due to carry passengers in 1975./*BRB*

Plate 30 *Sea Freightliner II* being unloaded at Zeebrugge Freightliner Terminal./*NFC*

Plate 31 Floating crane *London Leviathan* of the Port of London Authority./ *Port of London Authority*

5 · Motive Power

Introduction

At one time transport relied on natural power for propulsion — sea transport on the wind and road and inland water transport on animals. The advent of the steam engine and later the internal combustion engine revolutionised methods of propulsion to the extent that there is now no place in commercial transport for power in its natural state. The raw materials of artificially produced power are mainly coal and oil and for this purpose it may be either on the transport unit itself, as for example, on a bus or a railway steam or diesel locomotive, or in the case of electricity converted at some remote point and transmitted to the system, be it railway, tramway, or trolleybus, by cables and other conductors. This distinction is fundamental.

The form of motive power used is determined by local conditions and operating costs. In some countries oil may be plentiful and cheap, in others water may be almost unobtainable. A certain type of fuel might be subject to heavy taxation or the transport authority might for example also be the electricity authority. Considerations such as these can influence the choice of power and an examination of the manner in which these principles are applied in practice follows. The chart at Fig 6 illustrates the forms of transport which use these different types of power.

All forms of power emanate from natural sources. Steam is raised by heating water for which the most widely used fuel is coal. The steam may be used direct in the form of a steam engine or it can be used to generate electricity. Electricity can also be produced from water power or even from wind power although the latter is not very reliable and is not likely to be used commercially. Engines burning petroleum or diesel fuel are used in their thousands as a direct source of power but again, the diesel engine is also adapted to generate electricity. However, natural power in this context refers to its direct application without any form of artificial conversion. Such methods have now been largely overtaken by events but reference to them is nevertheless included if only for the sake of completeness. For this reason, as far as natural power is concerned, the different modes can be dealt with collectively but when considering mechanical propulsion, a separate examination of each form of transport will be more appropriate.

Natural Power

Animal Power

Animal power may be described as the moving force produced by direct physical exertion of either animals or humans.

Road transport saw its beginnings with horse-drawn carts and buses plus the occasional bullock, camel or other animal according to local conditions. The advent of the internal combustion engine has rendered horse-drawn vehicles

Source of Power	Type of Power / Means/Method of Propulsion	Road	Rail	Inland Waterway	Sea	Air
Natural						
Animal	Horse, ox, camel, etc	Carts, buses, etc, but now largely obsolete	Physically possible, but with isolated examples only	Canal barges, but now largely superseded	Impracticable	Impracticable
Human		Bicycle, pushcart, rickshaw, etc	Platelayer's **hand** trolley, etc	Rowing boat, punt etc	Rowing boat	Very limited possibility, with pedal-operated light aircraft
Wind		Land yachts for sporting purposes, but no commercial application	No commercial application	Sailing boat, but now obsolete for commercial purposes	Sailing boat, but now obsolete for commercial purposes	Glider for sport and military purposes
Artificial and carried on the vehicle, etc						
Coal, etc to produce	Steam	Traction engine, steam roller, steam bus, etc, but now obsolete	Steam locomotive, but now being superseded	Steam tugs, etc	Steam reciprocating engines	Impracticable
Oil	Petrol and/or Diesel Oil Engines	Private and commercial vehicles	Diesel locomotives and multiple unit trains	Diesel powered tugs, etc	Motor vessels, etc	Piston engined aircraft. Also kerosene for jet aircraft
Coal, etc to produce electricity	Storage battery	Light vans and passenger vehicles. Emergency operation for trolleybuses	Limited use for railcars, multiple unit trains and special locomotives	No commercial application	No commercial application	Impracticable
Artificial but not carried on the vehicle, etc						
Coal, water, power, etc to produce	Electricity	Street tramway, trolleybus	Electric locomotives and multiple unit trains	No commercial application	Impracticable	Impracticable

Fig 6. Various types of power as applied to different forms of transport.

obsolete and they are now no longer able to hold their place satisfactorily in present day traffic conditions. Also reduced to a museum piece is the tricycle barrow at one time used by ice-cream salesmen and others although the "passenger" version, being the pedal bicycle which is propelled in the same way as the "commercial" tricycle has survived as a means of transport and to a limited extent even for commuting purposes.

Inevitably, the use of animal power on the railway has been less extensive. Apart from the obvious impracticability of a fast main line service, the steam engine appeared on the scene before the internal combustion engine and at a time when horse-drawn vehicles were still virtually the only means of transport by road. The same need did not, therefore, arise. Nevertheless, rail transport has some record of animal power. It was seen in Chapter 2 that resistance to rolling is reduced if vehicles are fitted with steel wheels to run on steel tracks. It follows that a horse could pull a greater weight under these conditions, hence the advantage of the horse-drawn tram (or street railway) over the bus. Rail-borne transport worked by animal power was, therefore, developed in the form of street tramways until electrification and at least one system, that at Douglas in the Isle of Man, survives to this day. The service on the Fintona branch of the erstwhile Great Northern Railway (Ireland) remained horsedrawn until closure of the line in 1957 and a horse was used for shunting purposes at Newmarket Station of British Railways until very recent times. Similar examples but with elephants are occasionally found on railway systems in the Far East. Platelayers' trolleys worked manually with a lever are yet another example of animal albeit human power on the railway.

As was the case with the tramway, so also was the case with the canal. Because it requires less energy to pull a load on water than on a road, a horse can haul a considerably greater weight over a longer distance per day by waterway than on land. This was the justification for the construction of the narrow canals in Great Britain which came even before the steam engine was thought of. A walkway or "towpath" was constructed on the canal bank along which horses were able to walk and tow laden boats. The human counterpart is the rowing boat or punt. These boats are of necessity very small and apart from the occasional ferry, their uses are mainly for pleasure purposes or fishing.

In the air experiments have been conducted with treadle machines although in transport terms (and even in sporting terms), these aircraft have no significance.

Modern technology has rendered animal power obsolete and the one time extensive use of horses on the roads and alongside the canals has now fallen to negligible proportions. Only the pedal bicycle is still to be seen and this is no more than a private conveyance with no commercial application.

Wind Power

What animal power was for the canal and the road, wind power was for the sea. The wind was the driving force of the seagoing sailing ships which spread commerce across the world. These vessels are now dated and have gone. Nevertheless, wind power is still accepted as a moving force on water, be it the sea, lake or river, but for pleasure and sporting purposes. Given suitable terrain, wind power can also be used for movement on land. A land yacht, which is a wheeled vehicle with a sail, is used in this way, again for sporting purposes.

As far as the air is concerned, it is not essential for a suitably constructed aircraft to be fitted with any artificial means of propulsion once it has become airborne. The glider relies entirely on wind currents and in so doing it can remain aloft for considerable periods of time in smooth, silent flight. But aircraft which rely on this natural power have little commercial value. They are attractive to sportsmen and possess a limited military value.

Artificially Produced Power

Road Transport

Animal power was gradually replaced by the internal combustion engine (initially petrol fuelled) in the period before and immediately after World War I when steam and petrol-electric vehicles were also in use. From the mid-1930s petrol as a fuel was gradually replaced by diesel in the heavier vehicles which included buses and the larger vehicles used for haulage purposes. To-day the diesel engine is the most common source of power for the "heavies". Petrol engines are fitted to cars and light vans and vans in the medium size range are generally available with either petrol or diesel engines.

The qualities of petrol and diesel engines are well known. According to the individual designs and capacities, they have good acceleration, are capable of sustained speeds, are relatively economical in operation and with a conveniently sized fuel tank have an acceptable range. There are, however, alternatives. Propane, which is one of those gases contained within the generic term "Liquefied Petroleum Gas" (L.P.G.), can also be used as a fuel for internal combustion engines. It is derived from petroleum and is readily liquefied under pressure. A vehicle with a suitably adapted engine must be fitted with a heavy pressurized fuel tank. A satisfactory performance can be achieved but fuel leakage could be hazardous, which calls for careful maintenance. Although it is unlikely that propane will become widely used as a fuel for road transport, it has some potential in areas where adequate supplies are not only available but suitably marketed. A part of the bus fleet of the Chicago Transit Authority, for example, works on propane.

The electrically operated battery vehicle is another alternative and one which has been in use for many years. Whilst mechanically it is relatively simple with easy maintenance and there is no reliance on oil, the vehicles that have been in use so far have had serious deficiencies. They have a low maximum speed and the range between re-charging of the batteries is limited. Furthermore, the batteries are heavy and the weight must of course be carried around on the vehicle. To date the battery vehicle has been found to be most suitable for local delivery work which entails frequent stopping and starting such as, for example, a milk round. Considerable research is being undertaken in the field of electric vehicle technology. However, before a vehicle of this type can become accepted for general purposes, it must have a higher power-to-weight ratio to meet acceleration and performance requirements and a higher energy density to give it a reasonable travelling range between charges. It is for this reason that a great deal of research is going on to develop new and advanced batteries that would be capable of meeting these requirements.

Similar research is being undertaken into the development of the gas turbine. The turbine can be run on various fuels including kerosine and with a rotary instead of a reciprocating movement, the engine vibration is minimised. It also has good torque characteristics which means more power at lower engine speeds. These features suggest that turbines might have some potential for buses and other heavy vehicles.

Steam as a form of motive power has prominence in railway and water transport, although there were steam operated vehicles on the roads in the early 1900s. Like the railway locomotives, these were mostly coal burning vehicles and they had their use for heavy work. Tractors and road rollers were powered in this way. To-day, experiments are under way with steam engines installed in cars and buses of conventional appearance. Diesel fuel can be used to heat the boiler which produces high pressure vapour. The expansion of this high pressure vapour drives the piston in the expander and the steam exhausted from the cylinder is piped to a condenser for water recovery. The steam power plant is bigger and heavier than a comparable internal combustion engine and difficulties arise with lubrication and when temperatures fall below freezing point. The lubricating and freezing problems amongst others have led to the consideration of using fluids other than water sealed in the engine and heated from an external source to expand, drive the piston and hence develop power. With no combustion within the cylinder, this external combustion engine operates very quietly but there is little evidence to suggest that it is capable of development to the point where performance would engender general acceptance.

An objection to petrol and diesel engines and one that is causing increasing concern, particularly in North America, is that they emit a poisonous exhaust which is polluting the atmosphere. This is one of the reasons that is prompting research into alternative methods of propulsion although for other reasons these alternatives may not in the ultimate offer the best solution. Emissions of hydrocarbon and carbon monoxide are lower from an L.P.G. fuelled engine than from an engine with a standard fuel system. The gas turbine has a very low emission potential and experiments with the steam engine show a similar advantage in this respect. The relationship between the battery vehicle and air pollution is interesting. Whilst running, the battery vehicle does not, of course, emit any exhaust at all and it is frequently hailed as the answer to atmospheric pollution. Nevertheless, batteries must be re-charged and the electric power supply that is necessary for this purpose must be produced. Most power stations to-day burn either coal or oil and whilst emissions of hydrocarbons or carbon monoxide are negligible, they do emit air pollutants such as oxides of nitrogen and sulphur dioxide, although not, it is true, necessarily in built-up areas and at ground level as is the case with cars. Power stations can be located away from population centres and the emissions can be discharged high into the atmosphere but pollution is, nevertheless, there. Even after accepting that emissions from power stations can be controlled, research undertaken by the General Motors Corporation of the U.S.A. suggests that when compared on an equivalent basis, pollutant emissions that would be caused by use of a developed electric car might well be greater than that produced by its internal combustion engined counterpart, at least as far as the power stations which burn coal or oil are concerned. If this is the case, then the general impression that this form of motive power would solve the air pollution problem of the car is erroneous. The view is expressed by General Motors that for, say, the next 10 years, suitable emission control devices on I.C. engines might be the most satisfactory solution but the subject is discussed further in Chapter 14.

Trams and Trolleybuses

Mention was made at the beginning of this chapter that fuel may be either carried on the vehicle or power transmitted to it from an outside source. Road vehicles in the form of electric trams and trolleybuses (and also electrified railways which are discussed below) come within this second category. Electricity is fed to the system and to the individual vehicles through cables, wires and other conductors, hence the necessity for a specialised way as has already been described.

Trams and trolleybuses are of necessity tied to their tracks. They are, therefore, inflexible, as will be discussed in Chapter 6. To lessen the effects of this inhibition, an interesting development is under consideration in San Francisco in the U.S.A. with a trolleybus capable of travelling free of its overhead wires for extended distances and periods of time. Using kinetic energy, a trolleybus running in the normal way would use some of its power to keep spinning a heavy flywheel located underneath the vehicle. The shaft of this flywheel would form part of an electric generator and when the trolleybus required to leave the overhead wiring system the energy of the spinning wheel would be tapped for motive power. Normal speeds could be obtained in this way.

Whilst the great majority of the tramway systems that exist to-day are powered by electricity, alternative methods are possible and reference has already been made to a horse-drawn system. Trams could be propelled by petrol or diesel motors on a similar principle to diesel railcars. Cable lines which were mentioned in Chapter 2 may be adapted for anything from a lift to a street tramway. A classic example of the latter is again at San Francisco, a city that is particularly favourably disposed to electric traction for urban transport. Although the cable cars themselves are hauled by gripping the cable, the cable is kept continuously in motion by electric motors in a central carhouse. In addition to the cable cars, an illustration of which appears at Plate 8, the San Francisco Municipal Railway (known locally as the Muni) operates a fine fleet of conventional trams and trolleybuses.

Railways

Motive power has followed the lines of general development which, for reasons of output and working convenience, has led the railway industry as a whole to make use of modern forms of energy, namely electricity and heavy oils. The various forms of motive power suitable for use on a railway are as follows:

Steam

By this means, steam is produced from a boiler and is supplied to a reciprocating engine, which is an engine with cylinders in which pistons move backwards and forwards. There are no gear wheels, power being transmitted to the wheels direct via the piston connecting-rods, etc. Steam is normally raised by burning coal, although this is not necessarily universal. Locomotives have been adapted to burn wood and other fuel. The steam engine is self-starting and in so doing can exert a pull sufficient to deal with heavy trains. Sustained energy, however, depends on the size of the boiler and much of the power is absorbed in moving the heavy weight of the engine and its tender. This is a disadvantage of the steam locomotive. Other disadvantages are that it is extravagant in the use of coal in relation to power produced, adequate supplies of water must be available at strategic points along the track, the boiler fire needs constant attention, frequent cleaning and greasing is necessary and whenever the locomotive is in steam it must be supplied with fuel irrespective of whether there is actual movement. For these reasons, steam as a form of motive power is rapidly giving way to diesel oil and electricity.

Diesel
Diesel oil as a form of power is approximately four times more efficient than that of steam. Diesel engines do not require the same attention as steam locomotives and can if necessary be kept in service for up to about 21 hours out of the 24, whereas the steam engine is available for on average about 12 hours a day. Both a driver and a fireman are necessary to work a steam locomotive, but with diesel, in many cases only one man is necessary. One disadvantage, however, is that outside the oil producing areas the system relies on imported fuel which, in an emergency, could prove an embarassment. The diesel engine works most satisfactorily at a constant speed and when applied to movement by rail (and to road as well for that matter) there must be some kind of transmission between the engine and the driving wheels. This may be either hydraulic, electric (in which case the locomotive is known as a "diesel-electric" being propelled by electricity generated by the diesel engine), or, like the road vehicle, mechanical in the form of a gearbox.

Battery
This is the third form of propulsion where movement is not dependent on some external source when actually in motion. Power is contained within the vehicle itself and it is therefore still a locomotive within the true definition of "having power to go from place to place". The battery locomotive is driven by electricity taken from large storage batteries as are the electric road vehicles. The batteries must, of course, be constantly recharged and this type of locomotive is not suitable for particularly heavy or continuous work. Perhaps the best example of the use of battery locomotives is on the London Transport system where they handle special trains for maintenance purposes during the night when current is switched off. Some alternative to electric traction is necessary at this time and as a large part of the system is in tunnel, diesel locomotives would not be suitable on account of the exhaust. This form of propulsion may also be applied to the movement of passengers on services where power consumption is not abnormally heavy; avoiding, for example, routes where there are frequent stops or steep gradients. Providing there is sufficient stand-time, batteries may be recharged at terminal stations and this type of train gives a particularly quiet and smooth ride.

Electricity
Electricity as a means of propulsion has already been mentioned, power being generated by a diesel motor or supplied from storage batteries. But railway

electrification implies bringing electrical energy to the track from some external source to be transmitted to the train through conductor rails or overhead catenary. Strictly speaking, therefore, the pulling unit cannot, in this case, correctly be termed a locomotive, as it is not self-propelled.

A fundamental advantage of electricity in countries which produce coal but not oil is that power may be obtained from national resources. In addition, it enables use to be made of waste products or low-grade coal which can be burnt only in the large furnaces of generating stations. Furthermore, the average output of an electric locomotive may be more than twice that for its steam counterpart. Energy produced on the locomotive itself, irrespective of its method of propulsion, is inevitably limited, but there is virtually no limit to the amount which can be fed to an electric train, hence it is able to exert a tremendous power.

Railways may be electrified on either direct or alternating current. The former has the advantage that the direct current motor is eminently suited for traction purposes. The power must however, be fed to the locomotive at the same voltage as it is consumed. To transmit a large amount of power at a sufficiently low voltage, it is necessary to instal a heavy cross-section catenary or even conductor rails, together with numerous and costly sub-stations. With alternating current it is possible to reduce the voltage on the locomotive itself. The catenaries therefore may carry a high voltage; and catenaries constructed for high voltage can be lighter and hence more economical in cost. For technical reasons, however, an ac motor using current at 50 cycles per second — which is the universal current as supplied through the national grid — was not, at one time, used for traction. It was on the initiative of the French National Railways that technicians undertook and succeeded in the task of perfecting a locomotive able to accept alternating current of 50 cycles at 25,000 volts. Not only does this permit lighter catenary, sub-stations are reduced to a minimum and current can be taken direct from the grid. The advantages are therefore substantial. British Railways electrification is now also based on the high voltage ac supply, but in this case current is transformed and rectified on the locomotives which are equipped with dc traction motors.

There is, therefore, much to commend electricity as a form of motive power. But although capital equipment is kept to the minimum by the use of high voltage alternating current, the initial cost is nevertheless high. For this reason, electrification is undertaken only where traffic is sufficiently heavy to justify the capital cost involved. Diesel traction requires no such costly installation and is therefore likely to remain a practical alternative.

Air Transport
Of all forms of transport, movement by air has developed most rapidly and radically. Although every sustained flight since aviation began has been made with petroleum fuels, the piston engine remained unchallenged for commercial flights until the immediate postwar period when in 1952, BOAC opened the world's first pure-jet air transport service between London and Johannesburg with the Comet I airliner.

A turbojet engine consists basically of a shaft, with a compressor at the forward end and a turbine at the rear. Air, in immense volume, is drawn in at the front, compressed and then fed into the combustion chambers, mixed with fuel vapour and ignited. The hot gases are then directed into the turbine which, in turn, spins the compressor. The resultant gas flow passes into the jet pipe, expands and is expelled at great velocity creating thousands of pounds of "thrust" — the unleashed energy which propels the aircraft. The conventional type of propeller is not therefore necessary.

The advantages of jets over piston-engined aircraft are speed, the absence of vibration producing smooth flight and greater power which permits larger aircraft with greater payloads. The cruising speed of 460 mph of the jet-propelled Comet I in 1952 compared favourably with the 300 mph of piston-engined aircraft. This factor coupled with greater comfort has produced a marked passenger preference for this type of aircraft.

In the by-pass type jet engine, only about one-half of the compressed air passes through the combustion chambers. The other half — less highly compressed and therefore much cooler — bypasses the high-pressure compressor, the combustion chambers and the turbines and only then enters the tailpipe and mixes with the hot exhaust gases. The result is a jet of cooler air moving at a much lower speed, which in turn results in greater propulsive efficiency, lower fuel consumption and reduced noise at all times. A diagram of a jet engine incorporating the by-pass principle appears at Fig 7.

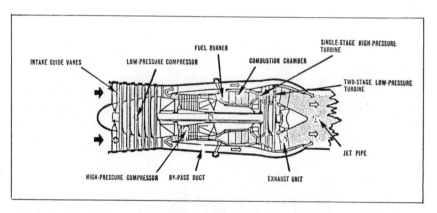

Fig 7. Diagram of a Jet Engine incorporating the By-Pass principle on which the Rolls Royce Conway is based. [*Reproduced by permission of the British Airways Board.*

Water Transport

The principal methods of propelling water-borne craft are the steam turbine, turbo-electric, diesel and diesel-electric, whilst the gas turbine and even nuclear power are in the process of development. It is not proposed even to touch upon the subject of marine engineering, the technicalities of which go far beyond this study. The reader should, however, at least know that ships are in the main propelled either by steam, a diesel engine, or by electricity generated by a diesel motor or a steam turbine. Looking at it in these elementary terms it will be seen that the methods of propulsion are not so very different from those of the railway. The choice depends on the economical and technical factors involved, but if steam is required it is now almost a foregone conclusion that the boilers will be oil-fired. The use of oil for ship propulsion was first attempted in warships at the beginning of the century and it soon became clear the compared with coal, oil allowed considerably greater radius of steaming, eased handling on board ship, required fewer stokers and took up less storage space. Its introduction greatly simplified and accelerated bunkering to which reference was made in Chapter 3 and by 1914 the use of oil by merchant vessels was becoming established. The impetus given to oil-firing by the subsequent war brought about a further rapid increase in the use of oil at sea and in the early twenties the development of the diesel engine also began to make itself felt. As the years went by, an increasing proportion of new tonnage was equipped with oil engines to the extent that by 1939, less than half of the total world merchant shipping tonnage was coal burning. The remainder consisted of oil-burning steamers and motor vessels. The decline of the coal-burning ship continued rapidly after the end of World War II.

Pipelines
The reference to pipelines in Chapter 2 noted that whilst the pumping station could be regarded as a part of the way, it is, of course, also the driving force as far as conveyance by pipeline is concerned. Some elaboration on the equipment used is, therefore, appropriate in this review of motive power. Pumping station equipment is very varied. Reciprocating pumps, single and multi-stage centrifugal pumps used in series or in parallel on single or multiple lines have all been used. Prime movers may be steam turbines, electric motors, gas engines, large diesel engines, diesel-electric sets, gas expansion turbines, or gas combustion turbines. The choice of the prime mover depends upon the availability of fuel or driving medium, possibly also of water and the nature of the pumping duty.

Long lines having several intermediate boosting stations present operating difficulties as the pumping rates at the various stations are inter-dependent though not necessarily equal. The oil in an unburied line, for example, expands when the temperature rises during the first part of the day, and contracts later, so that, for a steady flow of oil into the line, the variation in output at the delivery end can be as much as 5 per cent on either side of the average. The automatic control of the pumps has, however, been developed to such a point that operation on the closed line principle, i.e., without balance tanks at the boosting stations, is possible even under these conditions. Such control is of course additional to safety cutout devices which trip the pumps should delivery pressure become excessive, suction pressure be lost, or bearings overheat.

During recent years a number of boosting stations has been commissioned for unattended operation. All the operations of starting pumps, opening or closing of valves, etc., are carried out by automatic sequence control. The sequence may be initiated by remote control from another station, or by instruments responding to line pressure at the unattended station.

The Conveyance of Gas
Natural gas may or may not be associated with the production of oil. In the USA and Canada, where there is this association, the producing wells are comparatively close to centres of population and natural gas is widely distributed by

pipeline for use both in the manufacture of petroleum chemicals and as town gas. With the advent of North Sea gas the conveyance of natural gas by pipeline has now also been developed in the United Kingdom but in this case, the gas is mostly non-associated with oil.

Design problems encountered in gas lines differ considerably from those of crude oil lines.

A simplification results from the negligible weight of the gas and the pressure in the line is virtually independent of ground elevation. On the other hand, the compressibility of the gas introduces a serious complication, the density decreasing and consequently the volume rate of flow increasing in the direction of flow. Whereas in an oil line of constant diameter laid on level ground the pressure decreases uniformly with distance, in a gas line it decreases according to a parabolic law, the pressure gradient becoming progressively steeper.

Another essential difference arises from the characteristics of gas compressors. Oil pumps can be made to generate any desired pressure, but gas compressors perform at their maximum efficiency within certain defined limits. A gas boosting station must, therefore, be sited in accordance with these requirements.

6 · Characteristics

It will be recalled from Chapter 1 that transport is a service. It is a service which has the objective of a safe arrival regardless of the mode. Together, the different modes constitute the transport system that is considered in Chapter 7. Transport collectively meets the demand for movement of men and materials but the nature of these demands differs very widely. Each separate mode has its own peculiar characteristics and these characteristics determine its suitability or otherwise for the carriage of particular commodities. The traffics that are carried, be they passengers or goods, also have different characteristics. It follows that for optimum results, transport as a system must be judiciously used to ensure that each part carries that traffic for which it is most appropriate. In order, therefore, that this systems concept can be fully exploited, it is necessary to know for what purposes the different modes are most suitable. The characteristics of each will, therefore, now be examined.

Modal Characteristics

Road Transport

The great advantage of the road over other forms is the physical possibility of being able to provide a door-to-door facility. With exceptions such as the railway private siding and waterside premises, it is the only means which can give this service, hence travel by any other method invariably requires conveyance by road at the extremities of the journey. Apart, therefore, from its value as a means of trunk movement, the road is, by and large, essential for feeder purposes for rail, water and air. Because of the speed and vehicle size limitations naturally imposed on road transport as a result of the way being shared by all users, a feature to which reference was made in Chapter 2, the road is most suitable for short and medium distance traffic. It cannot directly compete in speed with rail or air but it is the road on which it is practicable for the individual to own and drive his own personal conveyance — the private car, the exceptional convenience of which has a very considerable (and rapidly increasing) public appeal. Similar considerations apply to privately-owned commercial vehicles for the conveyance of goods and for this reason long distance traffic by road throughout is now commonplace. Furthermore, the construction of fast motorways, both at home and abroad, is reducing the speed differential and thereby further popularising road transport for long distance travel. On the other hand and again as mentioned in Chapter 2, with sharing comes congestion. Delays through traffic congestion are becoming more and more an accepted part of travel by road and arrival times are becoming unreliable. Space and cost will prohibit the construction of highways sufficient to accommodate all of the vehicles that will wish to use them and some kind of restraint will have to be imposed. This feature of road transport is again referred to in Chapter 14.

Street Tramways

The street tramway was a satisfactory means of urban transport at the turn of the century and it remained strong both at home and abroad until the 1930s. Being a railed vehicle, however, it is tied to its tracks and with the substantial increase in vehicular traffic, there were thoughts that it could no longer take its place in normal traffic flows without materially aggravating the congestion. It was partly for this reason that British operators swung away from trams, and there is now only one electric street tramway system in Great Britain, that of Blackpool Corporation which, incidentally, is an excellent example of the very close relationship between a street tramway and a light railway. The tracks of the route along the seafront from Blackpool to Fleetwood are in part laid in the street, in part on a separate reservation between the road and the Promenade paved with flagstones and part on a fenced in right of way with rails laid on sleepers. Furthermore, there is a physical connection with the lines of the London Midland Region of British Railways which can share the use of the tram tracks for certain mineral traffics.

In some towns on the Continent of Europe and elsewhere, the natural advantages of the tram have been fully exploited and a number of highly efficient systems remains. Although the tram is inflexible — it cannot be temporarily diverted, extended easily to meet new demands, or even pass another vehicle, etc. which obstructs its special way — it does have advantages. It does not rely on oil for its source of power; it can be driven from either end and does not, therefore, require special turning facilities; a reversing movement can be effected wherever there is a suitable crossover in the track, which can even be in the centre of the road; it is smooth running, exhaust free, and has a high carrying capacity. In a number of Continental cities, these benefits have been preserved by the retention of the tram on a specially reserved way. At this stage, as at Blackpool, the tramway becomes very much akin to a light railway as described on page 28 and legally there is no clear definition between the two. The likeness becomes even greater with the use of trailers with trains of trams running on reserved railway (or tram) tracks. The reserved track allows the tram a free run clear of road congestion, but at the same time, frequent stops preserve the door to door characteristic of road transport. A further refinement as adopted in Brussels for example is to take the tramway underground into shallow tunnels at busy road intersections.

It is fair to say that the tram still has a legitimate place in inland transport, although this is not apparent if studies are confined to British practices.

Trolleybuses

The trolleybus is a hybrid — an attempt to combine the flexibility of the motorbus with the electric propulsion of the tram. Large-scale development of this type of vehicle came between the wars. The idea was to replace the street tramway with some vehicle which, unlike the tram, could avoid obstructions, pick up and set down passengers at the kerbside and eliminate the congestion and danger caused by trams fixed to their tracks in the centre of the road, but at the same time preserve the then low running costs of electricity. The result was a vehicle as illustrated at Plate 5, similar in outward appearance to a motorbus, but equipped with trolley poles for the collection of electric current from overhead wires. It is, however, still confined to special tracks, but not rigidly tied and in an emergency it can travel short distances independently on its batteries. Manœuvrability is possible within the limits of the trolley booms and dewirements are not frequent. Note in passing, however, that such dewirements as do occur are apt to happen at the points where routes diverge. This, of course, is at road junctions where an immobilised vehicle causes most embarrassment. Diversions and extensions cannot be undertaken at short notice and are costly; special turning circles are needed which the tram does not and the rising cost of electricity has tended to outweigh the advantage of cheaper running costs, notwithstanding the heavy taxation on diesel oil. There is now, therefore, less ground on which to justify the expense of maintaining two separate systems — the motorbus and the electric trolleybus. The trolleybus is silent, it has good acceleration, it is able to pick up and set down at the kerbside, it does not emit poisonous exhaust along the highway and it does not rely on oil as its source of power; but with two separate fleets so fundamentally different, it is impossible to reap the economies of standardisation and complete integration. The trend, therefore, is to abandon trolleybuses in favour of diesel-engined buses, but note the possible development in San Francisco of a more versatile trolleybus using kinetic energy as was described in Chapter 5.

The Railway

By the very nature of their service, railways must provide their own permanent way, stations, signalling and all necessary apparatus to ensure the safe passage of trains. In consequence a large part of their capital expenditure is spent on the provision of the way. Equipment must be kept in good working order, hence maintenance is also a substantial item. Because of these expenses, overheads represent a high proportion of the total costs. On the other hand, the way is private inasmuch as railway track can be used only by the specialised vehicles. In contrast to road transport, the railway alone must bear the entire cost of its way, but it is not required to share it and being the sole user, it does enjoy certain operating advantages. Railway management has complete control of all movement along its lines and is thus in a position to enforce a strict code of operational discipline. Subject to a satisfactory system of signalling, high capacity vehicles (or trains of vehicles) may be used to work a frequent service at fast speeds, which is in sharp contrast to road transport as noted above. The larger vehicles also enable the provision of more elaborate passenger amenities such as restaurant cars, sleeping cars, luggage accommodation and toilet facilities, and the high capacity substantially reduces the need for pre-booking. The railway is therefore eminently suitable for medium and long distance traffic, but it is a bulk carrier and its expensive equipment must be kept constantly employed if the service is to be viable. It follows that both distance and density must be features of railway traffic, hence the policy to close branch lines and intermediate stations in rural areas and to concentrate on through traffic in large consignments or numbers for which the railway is competitive in both speed and comfort. Physically, if not economically, the railway is also very suitable for meeting heavy surges of traffic for special events and for the concentrated morning and evening peak business movements in large towns. By catering for this traffic, the railway fulfils an important social function. There are many instances where the parallel road system could not accommodate without serious or even chaotic congestion that portion of the peak hour traffic which is at present carried by rail. In the event of continued development around existing centres combined with the absence of any remedial, albeit unpopular, measures such as compulsory and widespread staggering of hours, the problem of the peaks can only become more intense. It is a problem to which part of the answer, although costly, could lie in the construction of new railways in some form, perhaps underground as is considered in Chapter 14. Such new lines would not be profitable but, depending on local circumstances, they might reduce the need for otherwise expensive roadworks. Reasons other than purely commercial factors could therefore influence railway development.

Except in thickly populated areas likely to support a concentration of local suburban lines, passenger traffic is ideally channelled into a relatively few main trunk routes stopping only at stations serving the larger towns and fed not by railway branch lines but by road services. The limited demand for intermediate stopping trains rarely justifies their operating costs and looked at in isolation this traffic can usually be catered for more economically by road. It is for these reasons that British Railways has pruned its system. Outside built-up areas, branch line trains and stopping trains on the main lines in effect serve only rural areas as intercity traffic invariably travels by the faster trains. Revenue from the slow services therefore falls far short of the costs of operation. Even if the service is maintained with the cheapest possible vehicle — a diesel railbus, the track must still be maintained at a cost beyond all comparison with the annual vehicle tax of a road vehicle, to say nothing of signals, stations, level-crossings, etc, which might be necessary. True, a replacement bus service could also incur a loss, but not to the same extent as the railway. It was a historical accident that the steam engine was developed before the internal combustion engine and hence the possibility of fast travel by railway at a time when the road vehicle was still being pulled by a horse. The bulk of our railway system was, as a result, constructed at a time when there was no satisfactory alternative. Had this not been the case it is very probable that much of the system as we know it today might never have been built, but it was only the serious financial position of the railways that brought the matter to the public eye. Even so, there are other factors which could justify a railway network as will be seen in Chapters 13 and 14.

As far as freight is concerned, it is not only the type of goods but also the type of journey in relation to quantity which spells profit or loss for the railway. Like passenger traffic, intermediate sundry traffic is expensive operationally because of the need to provide full facilities at wayside stations to meet small and irregular demands. Again, therefore, traffic must be concentrated along main lines to centralised traffic points, hence the zonal system of collection and delivery as was explained in Chapter 3. As a word of explanation, sundry traffic is to the railway regarded as miscellaneous traffic carried by goods train. This, to British Road Services, for example, would be regarded as parcels traffic. Parcels on the railway represent miscellaneous goods consigned by passenger train.

Air

The outstanding characteristic of air transport is speed. Not only is the aircraft itself very fast moving, it is able to follow a direct line of flight unhindered by the physical barriers experienced by surface transport. Seas, mountains, deserts, sandbanks, jungle swamps, etc. offer no resistance to the aeroplane, but aircraft require a considerable length of runway for take-off and touch-down. It was seen in Chapter 3 that air terminals are extravagant on land space and cannot conveniently be placed in the immediate vicinity of large towns. It follows that there must often be lengthy journeys by surface transport between the town centre and the airport, which are time consuming and the portion of air travel must be of sufficient length to make the overall journey time competitive with more direct travel by surface transport throughout. For this reason, unless there are special circumstances, air transport seldom offers advantage for distances of less than say 100 miles, although any large scale commercial development of the helicopter or other vertical take-off aircraft might alter the position. Air transport is nevertheless ideally suited for the long haul and it is also highly competitive for short journeys over country which is difficult for surface transport or where a change from one form of transport to another would otherwise be necessary as, for example, the cross-Channel services from London to Paris etc.

In general characteristics, there is a remarkable similarity between air transport and shipping for the following reasons:

(1)   Both operate national and international routes for passengers and freight.
(2)   The way is natural in each case and operation is therefore flexible. No capital is invested in the way as such.
(3)   Both require extensive navigational aids.
(4)   Both require elaborate and expensive terminals such as docks and airports which the operators do not generally own.
(5)   Both are operated to a large extent under international agreements, either government or private.
(6)   There is a large charter market for each type of transport.

But there the similarity ends. In other respects the two are entirely different, particularly in terms of speed.

Sea

Some of the characteristics of sea transport have just been mentioned in the previous paragraph when discussing certain similarities with air. A very large part of seaborne traffic is of an international character, much of it being carried over very long distances. For natural reasons, international shipping lines give a service which could not be accomplished either easily or at all by any other means of surface transport. Vessels are large, and apart from the influence of the elements, provide a high standard of comfort. But sea transport is predominantly slow, hence a considerable part of the passenger business has now been lost to air. Nevertheless the great capacity of seagoing vessels tends to offset their high cost of construction as it is physically possible to carry a good payload on each trip. Shipping rates can therefore be maintained at a reasonably attractive level. Because of this and because of the available capacity, sea transport remains strong in the movement of merchandise in cases where the journey cannot readily be made by any other form of transport except air. Coastal shipping around Great Britain is of declining importance because of the small size and shape of the country and competition from rail and road. Where land masses are large, coastal traffic may still be important.

There is, however, one feature that has particular significance to sea transport. It was stated in Chapter 1 that transport is a service activity that usually stems from a derived demand. It was noted in that context that perhaps the best example to the contrary is a sea cruise. Travel in this way in the right weather at the right time of year can be enjoyment in itself and has widespread appeal, so much so that shipping lines now tend to concentrate on this type of traffic, having lost most of the passengers from their long distance point to point liner services to the very much faster and hence highly competitive airlines.

Inland Waterways
The average speed of a narrow boat on a British narrow canal is only about 3 mph, but the service is not quite as slow as this figure suggests as canals do not suffer from congestion as do roads. Nevertheless it cannot be denied that the canal is more suitable for the conveyance of lower classes of goods of a non-perishable nature, standing stocks of which are subject to continual replenishment and for which there is therefore no real sense of urgency. Coal lends itself to this form of transport, followed by such commodities as petroleum, grain, flour, timber, chemicals, iron and steel. Inland water transport has been found to be specially suitable and efficient for:

(a)   Traffic imported and for shipment in ports connected with the inland waterway system, particularly in those instances where overside delivery from ship to barge or vice-versa takes place;

(b)   Traffic which can be carried from point to point in barge loads;

(c)   Traffic conveyed to or from waterside premises;

(d)   Petroleum and liquids in bulk;

(e)   Traffic requiring bulk movement and storage in canal side warehouses;

(f)   Trunk haul to river or canal waterheads with subsequent delivery by road.

It is of course unfortunate but inevitable that the economies of bulk consignments apply equally to other branches of transport. It is precisely this traffic which railways are also trying hard to obtain.

Apart from the initial cost of construction of an artificial canal, it is not one of the most costly forms of transport and it is capable of carrying heavy loads but like sea transport, movement by canal or navigable river is not rapid.

Although reference has so far been confined to the movement of merchandise, the carriage of passengers has a limited place in this mode of transport. The reader will of course be familiar with the many different types of ferry boat which link the opposite banks of waterways and which range from the small flat bottomed manually-propelled punt to the large steam or diesel floating bridge (from which as we saw in Chapter 4, the roll-on roll-off ferry has developed) capable of accommodating heavy vehicles. Strictly speaking, however, the function of these craft is not relevant to the subject under review as the waterway is in this context little more than an impediment to another form of way. The purpose here is to consider the waterway as a line of communication in its own right and as such it has only a limited application to passenger transport. As a form of transport it can assume importance in cases where a naturally navigable river passes through tropical jungle or such other type of country, which renders the construction of a road or railway very difficult. Even so, it is likely that air transport would now be a more attractive alternative. By and large, apart from ferries, the passenger boat caters for the pleasure traveller and is seasonal. Given fine weather, a boat trip has appeal in its own right, particularly if the waterway passes through scenic country. The major ship canals serve a different purpose, as was explained in Chapter 2 and there could be in this case a considerable (but not necessarily local) passenger movement.

Pipelines

What are the characteristics of the pipeline and how does it differ from other forms of transport? Can, in fact, the pipeline legitimately be classified as a form of transport or is it only a means of internal communication like the conveyor belt in a factory? Chapter 2 has answered the second question. Technical development has not only given the pipeline a legitimate place but also, subject to suitable conditions, a competitive place in the transport industry. With regard to the first question, the pipeline is unique in that the way is also the carrying unit, thereby producing a transformation from batch-handling to continuous flow. It is purely artificial and requires expensive capital equipment. It is inflexible, as once laid its position cannot be altered easily, which calls for a sustained demand between fixed points. It is not therefore suitable where the movement pattern is liable to change. Furthermore, its use is very specific as, for example, surplus capacity of an oil pipeline would not be used for the distribution of beer. In other words, it is necessary to be selective in grouping materials for conveyance through the same tube, although this does not rule out the possibility of a multi-user pipe carrying different fluids. There is no reason why a delivery of motor spirit should not be followed by a dispatch of say paraffin as it is technically possible to separate one product from the next so that there is virtually no mixing in transit. But the characteristics of the pipeline are certainly not all negative. It offers many advantages compared with the more orthodox forms of transport. As the way is also the carrying unit, no packing is necessary and hence no returning of empty containers. Nothing moves except the commodity being transported. The problem of a return load does not arise and traffic remains unaffected by road congestion, transhipment points or difficult terrain. The elimination of a separate carrying unit and the absence of handling makes the pipeline very light on manpower. It has, therefore, much to offer in return for its high capital cost and general inflexibility.

The cost of batch road or sea transport between any two points does not vary materially with the quantity transported once the largest possible vehicle or vessel is kept fully employed. Costs are then at their lowest limit and any variation in traffic means only a larger or smaller number of carrying units. The cost of pipeline transport drops rapidly with the quantity moved until saturation of the line's capacity is reached. The high initial capital cost then becomes spread over the maximum volume of traffic. Owing to its static nature, operating costs are relatively low and are largely made up of fixed elements such as labour, maintenance, way-leaves, etc. Conversely, capital costs are high as have been shown. It follows that the optimum operating costs can be obtained only if the pipeline operates continuously at full capacity; unit costs rise rapidly as the actual throughput falls below the maximum. This theory is of course neither new nor unusual as for each form of transport, for maximum economy, traffic must be constant and sufficient to keep the resources fully employed. The pipeline is no exception to this rule. However, once the initial cost of construction has been met and providing the pipeline is used to maximum capacity the direct operating costs compare very favourably with other forms of inland transport.

The use of pipelines for the bulk transport of oil and natural gas has been a major development in the oil industry. Gas in any quantity can only be moved conveniently by pipe and, incidentally, at a greater cost than for the conveyance of oil of similar heat value. Nevertheless, the transport of gas by pipeline is very economical. For the transport of oil, however, pipelines are only an alternative to batch transport, either by seagoing or coastwise tanker, barge, or rail or road tanker. Except for very small quantities of oil, the cost per ton-mile is lower by pipeline than by rail or road transport, but even with the biggest pipeline capacities practicable today, the cost does not come down to the level of ocean-going tankers for the same length of haul. Unless the pipeline is operated continuously at something approaching full capacity, the cost per ton delivered is much in excess of that by sea transport for the same distance. Pipelines can as yet only compete with tankers if the pipeline route is considerably shorter than the tanker route, or if sea transport is subject to exceptional charges such as heavy canal dues.

These reasons explain why the principal use of pipelines is to connect inland oilfields with big refining or shipping centres and why their use for distribution of products to the market is not nearly as frequent. By far the largest user of the product line is the USA, whose large continental area contains a number of centres of very heavy consumption.

Traffic Characteristics

The foregoing has described the characteristics of the different modes which all have one common objective, that of a safe arrival. Together they form the overall transport system.

The traffic carried also has its characteristics. The fundamental distinction is, of course, that between passengers and goods, so much so that some carriers, and almost all in road transport, specialise in one branch or the other. Not only the vehicles but also the operating techniques are often entirely different and even in undertakings which carry both types of traffic such as a railway, administration of the commercial aspects is likely to be separate. Traffics within these two broad divisions however also have their different characteristics.

Passenger Traffic

People use transport services for a variety of reasons. They use it for travel between home and their place of work or to school and they may travel in the course of their duty. This is usually regarded as the essential traffic. Then there is the optional traffic which consists of those passengers who are not travelling in connection with their work but are doing so for personal reasons. These reasons could include shopping or hospital visiting or travel purely for pleasure such as to visit relatives or friends, the cinema, places of interest or of high scenic value, to attend sporting events or even, in a few instances, just for the enjoyment of travelling. The demand for optional travel is, to use an economic term, elastic. This means that it is more likely to respond to the quality of the facilities that are provided. People in this category do not have to travel. They could shop locally and they could follow alternative pastimes, even to the extent of staying at home and viewing television, etc.

Distance is another characteristic. Works and schools traffic are local and the journeys are generally short. Office workers sometimes travel a little further and the same might perhaps be said for some shopping expeditions. Travelling in the course of business, for recreation or for some special purpose could amount to anything from a local trip to something embracing the length of the country or the circumference of the earth.

It is unfortunate from the point of view of transport economics but nevertheless inevitable that the demands for these various categories of travel are not easily spread in terms of time. There are peak periods of heavy traffic concentration. As far as the daily peaks are concerned, business and schools traffic is likely to clash to create a heavy unidirectional demand in the morning with an almost as heavily concentrated return movement at night (schools are often ahead of the business traffic on the return journey). In Great Britain, traffic into the big towns between 8 and 9am and out again between 5 and 6pm is traditionally heavy. Large numbers of vehicles and operating staff are required for work in these two short periods of the day (and at that only on five days per week) and operators are at a loss on how to use those resources profitably at other times. The urban services of both road and rail are particularly susceptible to these daily peak fluctuations. Other types of traffic have a more seasonal demand. Holiday travel strains the resources of the longer distance road, rail and air services on summer Saturdays and on Bank Holiday weekends. Sporting events create short but heavy demands although if held on a Saturday or in the evenings,for, say, dog racing or football by floodlight, it might help to find badly needed work in what might otherwise be a slack period.

It is clear, therefore, that an intensive peak is highly uneconomical, even though vehicles may be filled to capacity (in one direction) at the crucial times. Furthermore, passengers are subject to discomfort resulting from pressure of numbers. The problem of the peak is indeed a very real problem for providers of all forms of transport — passenger or goods. A number of methods is adopted to help lessen its severe effects including the following:

(i) *Staggering of hours*
Local organisations or transport groups are approached to encourage large employers to stagger between themselves the hours of their workers. If successful, this spreads the peak movement over a longer period and makes it less intense. Vehicles can make two or more effective trips and a reduced fleet can thus cater

more efficiently for the same traffic. But there is a limit to what people can be asked to do. It would be unreasonable to expect a 6 o'clock start or an 8 o'clock finish as part of normal office routine. Staggering as is practised today certainly helps bus and local railway services in urban areas. It lessens but by no means eradicates the problem.

(ii) *Larger vehicles or aircraft*
It is in the peaks when full advantage can be taken of a high capacity vehicle. Although the use of a large vehicle means empty seats being carried around for most of the day, which, in itself, is uneconomic, in the circumstances it is often justified. Clearly, separate fleets of vehicles could not be kept for peak and slack working, hence, if the larger vehicle is required in the peak, it must be used throughout. Operators must select the optimum size and the tendency is to run those vehicles which offer maximum accommodation. Physical difficulties may, however, preclude the operation of the largest vehicles, etc., throughout the system, in which case, standardisation on one type, even selectively for each class of traffic, becomes impossible. These circumstances must be taken into account when vehicle specifications are being considered.

(iii) *Express buses*
A limited-stop service runs at a faster average speed than normal stopping services. Vehicles used on an express service might therefore be able to make an additional effective trip in the peak period, but care must be taken to ensure that the stops observed are convenient for the majority of passengers. It is useless to waste capacity by allowing buses with empty seats to pass queues of people, and this is a distinct danger with an express service.

(iv) *Special off-peak fares*
Special off-peak fare reductions encourage those people who do not have to travel at set hours to make their journeys at times more convenient to operators. Again, this produces some relief in the peaks, but only at the expense of lower receipts.

This approach is widely adopted in all forms of transport although perhaps in a slightly different form by charging extra during popular periods. The same principle can, of course, apply to days of the week or weeks of the year.

As indeed was noted in Chapter 1, unlike a manufactured product, transport as a service cannot be stored. A manufacturer of fireworks, for example, is able to spread production over the entire year for peak sales in November. Once produced, seat miles must be either sold or wasted which is a fundamental characteristic of all transport.

Goods Traffic
The characteristics of goods traffic are very different from that of passengers. It has been shown that passengers travel for a variety of reasons but their demands and expectations can be assessed accordingly. The passenger is a standard unit; he loads and unloads himself and he asks for no more than a seat (or perhaps only a place in which to stand). The comfort expected of that seat may vary but even so, the degree of vehicle specialisation is nothing like that which is required for the carriage of freight.

Goods may be in a solid, liquid or gaseous state, they may be inert or highly volatile, they may be durable, fragile or perishable and they may be dead or alive. They may be of an infinite variety of shapes, sizes and weights. Much of the traffic requires specialised vehicles or vessels and some goods cannot be mixed with others. Although, therefore, the purpose built vehicles and vessels may well be fully laden in one direction, there is often little possibility of a return load. On the other hand, goods that are not so exacting in their requirements and which can be accommodated in general purpose vehicles could be very awkward in shape and hence very demanding in space. This type of traffic denies the operator a proper payload, at least as far as weight is concerned.

This brings into focus the term "loadability" which is a characteristic of goods traffic. Traffic that has good loadability has the property of being able to accommodate itself within and make maximum use of the space that is available in the vehicle, vessel or aircraft in which it is being carried.

For the following reasons, coal may be cited as an example of a type of traffic which can be carried comparatively cheaply:

(a) It does not require a specialised wagon – on the contrary it requires nothing more than the simplest open truck.

(b) It is not perishable. It may be stockpiled and is therefore seldom urgent.

(c) Its size and shape allows maximum use of wagon space (i.e. good loadability).

(d) It is suitable for loading and (if delivered in sufficient quantities) unloading by mechanical means.

(e) It is a constant traffic. For industrial purposes it is not subject to serious seasonal fluctuations.

(f) It is dispatched in full truck loads (or full train loads).

Contrast this with, say, bulky and fragile, although not necessarily heavy, pieces of machinery. Consignments such as this might possess none of the advantages listed above. It is not difficult to visualise why costs vary accroding to the class of traffic and why in consequence a scale of charges based on weight alone would be inadequate.

Capacities

Reference has been made to the relative capacity characteristics on a modal basis. The railway, for example, being the sole user of a private way is able to operate large units at fast speeds. Given comparable circumstances, therefore, the capacity of a railway is likely to be greater than that of a road, the characteristics of which call for smaller vehicles and lower average speeds. But capacities vary within the mode itself depending upon the qualities of the way and the equipment used.

It has been said that a feature of any kind of railway is capacity. It is a bulk carrier and its provision can be justified only where the traffic potential is sufficiently heavy. But the traffic that is able to pass is much greater on some railway routes than on others. In fact, the features of different lines are such that capacities vary enormously. The first and obvious reason lies in the number of tracks that are provided. It may be a single track, a double track or more and if it is a single track, line capacity will vary according to the number of passing loops that are available. Reference was made in Chapter 2 to railway signalling which splits the line into sections. To avoid collisions it is necessary for trains to operate on the basis of at the most one per section. The shorter the sections, the greater is the number of sections that can be provided and hence the number of trains that can be accommodated on any given stretch of line. A correspondingly greater number of signals would also, of course, become necessary. Again an obvious indication of capacity is size and design of rolling stock. Overall dimensions depend on the loading gauge to which reference was also made in Chapter 2 and in the case of passenger vehicles, to the standard of comfort that is provided. Generally speaking, the greater the comfort, the less is the capacity. The length or number of coaches per train do, of course, have a direct relation to the capacity of each train as a unit but not necessarily of the line as on high density routes, train lengths are apt to have a bearing on frequencies, if only because of the need to have signalling sections (or blocks) long enough to accommodate the longest train. In terms of overall capacity, under certain circumstances it might be that a very frequent service of short trains is superior to a less frequent service of longer trains. Speed is another factor which influences capacity and very closely allied to speed is acceleration. These qualities depend on the type of motive power and the stock itself, but the faster the average speed, the greater is the number of trains that can pass in a given time, always remembering that the maximum speed on the line is determined by the speed of the slowest train. A line with mixed traffic with some slow trains is not likely, therefore, to achieve maximum capacity. It is for this reason that rapid transit lines are completely self-contained on their own right of way, separated even from other services of a similar mode.

Turning to road transport, highway capacities in terms of vehicles are determined very largely on road widths or the number of traffic lanes that are provided. Capacity in this respect is interpreted as vehicle capacity at any one point. The number of vehicles that can pass between any pair of points is also, of course, like the railway, influenced by speed and motorways where, emergencies apart, there are no stops, have a higher capacity in this respect than a corresponding dual-carriageway road of the conventional type on which traffic is frequently required for a variety of reasons to reduce speed or stop. It is on the road that vehicle size has a very material effect on overall capacity in terms of loads. It was seen in Chapter 4 that a bus can comfortably seat up to about 80 people and in peak periods in urban areas it frequently does just that. A vehicle of this size occupies about four times the road space of a private car, the average occupancy of which is about 1.5 persons. In other words, to move the same number of people, the private car does in reality take up about thirteen times as much road space as does the bus. Similar considerations apply to the carriage of goods although in this case wastage of capacity does not compare with the private car. Nevertheless, a large number of slower moving heavy goods vehicles restrict the passage of passenger vehicles which must, in turn, influence capacity at least as between goods and passenger traffic. In short, the capacity of a highway can only be judged in relation to the vehicles that use it. It can be assessed in terms of vehicle numbers but the loads that can be carried depends to a great extent on the types of vehicles that are used.

With inland waterways it is the width and depth that determines capacity as it is these factors that govern the size of vessels. In practice, it is often the locks that are the "pinch-points". This feature was noted in Chapter 2 when the British narrow canals were discussed. The restriction in size of the boats that can use these canals is a very serious limitation on their capacity.

The different features that have been considered make it possible to assess the capacities of artificial ways. In the case of the two natural ways, sea and air, the capacity as far as the way is concerned is virtually unlimited. Air space covers the world and the sea covers something approaching three quarters of it. Certainly over these great expanses, lines of communication have been developed from the one time trade routes to the now heavily used channels and some of these traffic lanes can become congested. Nevertheless, exceptions apart (and much mention has been made of congestion in the Straits of Dover, for example) it is not really the way as such that is the inhibiting factor in the capacities of either air or sea transport. Neither is it the size of the craft that use these ways. Aircraft can now seat nearly 500 people and larger ones can be expected if they can be justified for other reasons. Tankers of nearly 500,000 d.w.t. are now on the seas and again this is certainly not the limit. Capacity limitations of sea and air transport really come at the terminals and the approaches to the terminals which, of course, include the air space above and around airports and the depth of water channels into ports. Reception facilities for the ships and aeroplanes and for the traffic that use them must be adequate and it is here that limitations arise. Air services into London, for example, are limited in the main to the capacities of Heathrow and Gatwick Airports. Forecast demands indicate a future need for facilities beyond what these two airports will be able to provide, hence the plans for a third London airport. Landings and take-offs are always physically restricted by the available runways, navigational aids and air approach lanes. The capacities of runways are not, however, determined only by their size. Landing and take-off technology also affects capacity, which means that the position might be different in, say, twenty years time to what it is now. This matter is further considered in Chapter 14. There is also a limit to the number of passengers that can be received at any one time. This is governed by the terminal facilities.

These are the features that determine the capacity of a system.

Service Characteristics

When considering the characteristics of a service, the fundamental distinction between that which is provided for passengers and that which is provided for goods is again apparent. Compared with the traffic classifications, the distinction becomes a little blurred when, as is so often the case, many vehicles, vessels and aircraft that are designed primarily for the carriage of passengers also carry some freight and conversely, when those designed for the conveyance of goods or cargo do sometimes carry a few passengers. There is, nevertheless, a basic purpose and use for the services that are provided, be it for passengers or for goods, but it is not necessarily an exclusive use. Bus services to a small extent and passenger trains to a much greater extent carry unaccompanied parcels. Passenger ships and aircraft are able to carry a limited amount of cargo. Instances of the converse situation can also be found. Services planned primarily for the carriage of mail are likely to be available for passengers also and cargo ships are permitted to carry up to 12 passengers without a special passenger certificate.

Another basic characteristic is that between a pre-scheduled service and one that is provided on a pre-booked or contract basis. A scheduled service is one that is planned and advertised in advance and will operate regardless of the demand at the time. In sea transport, pre-scheduled shipping services are known as liner services. A feature of the "Freightliner" trains of the National Freight Corporation is that they offer an advertised facility. All of the normal service workings on the passenger sections of road, rail, sea and air are pre-scheduled and they operate regardless of the actual demand at the time of departure although on many of the longer distance services, a system of pre-booking of seats is in operation. This not only guarantees the would-be passenger accommodation but enables the demand to be pre-judged. To this extent, therefore, actual provision may be matched to demand at the time of travel, even on pre-scheduled services, by the operation of additional unscheduled journeys as duplicates to the normal service departures.

Alternatives to the pre-scheduled service may take the form of a charter or contract operation whereby the vehicle, vessel or aircraft is hired for the exclusive use of a party of people or movement of freight. In this case an inclusive charge is levied to cover both the direct and indirect costs of the complete operation regardless of the number of people or the load that is carried. Responsibility for solvency is in this case on the hirer and not on the operator who is assured of his return. This type of operation is the basis of package holidays. By an intricate system of bloc booking of both transport and hotel facilities, organisations are able to utilise to the maximum all available resources. There are no empty and hence wasted seats. Costs may, therefore, be spread over the maximum number of people which means that the charge to the individual can be attractively low. An excursion or tour is something between a charter and a normal service. Often organised by the operators themselves, excursions and tours are pre-advertised and seats are sold separately. Even so, if sufficient patronage is not forthcoming, a tour programme is liable to be altered at very short notice, which might involve cancellations and transfers of passengers.

It is not inopportune to mention at this juncture the taxi and the characteristics of the service that it provides. The taxi is hired by the individual for his own specific purpose. Its use is well known and well used for local journeys by road but this is not the only place for the taxi. Water taxis are often available where geographical conditions happen to suit and light aircraft are used as air taxis for a rather limited clientele. The principle is, nevertheless, the same regardless of the mode. It is a refinement of the charter system and is really a part of public transport offering its facilities to all who wish to use them. However, once the vehicle or whatever it may be becomes engaged, the hirer is in the same position as if he were using his own private transport, the characteristics of which are considered later in this chapter. Once again, distinctions become blurred. This time it is between what may be regarded as public and what is really private transport. The company that publicly offers self-drive cars for hire takes the process one stage further. If the taxi can be classified along with private transport then this must certainly be the case with the self-drive car.

Frequency, regularity and speed are the characteristics which users tend to employ in a discriminatory manner to measure the qualities of a particular service. For a local journey in an urban area, a frequent bus service is likely to be regarded as one which produces a departure at least, say, every five minutes. For a rail journey of 100 miles, two trains per hour might be accepted as frequent. Regularity is generally considered in terms of frequency as being the time that elapses between successive vehicles or, in other words, the headway. But a regular headway that is exactly repetitive in each hour is really more than a regular service, it is a regular "clock-face" service. Odd bus journeys may run for works or school purposes, a shipping line might run a vessel per week or per month on a liner service, but these are all nevertheless regular services even though the headways may be nothing like regular. Speed is another characteristic and again this can be looked at in two ways. It was seen when the modal characteristics were considered that some forms of transport have a greater speed potential than others. But some services may be regarded as fast and others as slow regardless of the mode and these considerations are often in contradiction to the generally accepted modal characteristics. This could arise, for example, where a change of vehicle is required by one mode of transport but not by another.

We are now coming to the point that in judging qualities, no one service is likely to be considered in isolation. The users require to move either themselves or their goods between two points. They are concerned with the overall movement from the beginning of the journey to the end of the journey. Each individual service constitutes only one part of that journey; to the operator(s) several services may be involved but to the user it is one journey. In other words, users are interested in the assortment of services that are provided, not individually but collectively as a system. This systems concept is further considered in Chapter 7.

The systems concept and the judicious use of transport modes for the purposes for which they are most appropriate as was mentioned in the first paragraph of this chapter brings back into focus from Chapter 1 the justification or otherwise for the availability of choice. Doubt was expressed in Chapter 1 on the validity of any economic justification for the availability of choice, particularly in the carriage of goods including parcels and mail. The justification is perhaps stronger in passenger transport as people are more discerning about safety and comfort. Preferences on grounds of safety are, nevertheless, rather more imaginary than real. Everybody, of course, looks for safety, both for themselves and for their goods and in this respect, a safe arrival (which, remember, is the objective of all transport as was stated in Chapter 1) means not only an arrival free from personal injury but also from damage or loss of merchandise. Nevertheless, people do not really have to look for safety. As far as public transport is concerned, to the extent that is humanly possible, they get it. No operator runs his business in a dangerous manner and in any case there is legislation to prevent him from doing so as will be seen from Chapter 8. Even so, human nature is such that individuals might have more confidence in one form of transport than in another. Travel by air is still considered by some as a hazardous pursuit but those same people are often keen motorists regardless of the fact that casualties involving occupants of private cars are very great in comparison with air travellers. Comfort, of course, involves considerations not only in terms of the quality and size of the seat and the smoothness of the ride but also the need for changing vehicles and the extent of walking and waiting at interchange points.

Reliability is another characteristic of the transport service and with it, punctuality. Nothing can foster goodwill more than a reputation for a consistently high standard of reliability. It was seen earlier in this chapter that road transport is experiencing delays due to traffic congestion. Speed and punctuality is thereby suffering. Furthermore, delays cost money as proper use cannot be made of either vehicles or staff. This increases the working expenses which must be recovered by the imposition of higher fares and this in turn makes the service even less attractive because the price is no longer right. Reference is made in Chapter 12 to staff negotiation and consultation but it can be said here that over the past 25 years trade unions have become stronger, often as a result of compulsory membership by the staff, and the staff themselves have become more militant. The working population (and this does not mean only transport workers) is demanding improved standards of living and hence wages in excess of what their respective industries can economically support. Along with this there seems to have disappeared the pride in the job and the will to give service. Such things as bad timekeeping, incorrect display of destination blinds, insolence and shabby appearances are all too often experienced. Local supervisors become frustrated in their endeavours to maintain proper discipline through lack of support from managements who must at the same time maintain working relations with very powerful trade unions. Those workers who are still strong for service and, to be fair, there are some, are similarly frustrated by the attitude of their colleagues and the trade union membership generally of which they may be forced to be a part. Wage demands are not only frequent but are often accompanied by strikes and go-slow tactics. Nevertheless, it is not intended to castigate any one section of the community. It is probably true to say that during the early years of the present century and before, the working population was quite literally overworked and underpaid. Perhaps we are now gathering the fruits of the policies that were followed in those times. But, be that as it may, this is not a discourse on the history of industrial relations. The subject is reliability and the allegations that have been made, even though they are not valid in every case, have resulted in conditions that have not been conducive to the maintenance of a good image. Some public services are now no longer seen to be dependable. Let it again be said, there is no more valuable asset to a transport undertaking than the tag of reliability and for one reason or another it is unfortunate that standards have so often deteriorated. This is one of the reasons why many individuals and industrialists have turned to their own private transport.

Private Transport

Private transport, like public transport, falls into two classes, that which is used for the carriage of passengers and that which is used for goods. On the passenger side, it is, of course, one's own private means of conveyance, the private car.

Mention was made earlier in this chapter that the road is particularly suited for private and personal vehicle ownership for both passenger and goods transport. There are two special reasons for this:

(a)   The capital cost of a road vehicle is within reach of the individual.

(b)   It is not difficult to attain the necessary skill to drive a mechanically-propelled road vehicle.

For passenger transport, therefore, a small private car is a convenient alternative to public road and rail services and is within the means of a large number of people. For the conveyance of goods, private road transport is a practical alternative, even for small-scale enterprise, to the employment of public haulage facilities. The railway is not appropriate for this type of use and the very occasional privately owned coach or the more common privately owned wagon (the movement of which is controlled by the railway authority and not by the owner) is the nearest example that is likely to be found. Similarly with sea transport, privately owned ocean-going vessels are the exception rather than the rule and are the playthings of the minority where money is no object. Lighter craft for use on inland navigations and other sheltered waters are more widely owned, but the purpose is more for sport and recreation than for transport. Privately owned aircraft have a much greater transport value and light aircraft are owned and used in this way. Although this type of operation is very limited in Great Britain, it is more common in North America.

For the carriage of freight, this type of private operation is found in sea transport. The major oil companies have their own private tanker fleets and other purpose built ships are used in certain other specialised industries such as, for example, the importing of bananas. It is however the road that is particularly appropriate for "own account" operation. Manufacturers and others who have a constant need for commercial transport are able to consider the advantages of a privately-owned road vehicle or vehicle fleet as against use of the public services and make their choice according to circumstances. For the larger users, advantages and disadvantages of private transport may be summarised as follows:

(i)   The user has greater control over driving personnel as they are a part of his own staff.

(ii)   Vehicles and staff are entirely at his disposal, which is an advantage in emergencies, etc.

(iii)   The operation of a private transport fleet is an added responsibility. Unless the work involved is sufficient to justify the employment of a specialist transport manager, it might be better left in the hands of professional hauliers.

(iv)   In the case of a private fleet, the manufacturer must bear not only direct running costs, but also the entire overhead expenses. Work must therefore be sufficient to keep vehicles and staff constantly engaged. Public transport is paid for only as it is used.

(v)   A private vehicle fleet carries the trade name of the manufacturer, which has advertising and prestige value. This function, however, can also be met by the public haulier. British Road Services, for example, operates a contract hire service whereby vehicles bear the customer's livery. The drivers are also supplied; they act as if they were part of the customer's staff. At the same time, by contract hire, the user avoids

capital outlay together with the problems associated with vehicle operation and maintenance.

The great advantage of private transport for both goods and passengers is convenience and the numbers of vehicles in this class grow year by year. Roads
become more congested as private motoring gains popularity even though the
strain of driving becomes greater. This ever increasing competitive force is indeed
a challenge to public transport.

7 · The Transport System

Introduction

In Chapter 1, the role of transport was examined from the standpoint of elementary economics. The purpose of this chapter is to show briefly the build-up and provision of transport facilities in toto, the repercussions on international traffic with particular reference to air transport and finally the bases on which charges may be levied for the use of the facilities that are provided. Transport as a system or in "total" terms will, therefore, now be considered, not in any abstract sense but as a tangible service to the community.

The Developing Period

Transport facilities were pioneered by private enterprise and all have sprung from very humble beginnings. On both land and water, propulsion was in the first place by natural power (either human power or the wind on the sea and by animal power on the roads and inland waterways). This was followed by the advent of the steam engine and the birth of the railway. The steam age spread also to the sea and in due course came the petrol and diesel engines, first on the roads and then in further developed forms to rail and sea and finally to air. The evolution of transport from the steam operated railway trains to passenger carrying air services was spread over a period of about 100 years and services were built up in accord with technological developments of the time. Steamship, canal carrying, railway, bus, road haulage and air transport companies came into being over the years to offer new facilities and so produce a return on capital invested by optimistic speculators. Some met a need, some created their own need as transport stimulated economic growth which in turn created a demand for yet more transport. Nevertheless, notwithstanding this economic necessity (which was explained in Chapter 1) the motive of the promoters (as distinct from the function or the objective) was profit. Each service or group of services provided by any one undertaking was, company-wise, a self-contained competitive unit. There was no connection with "the firm next door" and as the population grew larger and the economy grew stronger so these facilities were extended until they overlapped and duplicated each other.

Public transport considered collectively reached its zenith around the 1950's. Movement in relative comfort, speed and safety by land, sea and air had become a reality whilst wartime conditions had retarded the growth of private transport (a situation that has been remedied in subsequent years!). A wide range of public facilities were provided which met the different demands as considered in Chapter 6. In Great Britain, pairs of towns were still often linked by two separate and quite distinct main line railway systems which, by this time, were no longer competitive in the accepted sense but neither were they co-ordinated. Rail-borne goods were conveyed albeit uneconomically to most wayside stations and bus services paralleled local railway lines. Interchange and connectional facilities were sometimes very poor. Examples of such conditions can still be found but over the years and subject to the remarks on the competitive element which follow later in this chapter, transport has now come to be regarded not as an assorted collection of services but more as a unified comprehensive system.

The Systems Concept

The point has been made in Chapters 1 and 6 that maximum economy can be obtained if the different modes of transport are utilised for the purposes for which they are most appropriate. Transport does not, however, necessarily mean public transport or, in other words, the pre-advertised public services that are available for all who care to use them. Private transport cannot be disregarded as part of the overall transport system. Indeed, in Great Britain something approaching 90 per cent of the road haulage vehicles are employed on an "own account" basis and the ratio of buses and coaches to private cars is about 1 to 150 although to put it into proper perspective, be it noted that this is in terms of vehicles and not vehicle seats. Private transport is, therefore, now very much a part of the overall transport pattern. Both play their part in taking people to work and on holiday. Both carry essential supplies and both perform a service without which the economic life of a nation would no longer be sustained. Those responsible for the preparation of traffic and transport plans must consider the needs of private as well as public transport, although in the conurbations, there is a limit to the number of highways and car parks that can be provided and if greater use is not made of public transport, that limit will be reached in some places. This does not mean the demise of private transport but it does mean that the two will become more and more complementary. "Park and ride" and "kiss and ride" are but examples of private transport feeding into public transport. Further afield, the roll-on roll-off ferry and the "piggyback" train are examples where private vehicles are conveyed by a public transport service.

To return to the systems concept, having established that it concerns both public and private transport, there is now an increasing trend to co-ordinate the different modes to produce through facilities. Certainly odd examples of through tickets and road/rail connections have been with the industry for many years but through transport in its real sense is something much more than that. In fact, there is no better example than to quote again the roll-on roll-off ferry which does, in effect, provide a through route for passengers and goods between inland destinations of two or more areas or countries that are separated by water. A feature of the transport of general merchandise is the time taken to load and unload. A ship is a particularly large unit and its high capacity magnifies the time spent to turnround at its terminal. The economic advantages of reducing this time have long been realised and the various forms of mechanisation in the ports described in Chapter 3 have each made their contribution to this end. The turnround time is most noticeable on short sea crossings as it then shows up very unfavourably in relation to actual sailing time and it is here that this type of vessel has maximum advantage. Another example and again one that has already been mentioned is the piggyback train. In each case there is a through route for road vehicles and their loads using different transport media but without the need for transhipment. It was said in Chapter 1 that the objective of the transport industry is a safe arrival, and this means that goods must be delivered without loss, damage or delay. It is at the points of transhipment where these three possibilities are most likely to arise. This is the vulnerable point and a through facility which eliminates physical transfers between one mode of transport and another can only instil confidence and enhance the quality of the service. This is one of the reasons why the use of the container has developed so rapidly in recent years.

The Container

The principle of the container was considered in Chapter 3. It is a transport facility that has evolved which offers a door-to-door movement able to take maximum advantage of each mode according to the geography of the journey. It offers a through facility and one in which even own account operators can participate. To the customer there is no transhipment of goods and it has, therefore, similar advantages to those of the roll-on roll-off ferries referred to above but with less complex carrying units, as mentioned in Chapter 4. Attention was drawn in Chapter 3 to the special terminal facilities that have become necessary as the container concept has developed but with the spread of this system across the world, valuable through facilities, with delays at the transfer points between the modes reduced to the absolute minimum, have come into being. In Great Britain, Freightliners Limited, a subsidiary of the National Freight Corporation with a British Railways interest, has developed a nationwide system of container services whilst various consortia of shipping companies have made possible through facilities, not only to the Continent of Europe, but also to America and beyond that to as far afield as Australia and New Zealand. There is every reason to believe that the container concept will continue to develop.

Physical Distribution

It is now opportune to turn again to Chapter 1 and to recall that production is something that embraces any activity that yields value. It was found that distribution added value because goods are worth more if they are in the right places, being the places where they are needed for consumption or use. Transport supplies that utility of place but transport or movement is only a part of distribution. Remember the example which depicted timber and the process of furniture manufacture with the timber beginning as a living tree and finishing as a table in the kitchen. Mention was made of manufacture and also of transport, but more than that is necessary to complete the cycle. The material in whatever form it may be, and reference is now being made to all types of merchandise, will have to be handled and there must be a selling organisation through dealers or middlemen thence to retailers, which is likely to bring with it a need for warehousing. The wholesalers and retailers must keep on hand bulk stocks according to the requirements of their trade, which means a stock control system with orders anticipating future needs. As the goods are moved from place to place they must be suitably packed according to their nature and bulk and method of conveyance. Although these are separate functions independent of each other, they are all, nevertheless, a part of the distributive system and to which "physical distribution" as a collective term, is applied. It is often regarded as a process that follows production but distribution occurs also in the movement of raw materials before manufacture and of semi-finished goods between stages of manufacture. Physical distribution, therefore, is an all embracing process playing a strong supporting role to manufacture. As a further development of the thoughts expressed in Chapter 1, it can be said that the cost of an article to the individual is made up of the values that are added by the processes of manufacture, selling and distribution. This leads to the topic of rate fixing within the transport industry which is considered later in this chapter.

Within the concept of this book it is important to understand that the transport system is but a part of physical distribution. All modes play their part but other facets of the overall distributive system may be influenced by the qualities of the transport facilities that are provided. For example, unitisation has been considered and exemplified by the container. Goods are stacked in a container and it is the container that is the unit carried, regardless either of the mode or what is inside. It can be transferred at will from one mode to another and this can and does have its impact on other parts of the distributive system. The container might, for example, eliminate much of the need for handling and for protection packing. It could also influence storage space and warehouse requirements. The development of air cargo with its characteristic high speed qualities could mean that it is no longer necessary to keep on hand large stocks, which removes the need for an elaborate system of stock control. Although the constituent parts of physical distribution are independent of each other to the extent that they require different skills, they are, nevertheless, interdependent as one does have its influence on another. A refinement of one part might even nullify the need for another but the one function that can never be dispensed with is movement or, in other words, transport.

The Competitive Element

Reference was made in Chapter 1 to the availability of choice. It will be recalled that in the interests of economy, a measure of support was given to the avoidance of the provision of duplicate facilities. This view has now been reinforced by reference to the systems concept and the theory that if maximum efficiency is to be achieved, the different modes and the different facilities within each mode should be complementary rather than competitive. Many of the facilities are, in fact, now being developed in this way to considerable advantage. But the availability of choice is still very much with us and to some people it is even a cherished possession, particularly in Great Britain. A potential customer is free to use public services or he may provide his own private transport for himself and for the carriage of his goods. The latter has even been facilitated by the 1968 Transport Act which has relaxed the licensing regulations on public road haulage and made own account operation a more attractive proposition by allowing surplus capacity on private vehicles to be utilised for the carriage of other peoples' goods for payment.

On the passenger side, a choice between modes is still available. Express services by rail and road link the same pairs of towns and both British Railways and the National Bus Company are endeavouring to promote travel by modern marketing methods supported by attractive publicity. Again, current legislation assumes the availability of choice as even though the British Railways Board and the National Bus Company are required to co-operate with each other (vide Section 24 of the 1968 Act) British Railways is still entitled to object through the traffic courts to applications for road service licences (and this includes applications submitted by the National Bus Company) vide Section 135 of the 1960 Road Traffic Act, but this is encroaching on Chapter 8.

Perhaps the interests and justification of both rationalisation and competition can be satisfied if the services that they provide do, in the event, generate a new class of traffic. The services themselves may duplicate each other but they might still cater for different demands. By custom and practice or personal preference, some people refuse to travel by one mode but accept another. If there is a fare differential (and there very often is) a section of the community might be able to travel who could not afford the standard fare charged on the basic service of either the same or a different mode. These are the people who are prepared to accept a cheaper type of service even though the quality might be inferior in one or more respects. It follows that there are different markets for travel between the same two places. Whilst, therefore, there may be duplication in transport terms, the different facilities that are provided have different qualities in terms of speed, comfort, convenience (including availability of pre-booking and time of travel), baggage accommodation and price. It is here that the competitive element has its place. Duplication of services with identical standards is one thing and the case of parallel main line railways has been noted, but alternative facilities with different standards is another. British Railways has now rationalised its system but the competitive road and air services remain. One view is that some competition is a spur to efficiency and that it stimulates business.

The Particular Problems of Air Transport

The foregoing has considered transport in toto, not only regardless of the mode but regardless also of the individualities of the countries through which the services operate. International transport produces political complications and this is particularly so in the case of air transport which is the one branch which attempts to provide a unified global network of regular timetabled services. It is for this reason that a special examination is now to be made of the various conventions and conferences that have taken place over the years in an endeavour to facilitate international operation and thereby enable the airlines to cater adequately for this class of traffic.

The Warsaw Convention

As much of air transport is international in character, it is natural that complications would arise if airlines attempted to observe only those laws made by its own national government, for they could not be enforced in foreign territory. Ideally, there should be some independent set of regulations agreed to and observed by all governments and it was for this reason that the Warsaw Convention was held in 1929. The Warsaw Convention did, in effect, produce a set of rules and regulations with particular regard to legal liabilities, which would apply to all participating nations upon ratification by their individual governments. Acceptance of the terms of the Convention was in fact made law in Britain by the Carriage by Air Act, 1932.

Although the basic principle of the Warsaw Convention remains, the Convention was held between the two world wars and at a time when air transport was in its infancy and its scope very different from what it is today. The agreements made at Warsaw have, therefore, been amended from time to time, principally by the Chicago Convention of 1944 and the Hague Protocol of 1955.

The Chicago Convention

The necessities of World War II produced a vast network of air services run for essential traffics without regard to political considerations. Such matters as territorial boundaries and agreed charges were of small concern to nations at war and it became apparent that many legal and commercial complexities would arise if these services were to be maintained on return to peacetime conditions. For this reason the Government of the United States of America convened a conference at Chicago in 1944 attended by representatives of allied and neutral nations. The outcome of this conference was

(a) The establishment of the International Civil Aviation Organization — referred to in Chapter 9.

(b) The Convention on International Civil Aviation, the purpose of which is contained in its preamble as follows:

"Whereas the future development of international civil aviation can greatly help to create and preserve friendship and understanding among the nations and peoples of the world, yet its abuse can become a threat to the general security; and

Whereas it is desirable to avoid friction and to promote that co-operation between nations and peoples upon which the peace of the world depends;

"Therefore the undersigned governments having agreed on certain principles and arrangements in order that international civil aviation may be developed in a safe and orderly manner and that international air transport services may be established on the basis of equality of opportunity and operated soundly and economically;

"Have accordingly concluded this Convention to that end".

(c) The setting up of the International Air Services Transit Agreement making provision for the aircraft of any signatory power to fly over or land for non-traffic purposes in the territory of any other signatory.

(d) The setting up of an International Air Transport Agreement, a more comprehensive agreement providing among other things for the carriage of traffic between member states.

These privileges have become known as the Five Freedoms which are:

(1) The right to fly over the air space of any contracting state without landing.

(2) The right to make a technical landing (e.g. for refuelling) in the territory of any contracting state.

(3) The right to set down traffic in the territory of any contracting state, providing it originated in one's own country.

(4) The right to pick-up traffic in the territory of any contracting state, providing it was destined for one's own country.

(5) The right to carry traffic between the territories of any two contracting states.

The first two of these freedoms have been generally adopted, but the remainder are the subject of bilateral agreements.

The Hague Protocol

A conference was held at The Hague in 1955 to make certain amendments to
the agreements made at Warsaw. These amendments, which affected the legal
side of the business, were based on recommendations made by the Legal Committee of the International Civil Aviation Organization. Although the United
Kingdom was a signatory to the Protocol, the terms were never ratified by the
British Government but they were incorporated subsequently in British legislation by the Carriage by Air Act, 1961.

Charging Methods

Under competitive conditions price is fixed by the interaction of supply and
demand freely operating in an open market. A perfect example is the Baltic
Exchange described in Chapter 9 where the charter price of tramp tonnage is
directly influenced by the availability of suitable facilities and the extent of demand at the time. For various reasons, it is often impracticable to allow transport
services to operate free from restriction and therefore subject only to this economic law of supply and demand, but disregarding for the moment any artificial
influences, there are broadly speaking two theories of rate fixing. Rates or
charges may be based on either the cost of the service or the value of the service.

Cost of service

The cost plus profit basis of charging is widely adopted in road transport, particularly road haulage where charges are not subject to statutory control and the
operator is free to quote as he wishes upon request. In this instance, to prepare a
quotation the proprietor estimates his operating costs, i.e. wages, fuel and tyres
based on time and distance, to which he adds a percentage to cover overheads
and a further percentage to allow a reasonable profit. The resultant figure is the
basis of his charge. The operator will rarely accept less than this figure and then
only in exceptional circumstances when either it suits his convenience or it is a
way of keeping goodwill. When business is brisk, demand may enable him to
secure a greater reward, but even then he might well prefer to keep to his standard rates and thereby maintain good customer relationship. On the road passenger side, as in air, prices are subject to control and must therefore be determined
(and officially approved) in advance, but here again the principle of cost plus
profit is a basis for the calculation of fares. Such a method would, however, normally embrace the system as a whole. It would generally be quite impracticable
to introduce different scales based on the varying costs of each route.

Value of service

A system of charging based on value of service began on the canals and was later
developed by the railways at a time when they had a virtual monopoly of all
traffics. The system is more suitable for these forms of transport because:

(a)   Heavy overhead expenses necessitated by a costly specialised way make
it virtually impossible to calculate the exact cost of any one transaction.

(b)   The heavier the traffic the greater is the spread of overheads. Hence the cost of movement varies in inverse proportion to the amount of traffic carried. Although this is true of all forms of transport, the greater the overheads the greater will be the influence of traffic fluctuations on costs which accentuates the difficulty of calculating railway or canal costs.

(c)   Railways and canals are bulk carriers. They can often accommodate "a little more" without seriously increasing direct costs. On the other hand, marginal traffic, even at a lower rate makes some contribution towards overheads.

The system is based on differential charging according to the value of the service to the consumer. In other words, the charge is based on "what the traffic will bear" which cannot exceed the difference between the value of the goods at the loading point and at the destination. It is the supply of the utility of place which represents not only the function but also the worth of transport and if the charge for conveyance is in excess of the difference between these respective values then the traffic will not flow. Conversely, if the rate that the traffic can bear is below the cost of providing the transport, then in theory the service would not operate, but the issue is generally clouded by either cross-subsidisation from other more profitable services or by a statutory or moral obligation to provide a facility. Rates based purely on the concept of what the traffic will bear pay scant regard to distance, and this is not entirely illogical as transport costs do not increase in direct proportion to the length of journey.

Another aspect is the conveyance of different commodities over similar distances. Different materials bear different rates, as for example the conveyance of scrap iron and gold. Both may travel from the same place to the same destination but quite apart from any security risk, the greater value of the gold can stand a higher rate.

Such then are the bases of charging. However, as costs do not rise in direct proportion to distance, even on a cost basis there is a case for a tapering scale (i.e., a decreasing rate per mile as distance increases). Mileage does nevertheless influence costs and this aspect is not properly reflected in a scale based on value. Whilst therefore railway and canal rates have developed on a value-of-service principle, they are now much influenced by considerations of cost as are the charges on other forms of transport where true costs can more easily be determined. Thus has evolved the current railway fares structure in which mileage is a consideration. An alternative method is to charge a flat fare per journey irrespective of distance. Whilst this system simplifies administration, it does produce problems on services where distances travelled vary widely.

Special facilities

The previous two paragraphs described the theory of rate fixing. But there are many rates or fares which pay little or no regard to these principles. Exceptional rates and excursion fares are based on other considerations and are granted only when special circumstances justify a reduction.

The cost of constructing a railway system is very high, but once established, provision of extra trains within the limits of line capacity is relatively cheap. It has already been noted that because of the high proportion of overheads in the total costs there is a natural desire to secure any additional traffic even at a rate which makes only a very small contribution to overheads and if this traffic could be encouraged it would benefit the railway in the long run. The aim must be to spread on costs over as many units of traffic as possible. Occasions can therefore arise when the provision of a sub-standard agreed charge is commercially justified, as for example, to a customer who can guarantee a consistently heavy movement of some remunerative type of traffic or even for other business with that customer if only to retain his goodwill. A road operator could be similarly placed. He might find it possible to utilise at a lower rate a vehicle which would otherwise be idle, or on which there is surplus capacity as on a return trip. In the first instance any return above the immediate running costs (i.e., fuel, tyres, wages, etc) would be justified irrespective of the failure to cover overheads, while in the second case any sum however small would be beneficial. On the passenger side, special reduced fares in the off-peak are an example, but operators must always guard against accepting cut price traffic which would have been available anyway and which otherwise would have accepted the normal charges. To stimulate an excursion movement at the expense of normal traffic would result in a net loss and the commercial manager must exercise careful discretion when planning cheap trips or granting exceptional rates.

8 · Statutory Control of Transport Services

Introduction

Statutory control is an all embracing term. Such controls may be exercised direct through the provisions of Acts of Parliament and Statutory Instruments or, as a result of those Acts, administered through statutory licensing systems. There will invariably be some form of quality control, which could be nothing more than the obligation to observe adequate safety standards, but there may also be quantity control. Quantity control means that operators are not free to provide all of the services that they might wish to do or, for that matter, to reduce them. Approval must be obtained from a third party before alterations are made, with the power given to other bodies to object to applications that might adversely affect their interests. This ensures a degree of co-ordination, the avoidance of wasteful competition and greater security for established operators. On the other hand, quality licensing demands only the need for proper standards by the operators concerned and having satisfied the licensing authority on this point they are permitted to operate what services they please. Quantity licensing, therefore, controls the services whilst quality licensing controls the standards of the operator. Specific control for reasons of safety can also apply to each vehicle, ship or aircraft and to each member of the staff who may require some special skill.

In Great Britain until quite recently road passenger, road haulage and air were all subject to systems of quantity licensing within the strict meaning of the term. Now, that applicable to road haulage has been repealed (except for a minor point of academic interest only) by the Transport Act, 1968 and as a general principle but subject to regulations, that applicable to air by the Civil Aviation Act, 1971. Only that for road passenger transport remains. Regardless of the pros and cons of quantity and quality licensing, it is interesting to note that whilst the 1968 Act was introduced by a socialist government, the 1971 Act has come from a Conservative administration, which is somewhat indicative of national policy regardless of politics.

Although forms of ownership are dealt with in Chapter 10, it is appropriate to mention here that as undertakings have passed into public ownership (and in Great Britain this was the trend around the late 1940's), the new publicly owned administrations that emerged had certain terms of reference imposed upon them by Parliament. The Transport Act, 1947 was responsible, among other things, for the passing of railways and canals into public ownership together with the formation of the British Transport Commission. At that time the Commission was charged with the duty to provide an efficient, adequate, economical and properly integrated system of public inland transport and port facilities within Great Britain for passengers and goods, excluding transport by air. This all-embracing responsibility was however subsequently broken down by the Transport Act, 1953 which required the Commission to provide only:

(i)   railway services within Great Britain

(ii)   an adequate and properly co-ordinated system of passenger transport within what was then the London Passenger Transport Area

(iii)   other transport services, facilities for traffic on inland waterways and port facilities at places where such facilities were provided prior to a specified date before the passing of the Act, as the Commission deemed expedient having regard to the needs of the community.

The Transport Act, 1962, dissolved the Commission and split its undertaking into a number of competitive units in the form of public boards and a Holding Company. The current position, however, regarding the statutory duties of the major transport undertakings which were at one time a part of the British Transport Commission is governed by the provisions of the Transport Act, 1968, which re-directed certain responsibilities.

The Post Office is another large scale publicly owned organisation involved in the movement of a specialised form of freight — the carriage of mail. It has a monopoly of the carriage of letters under the Post Office Act, 1953 and of telecommunications under the Telegraph Act, 1869 which has been retained in the Post Office Act, 1969 and which sanctioned the reorganisation of the Post Office from a Department of State to a public corporation (see Chapter 10). The Post Office is, therefore, equipped with powers to provide letter and telephone services for the United Kingdom and to meet the needs of commerce and industry for inland and overseas communications.

The Effects of the Transport Act, 1968

The obligation of the British Transport Commission to provide an efficient, adequate, economical and properly integrated system of inland transport, built up by the 1947 Act and broken down (except for London Transport) by the 1953 Act, has not been re-imposed on the present authorities. However, the permissive powers of these undertakings in manufacturing, catering and other ancillary fields are now wider than they were before, subject to any such activities being conducted in a proper commercial manner.

Goods

A major change brought about by Section 5 of the 1968 Act was the requirement of British Railways to segregate the sundries (defined on page 89) and Freightliner businesses from the rest of its undertaking. Responsibility for these functions with the sundries side now trading as National Carriers Ltd was transferred to the National Freight Corporation along with what were the freight interests of the Transport Holding Company. Under Section I of the 1968 Act, the National Freight Corporation has a duty in conjunction with the Railways Board to provide a properly integrated service for carrying goods by road or rail in Great Britain and in so doing to ensure that goods are carried by rail whenever it is efficient and economic to do so. This in turn has had a limited repercussion on the statutory control of road haulage to which reference is made under the appropriate sub-heading below. The National Freight Corporation has, therefore, the power to carry goods by road and it also carries by sea and enters into arrangements with the Railways Board for the conveyance of goods by rail. British Railways is in effect shorn of its ancillary road haulage operations (although not its legal right to operate such services) and has become basically a "wholesaler" of that traffic which is conveyed by goods train, being itself concerned only with train-load siding to siding and Freightliner movements or wagon load traffic from private sidings. The National Freight Corporation is the "retailer" which as well as selling road transport processes traffic for the Freightliner train-load movements of British Railways.

New provisions for the British Waterways Board were contained in Part VII of the 1968 Act. The Board's waterways were divided into three groups, group (a) being mainly the big barge navigations and known as the commercial waterways, group (b) including many of the narrow canals and known as cruising waterways and group (c) constituting the remainder. The Board is required vide Section 105 to maintain in a suitable condition for use by freight carrying vessels only those few waterways which are regarded as having some commercial value and are included in group (a) and to maintain those in group (b) in a fit condition for the use of passenger boats. This is, of course, a less onerous responsibility than that required by the 1962 Act which gave to the Board an overall duty to provide services and facilities on all of their inland waterways. As far as the waterways in group (c) are concerned, the Board is now free to deal with them in the most economical manner possible subject to certain provisos to which reference is made under the inland waterway sub-heading below.

Passenger

The major change on the passenger side in the statutory control of the provision of services in the 1968 Act is in the form of the introduction of Passenger Transport Authorities and Passenger Transport Executives, again as described in Chapter 10. This development, which is covered in Part II of the Act, affects the system of licensing in areas that are so designated and reference to this aspect is made in the subsequent paragraph relating to buses and coaches. The Transport (London) Act, 1969 requires the London Transport Executive to provide, in conjunction with British Railways and the National Bus Company and within the limits of its financial duty, public passenger transport services to meet the current needs of London as interpreted by the Greater London Council.

There now follows a summary of the different types of systems control which includes quantity and quality licensing, a selection of controls made only in the interests of safety and a reference to the regulation of rates and charges, all of which as is applicable within Great Britain. It may be noted here that all forms of transport are and have long been subject at least to safety regulations regardless of whether they are or have been subject also to any other type of control. Undertakings which require a specialised form of private way are not subject to quantity control as such but the development of their systems as a whole is likely to require special authority.

Systems and Operational Controls
ROAD TRANSPORT
Buses and Coaches
Legislative control over the operation of buses and coaches came with the passing of the Road Traffic Act, 1930. This and subsequent acts have been consolidated

into the Road Traffic Act, 1960, and it is this enactment which today governs the licensing of road passenger transport, apart from the special provisions appertaining to Passenger Transport Areas as discussed below. Part III of the 1960 Act relates to public service vehicles and Section 117 states that a public service vehicle is a motor vehicle used for the carriage of passengers for hire or reward either at separate fares or, if not carrying at separate fares, adapted to carry eight or more passengers. Passenger vehicles are divided into three groups depending on the type of service on which they work, namely stage, express and contract carriages. Briefly, stage and express services are the normal bus and coach services as we know them, the only distinction being that the express service has no ordinary single fare less than eleven pence. A contract carriage is a vehicle which is not part of an advertised service and with certain provisos does not carry passengers at separate fares — in other words a private hire. The authority necessary to operate a stage or express service outside a designated passenger transport area is a road service licence which is granted at the discretion of the appropriate Traffic Commissioner vide Sections 134 and 135 of the 1960 Act. Great Britain is for this purpose divided into eleven traffic areas with full and part-time Traffic Commissioners (the full-time member being chairman) appointed by the Secretary of State for the Environment and it is their duty to consider applications for licences. In so doing they are required to have regard to:

(a)   The suitability of the route.

(b)   The extent to which the route is already served.

(c)   The extent to which the service is necessary or desirable in the public interest.

(d)   The traffic needs of the area as a whole and the co-ordination of passenger transport including transport by rail.

They also consider, at a public hearing if necessary, any representations from existing operators who fear that they might suffer some abstraction of traffic in the event of a competitor's application being granted. The commissioners are at liberty to grant or refuse an application or to issue a licence in a modified form, but any aggrieved party has the right of appeal. Details such as roads traversed, timetable, faretable and type of vehicle are stipulated on the licence and any variation however small must be formally applied for and approved.

An exception to the need for a road service licence has been made by Section 30 of the Transport Act, 1968. This Section enables stage carriage services worked by vehicles constructed to carry no more than 12 passengers or stage or express carriage services worked by any type of vehicle on a school service in pursuance of arrangements made under Section 55 of the Education Act, 1944, provided that service accepts also normal passengers if accommodation is available, to operate under a permit instead of a road service licence. The permit is granted by the Traffic Commissioner, who may attach certain conditions, but the applicant is not required to submit details of the service in the way that he is for a road service licence.

Another more important exception to the standard licensing system is made in the designated Passenger Transport areas and in the London area. Reference to the special circumstances applicable to these areas is contained in Chapter 10. The monopoly conditions created in the designated areas by the Transport Act,

1968, and perpetuated in the London area by the Transport (London) Act, 1969 make the standard system superfluous. Once an order has been made by the Secretary of State for the Environment, a road service licence will not be necessary for any services operating within passenger transport areas regardless of whom the operator may be. However, in such cases, the Passenger Transport Executive concerned has a duty vide Section 9 of the 1968 Act or, in the case of London Transport, Section 1 of the 1969 Act, to make provision for or to provide an integrated service within its area and for this reason no other operator (including the National Bus Company) may run a service within an area so designated without the agreement of the Executive. It is the responsibility of the Passenger Transport Authority (or, in the case of London, the Greater London Council) to approve any major revision of services and the general level of fares and charges, again of all services within its area, Executive or otherwise. To that extent therefore, provision has been made for Passenger Transport Authorities to assume the functions of the Traffic Commissioners within the designated areas, once the necessary orders have been made.

Road Haulage

The Road and Rail Traffic Act, 1933 first introduced a system of quantity licensing into road haulage and again the relevant provisions of this and subsequent acts were consolidated in the Road Traffic Act, 1960. However, Part V of the Transport Act, 1968, has by and large replaced Part IV of the 1960 Act which related to road haulage with the result that quantity control has now been virtually swept away and replaced by a system of quality control.

Section 60 of the 1968 Act requires a road haulage operator (which includes both public carriers and own account undertakings) to possess an "operator's licence". This licence is issued at the discretion of the Licensing Authority (which is, in effect, the chairman of the Traffic Commissioners but in this capacity known as the Licensing Authority) with a right of appeal to the Transport Tribunal. The fitness of an applicant for an operator's licence is interpreted basically as:

(a)   ability to maintain proper control of the business with proper provision for maintenance;

(b)   adequate financial resources and the prospect of sufficient traffic to sustain the business;

(c)   the employment of competent staff at the operating centre.

The granting of this licence is, therefore, dependent upon the applicant's ability to maintain and operate a road haulage fleet. Provision is made for the right to object on the grounds that the applicant does not satisfactorily meet this criteria but this right may be exercised only by employers' associations representing operators, the police, a local authority or appropriate trade unions. Once a carrier is granted an operator's licence he is free to run as he pleases as far as the licensing system is concerned. He is not now subject to quantity control as are passenger operators.

Users of vehicles with a plated gross weight not exceeding 3½ tons (for which an unladen weight of 30 cwt is regarded as an approximate equivalent) do not even need an operator's licence. These small vehicles are not subject to either quantity or quality control and goods may be carried in them at will (subject, of course, to the vehicle licensing regulations which are imposed more for revenue purposes).

The only reference to quantity licensing that is contained in the 1968 Act applies to goods vehicles of more than 16 tons plated gross weight engaged in hauls of over 100 miles or, in the case of certain materials which may be specified, for shorter distances. Own account vehicles of the same gross weight are included but goods vehicles under 16 tons gross (which is considered equivalent to an unladen weight of 5 tons) are not included. This provision was made to divert this type of traffic to rail wherever possible and the Act envisaged that application for a quantity licence would be made to the appropriate Licensing Authority. The only bodies able to object would have been the National Freight Corporation (through its Freightliner Company) and the Railways Board. The National Freight Corporation, however, would have been in the same position as other road hauliers and if any such operator became compelled to use rail for a particular journey, the same conditions would automatically apply to all other hauliers wishing to give a similar service, be they privately owned or NFC subsidiary. If the NFC made its own application, there would still have been British Railways as a possible objector, but in this context it must be remembered that NFC is under a statutory obligation to arrange for carriage by rail whenever it is efficient and economic to do so and the two undertakings are also required to co-operate with each other. The only basis for an objection by NFC or British Railways would have been that the road/rail service which they provide is as economically satisfactory as that of the applicant taking into consideration a combination of speed, reliability and cost to the consignor in relation to need. The decision of the Licensing Authority would have been subject to appeal to the Transport Tribunal.

This is the only provision for quantity licensing in road haulage that is contained in the 1968 Act. However, since the passing of that Act there has been a change of government and although the relevant sections have not been repealed, neither have they been implemented, and the successor administration has indicated that there is now no intention of doing so.

Trams and Trolleybuses

For this form of transport there is no quantity licensing as such since neither a tram nor a trolleybus is classified as a public service vehicle within the terms of the 1960 Act (Section 117). The licensing system for buses and coaches described in a previous paragraph does not therefore apply to trams or trolleybuses. To clarify this apparent anomaly, remember that the electric trolleybus is technically a development of the tram. It is trackbound for the purpose of power collection, but as the power line is overhead and the energy is transmitted to the vehicle through manoeuvrable booms, it is not confined rigidly to a fixed line as is a tram or railway train (hence the term "trackless"). This was a subject matter of Chapter 6 but here it is sufficient to note that legally the trolleybus is akin to the street tramway.

Like the railway, the construction of a tram or trolleybus system, or the conversion from one to another, requires Parliamentary authority and the individual Act appropriate to any particular system will contain the rights and the duties of the undertaking concerned. The tramway mania in the latter part of the 19th century produced a stream of requests for authority to construct and the Tramways Act, 1870, which was framed to assist the construction and regulate the working of tramways was in effect an authority or basis for subsequent local acts which authorised the construction of particular lines. The Tramways Act itself did not authorise actual construction but said that authority could be obtained by any local council, person, company or corporation subject in the case of a company or the like to the consent of the local authority and also of the road authority if a separate body. It also detailed the procedure for submitting such applications. A tramway as such was not defined, but reference was made to the type of track. Unless specified to the contrary, the lines were to be as nearly as possible in the centre of the road, the gauge should be the standard 4ft 8½in and the uppermost surface of the rail level with the surface of the road. The roadway between and up to 18in on each side of the tracks would be maintained by the tramway promoters. The type of motive power would be defined and the vehicle would not overhang the side of the track by more than 11in. One important feature of the Act was the opportunity afforded to local authorities to enter the tram (or trolleybus) industry even on a system already established through private development. Section 43 gave to local authorities the power to purchase systems owned by companies after 21 years from the time of authorised construction and the option came again after every further seven year period subject to government approval. In so doing they were required to pay only for the tangible assets (i.e. nothing for goodwill). This section is of historical interest, but as in the United Kingdom the remaining tram undertaking is municipally owned and all trolleybuses have been withdrawn it now has little practical relevance.

To summarise, therefore, the statutory control of tram and trolleybus services is contained in their respective local acts which are the result of legislation dating back to 1870. However, a more recent development *vide* the Transport Charges Etc. (Miscellaneous Provisions) Act, 1954, gave the Traffic Commissioners power to fix charges in respect of tram and trolleybus services and a similar power will be assumed by Passenger Transport Authorities under the Transport Act, 1968.

RAILWAYS
Parliamentary authority is a necessary prerequisite for the construction of a railway. Subject however to any clauses contained in a local act, the railway authority is free to operate the service it pleases. It is not therefore required to apply to any independent authority for a licence (although it can lodge objections to the applications of road operators). In these respects the railway is relatively free from restriction although some form of control has been introduced by Section 20 of the Transport Act, 1968. A Passenger Transport Executive in a designated area (which has already been described) may, at the discretion of the Secretary of State for the Environment, be given a special duty to keep under review the railway passenger services provided for meeting the needs of the area and enter into agreements with British Railways to the extent that the appropriate

Passenger Transport Authority considers to be necessary. Certain other controls may be exercised by the Department of the Environment in respect of grant aid services which are explained in Chapter 13.

Notwithstanding these recent and special arrangements in designated areas, there has over the years been strong competition from other forms of transport with, at one time, a very rigid control of charges. Although the history of railway rates is a subject in itself, even at this stage there must be some background knowledge if one is to understand the circumstances which have led to the freedom now enjoyed by British Railways. The control of railway rates is therefore dealt with later in this chapter.

A special procedure applies to railway closures which involves Transport Users' Consultative Committees and to which reference is made in Chapter 9.

AIR

The Civil Aviation (Licensing) Act, 1960, introduced a system of quantity licensing into air transport by the introduction of air service licences granted at the discretion of an Air Transport Licensing Board through machinery very similar to that which currently applies to road passenger transport and which has been described in a previous sub-section. However, new legislation in the form of the Civil Aviation Act, 1971, has repealed practically the whole of the 1960 Act and a new Civil Aviation Authority has assumed, *inter alia*, the responsibilities of the now defunct A.T.L.B.

The regulation of British civil aviation is now governed by the Civil Aviation Act, 1971. This Act created the Civil Aviation Authority which will be further considered in Chapter 10. In order, however, to explain the method by which control is applied to air transport, some encroachment on that chapter is necessary here.

The main responsibilities of the Civil Aviation Authority are:
(a)   The regulation of airlines and organisers of air travel.
(b)   The control of the safety of civil flying.
(c)   The operation of air navigation services.
(d)   The management of certain aerodromes in Scotland.
Of the foregoing, only functions (a) and (b) are strictly relevant to the present topic. Functions (c) and (d) together with other features of the 1971 Act are more appropriately a part of Chapter 10 and will be dealt with accordingly but some overlapping is inevitable as:
(i)   The Civil Aviation Authority is both a part of the structure of the industry in its own right (i.e., in its ownership and management of certain airports) and a controlling authority for airlines and
(ii)   Government policy regarding the existence of competing British airlines (both publicly and privately owned) is enforced through a licensing system which is administered by the Civil Aviation Authority.
The statutory regulation of carriage by air is contained in Part II of the 1971 Act. Section 21 requires the operator of an aircraft which is used for the carriage for reward of passengers or cargo to be in possession of an air transport licence which is granted at the discretion of the Civil Aviation Authority. In considering applications for air transport licences, the Authority is required to satisfy itself

(vide Section 22) that the applicant (or body corporate) is properly experienced in aviation, is suitably qualified to operate aircraft and has resources and financial arrangements adequate to discharge the obligation that would arise in the event of the application being granted. The licence may contain terms as the Authority thinks fit and this includes the stipulation of fares and charges. Provision is made in Section 24 for appeal to the Secretary of State for Trade and Industry should an applicant for an air transport licence be aggrieved by a decision of the C.A.A.

This is, of course, British law and applies to any flight in any part of the world by an aircraft which is registered in the United Kingdom. In considering applications for air transport licences, the Authority is required vide Section 3 of the 1971 Act and in addition to what has been said in the previous paragraph, to pursue certain objectives, which are, briefly:

(a)   to secure that British airlines provide services which satisfy within reason the main categories of public demand at the lowest charges consistent with a high standard of safety and an economic return and with securing the sound development of the civil air transport industry of the United Kingdom.

(b)   to secure that at least one major British airline which is not controlled by the British Airways Board (a subject to be considered in Chapter 10) has opportunities to participate in the provision of air transport services.

(c)   to have regard to a favourable balance of payments and the prosperity of the economy of the United Kingdom; and

(d)   to further the reasonable interests of the users of the air services.

On the face of things, Section II of the 1971 Act has replaced quantity licensing by a system of quality licensing and has done the same for air transport as the 1968 Act did for road haulage. Looking a little deeper, however, item (b) of the preceding paragraph introduces an element of discretion between operators which does not exist in road haulage. In practice, this is having a regulatory effect, particularly insofar as the State airlines are concerned where some traffic must inevitably be lost to a privately owned competitor, but again this is a matter for Chapter 10. Section 3 of the 1971 Act also provides for the Secretary of State for Trade and Industry to give guidance which amplifies and supplements the four aforementioned objectives and it is the duty of the Authority to follow this guidance. There is, however, a further feature in that the bulk of the services that are operated by British airlines are international in character and their operations must, therefore, depend on the consent of other countries or on agreements for the exchange of traffic rights (a matter which is a function of the International Air Transport Association as is discussed in Chapter 9). These considerations must necessarily limit the United Kingdom's freedom of action in practice and the licensing procedure as described and the objectives and guidance have to be set against the background of these limitations. The Civil Aviation Authority and the Department of Trade and Industry must, therefore, in any case work closely together in these matters.

The 1971 Act also provides for the regulation of the provision of accommodation in aircraft. This part of the Act affects air travel organisers and is designed to ensure that only those who act within rules that may be prescribed and who have adequate resources or financial arrangements may engage in the organising and wholesaling of air travel. The Authority has no power to regulate competition among travel organisers.

SEA

The commercial side of British shipping has remained remarkably free from statutory control. Legislation of other nations does however have repercussions as, for example, the practice of flag discrimination whereby countries insist on certain cargoes moving in ships of their own flag. The British Mercantile Marine is the champion of free enterprise and is, except in time of war, free to operate where it will and charge what it pleases subject only to any stipulation which might be imposed by a foreign government and to the economic law of supply and demand. Rates are in some cases subject to the deliberations of liner conferences, a voluntary arrangement described in Chapter 9.

INLAND WATERWAYS

Like the railways, canals are constructed under authority of special Acts of Parliament, although closure rather than construction of canals has greater relevance in Great Britain today.

To "close a canal to navigation" means to obtain relief from the statutory obligation attached to the original powers to build the canal. The enabling Acts of the canal companies usually created certain statutory rights of user (generally subject to payment of tolls) for canal traffic. Further, the Acts sometimes imposed specific obligations as to maintenance for navigational purposes, more particularly for railway-sponsored canals. Section 17 of the Regulation of Railways Act, 1873, restated and applied to all canals owned or managed by railway companies a general obligation as to maintenance for navigational purposes. This requirement was applied, by Section 61 of the Transport Act, 1962, to all of the waterways of the British Waterways Board, whether or not they were previously railway owned canals. These liabilities could be expunged only by amending legislation, which "closed the navigation", or by applying to the now Secretary of State for the Environment for a "warrant of abandonment" under the procedure laid down in the Railway and Canal Traffic Act, 1888. However, over the years, owing to lack of money, physical closures were in practice effected in advance of statutory authority, with the result that there remained a number of canals which although legally "open" were difficult or impassable for navigation. This unsatisfactory position was recognised by Parliament and Part VII of the Transport Act, 1968, facilitated closures by enabling the Secretary of State, after certain consultation with users, to "de-rate" a canal in accordance with the groupings referred to earlier in this chapter. The Secretary of State may also, by order, nullify the effects of Section 17 of the Regulation of Railways Act, 1873, regardless of whether the canal is owned by the British Waterways Board or any other undertaking. If a commercial waterway is to be de-rated, the Secretary of State will first consult any organisation operating freight carrying vessels and in the case of a cruising waterway, with the Inland Waterways Amenity Advisory Council, a body described in Chapter 9 and with functions similar in principle to those of the users' consultative committees in road and rail transport.

PIPELINES

The legal complexities involved in the construction of a pipeline were at one time similar to those which appertain to railways. In other words, it was necessary for pipeline promoters to introduce private Bills to Parliament. This procedure is now simplified by the Pipe-lines Act, 1962 which regulates and facilitates the construction of pipelines. Its main objects are:

(a) to regulate the development of pipelines in the public interest, to discourage their proliferation and to encourage the principle of the common user system.

(b) to set up a procedure for objections to be heard at local enquiries.

(c) to enable a successful applicant to obtain compulsorily the necessary land, rights, etc, without the need to promote a private Bill.

(d) to regulate the construction, operation and maintenance of pipelines in the interests of safety.

The 1962 Act also established that pipelines were rateable but this aspect is now covered by the General Rate Act, 1967.

There is, of course, a fundamental difference between railways and pipelines to the extent that railways normally require occupation of the surface of the land they cross, whereas pipelines do not. Pipelines, therefore, usually require the grant of an easement or wayleave rather than the purchase of land. Although item (c) above makes provision to obtain compulsorily, land, rights, etc., by late 1972, only six compulsory rights orders had been made and two of these were subsequently revoked. The four remaining orders covered less than ¾ mile of pipeline. No compulsory purchase order had been made and the rights required for the construction of pipelines authorised through the machinery of the 1962 Act were obtained by voluntary negotiation.

To summarise, therefore, the construction of pipelines in Great Britain is governed by the Pipe-lines Act 1962, which does not in itself constitute an authority for any particular project, but which has established a framework for applications to be submitted for consideration without the need to promote a private Parliamentary Bill. At the same time, the interests of landowners are protected. For the purpose of this legislation, a pipeline is interpreted in Section 65 of the 1962 Act as a system of pipes for the conveyance of anything other than air, water, water vapour or steam and not being a drain, a sewer, or pipes for heating, cooling, or for domestic purposes. The Act is administered by the Department of Trade and Industry.

Special exemptions from the provisions of the Pipe-lines Act are made for gas, electricity and atomic energy undertakings.

Safety Controls

The point was made in Chapter 1 that the end product of any transport system is the arrival and it is, of course, very much in the interests of operators as well as the users that it should be a safe arrival. Although most transport undertakings work to high standards in this respect, safety measures are costly and in this era of perpetually rising costs, the interpretation of what might be regarded as adequate is liable to vary between operators. At the same time, movement of any kind is bound to produce potential hazards unless satisfactory equipment is used, suitably qualified staff are employed and proper codes of operational discipline are enforced. Any laxity in safety standards could well result in serious loss of life, particularly in passenger transport, and successive governments have therefore sought to safeguard the interests of the community at large and the users in particular by the imposition of regulations made in the interests of safety and which have the backing of law.

In Great Britain, road and air transport safety requirements are enforced through licensing systems as have already been described. Additionally, vehicles and aircraft must conform to prescribed standards and the staff that operate them must be sufficiently skilled. Traffic Commissioners and the Civil Aviation Authority, for example, have responsibilities in this respect.

As has been seen, licensing systems as such are not applied in the case of railway and sea transport, but very extensive regulations have been introduced over the years, through various Acts of Parliament, which control construction and operation. Of particular interest is the work of the Railway Inspectorate, which is a branch of the now Department of the Environment and was formed originally by an Act of Parliament in 1840 although its responsibilities have been extended from time to time by subsequent legislation. The functions of the Inspectorate include the statutory approval of new works on railways carrying passenger traffic, accident investigations including the holding of formal enquiries, technical advice to the Secretary of State on general railway matters and the consideration of administrative and technical questions concerning the design, construction and operation of tram and trolleybus systems, although work in connection with this last mentioned item is not now particularly onerous.

Beyond what has been said so far, many of the national and international trade organisations that are to be described in the next chapter and of which most operators are members, have produced codes of conduct and other measures designed to further the interests of safety. International organisations have been particularly active in this field and this has, in many cases, achieved the observance of satisfactory standards in circumstances where national laws are either inapplicable or inadequate.

Safety legislation is a topic which goes far beyond the principles of transport and a detailed study is not appropriate in a work such as this. The Merchant Shipping Act, 1970, the Civil Aviation Act, 1971 and the Road Traffic Act, 1972 are but recent examples of statutes that have substantial bearings on the subject. Specialised Acts and delegated legislation such as the Railway Employment (Prevention of Accidents) Act, 1900, the various Merchant Shipping and Road Traffic Acts and Air Navigation Orders and Regulations are all concerned with safety in transport. Road transport vehicles are strictly controlled through Construction and Use Regulations. The Civil Aviation Act, 1971, created the Airworthiness Requirements Board, which consists of a team of specialists appointed by the Civil Aviation Authority with responsibilities in respect of standards of design, construction and maintenance of aircraft and the issue of certificates of airworthiness. The Board has assumed the functions of the former Air Registration Board. To encroach a little on Chapter 11, it is the Department for Trade and Industry that is the government department responsible for most matters connected with merchant shipping and under the Merchant Shipping Acts it administers many regulations for marine safety such as certifying the load-line (or Plimsoll line) to indicate that a ship is not overloaded, ensuring that standards of safety are observed in ship construction and maintenance and the provision of adequate life-saving, fire-fighting and radio equipment. The Department also administers the Coastguard Service and has certain functions concerning pilotage and lighthouses, which are again referred to in Chapter 10.

Control of Rates and Fares

The theory of rate-fixing was considered in Chapter 7. However, to ensure overall stability, governments have from time to time seen fit to introduce legislation providing for some form of control over transport charges. The extent of control exercised in Great Britain is now confined largely to road passenger transport through the granting of road service licences or the dicta of Passenger Transport Authorities and to air transport through the air transport licence machinery as has been described. The commercial freedom of the railway is of particular interest because it follows a century or more of control and, as has already been said, the historical background of railway rates justifies a brief review.

Ever since railways assumed importance as carriers, there has been a fear that they would exploit their monopoly and hence a feeling that the law should afford some protection to the users by ensuring that their services would be available to all at a reasonable cost. Remember that railways were constructed under authority of special acts which gave Parliament the opportunity to impose limitations on fares and charges on any particular line quite apart from other requirements in respect of methods of working, etc. But in the middle of the 19th century such legislation quickly multiplied and some form of general regulation became necessary, hence a number of Acts were passed covering methods of working, provision of reasonable facilities, etc. One of the first milestones in the history of railway rates was the

RAILWAY CLAUSES CONSOLIDATION ACT, 1845

which, among other things, prevented a railway company from charging beyond a certain maximum (as stipulated in its respective special Acts), although this maximum was admittedly very high and in any case well above the normal rates. The maximum charge applied only to the actual conveyance. Charges for terminal services were not controlled although they in their turn were required to be reasonable. But the maximum rates were still contained in the individual Acts, the number of which grew to some several hundred and to clarify the position, the

REGULATION OF RAILWAYS ACT, 1873

required the railway companies to maintain rate books at every station still with each rate subdivided into conveyance and terminal costs. (Until recent times the railways were obliged to publish their charges — a feature which severely restricted their competitive power in the movement of freight). It was however an inconsistent and very complicated structure. Hence, by virtue of the

RAILWAY AND CANAL TRAFFIC ACT, 1888

the then Board of Trade agreed a new classification for goods and revised schedules of maximum charges (terminal charges still being shown separately) which brought about a degree of simplification and unification. However, under the terms of the 1888 Act, there was no provision for any increase above the authorised maximum without reference back to parliament, although there was no restriction in making exceptional rates, that is rates below the normal standard, subject to there being no undue preference. It must here be explained that undue preference means the granting of a favourable rate only to selected customers. As this was prohibited, the railways were not in a position to generate the most lucrative traffic as they could not bargain with individual customers without publicising an exceptional rate and granting a similar concession to other people who might require the same service, irrespective of whether they were regular users of the railway. They were therefore placed at a disadvantage with their competitors (and this was felt particularly in later years when road transport became an attractive alternative) who were under no such obligation and who in consequence were able to encourage through normal business negotiation, the patronage of those customers who required the service which the carriers found most economical to provide. Nevertheless, the course was still open for the railways to raise their rates up to the legal maximum and in so doing, there were objections from the users which led to the passing of the

RAILWAY AND CANAL TRAFFIC ACT, 1894
which required the railway to prove the reasonableness of any increases notwithstanding the fact that they were within the legal maximum. This applied even to experimental exceptional rates and any form of commercial enterprise was by now completely stifled. These were the circumstances when the Government assumed control of the railways in 1914 upon the outbreak of war, firstly through the Board of Trade and then (from 1919) through the newly-created Ministry of Transport. The period of rising costs following a return to peace time conditions aggravated the already unsatisfactory position and a complete reorganisation came in the form of the

RAILWAYS ACT, 1921
some of the features of which are considered elsewhere. As far as railway rates are concerned, fares and charges were to be fixed by a newly appointed Railway Rates Tribunal. The principle of a legal maximum gave way to a system of fixed charges alterable upon application to and approval by this independent body, although provision remained for the granting of exceptional rates subject to there being no undue preference. The companies were still therefore unable to agree charges with individual traders on a personal basis. The principle behind the 1921 Act was a standard revenue based on income obtained in 1913, which was considered to be the last standard year. It was the duty of the Railway Rates Tribunal to fix railway fares and charges sufficiently high to permit the companies to earn this standard revenue but at the same time to bear in mind public interests. Thus some effort was made to ensure that the railways received an adequate return, but it was unfortunate that no account was taken of the rapidly expanding road transport industry in the mid 1920s. In the event, the standard revenue never materialised under normal conditions. Freedom to grant exceptional rates without the strings of undue preference was the real answer to this

increased competition, but as it was, such rates could not be granted without supporting publicity (i.e., in the form of an entry in the rate book) for acceptance by all who might care to do so. The result was that traffic offered to the railway was either of a low classification which according to "what the traffic can bear" theory carried a low rate or, alternatively, was that which could pass at an exceptional rate. The more lucrative traffic was frequently dispatched by other means. The classification of merchandise even precluded flat rate agreements based on weight, etc, on miscellaneous consignments. Some relief was afforded by the

ROAD AND RAIL TRAFFIC ACT, 1933

which permitted a flat rate as an agreed charge. But even this required approval of the Tribunal in each case and such approval would be withheld if the purpose could be achieved by the granting instead of an exceptional rate. The position of the railways became more distasteful as competition increased and in 1939 they launched their Square Deal campaign in the hope that the weight of public opinion would in the end free them from the shackles which so restricted their enterprise. But their cries were lost in the turmoil of the 1939-45 war when the Government again assumed control through the Railway Executive Committee. Wartime conditions brought new traffic to the railways and also curtailed the services of their competitors, with the result that, for the first time since the passing of the 1921 Act, the standard revenue and more was forthcoming. But at the end of hostilities history repeated itself and the railways were again in need of some form of reorganisation. Hence the

TRANSPORT ACT, 1947

which abandoned the standard revenue theory, but otherwise retained as a transitional measure the prewar system of approval by the Tribunal (now renamed the Transport Tribunal because of certain additional responsibilities), protection being given instead by restricting the railways' competitors. It was the ultimate intention that the by now British Transport Commission should produce area integration schemes. In the event, such schemes did not materialise as by virtue of the

TRANSPORT ACT, 1953

freedom was restored to road haulage. At the same time the railways were given much of the commercial freedom for which they had clamoured for so long. The system of approval of actual charges reverted to approval of maximum charges as it was in fact prior to the Act of 1894, but more than that, the law of undue preference no longer had effect. The Commission was required to publish only its maximum charges and it was able to use discretion in charging below this figure. The final eclipse of statutory control of railway fares and charges came with the

TRANSPORT ACT, 1962

which broke up the British Transport Commission into self-contained units each responsible for its own solvency. On the theory that the free forces of competition would discourage exorbitant rates (the restrictions in the past were, as seen at the outset, based on alleged monopolistic tendencies), railway charges in

Great Britain were freed from control except for passenger fares within the London Passenger Transport area (because of a statutory monopoly of passenger transport in London). These fares were still subject to the approval of a very much diminished Transport Tribunal. This freedom from control was retained in the

TRANSPORT ACT, 1968

except that in the designated passenger transport areas where services may be maintained as a result of agreements with the local Passenger Transport Executives, stipulations regarding fares might in this instance be applied. The PTEs become responsible for the general level of charges in their areas subject to the approval of their respective Passenger Transport Authorities as has been described and this could affect certain railway charges. On the other hand the PTA would take responsibility for paying grants for any continuing losses on the suburban railway services it decides are necessary as part of a comprehensive plan. Furthermore, a grant made by the Secretary of State towards the maintenance of any other unremunerative service may be accompanied by any special conditions as considered appropriate. The control of charges in the former London Passenger Transport Area is now broken down by the

TRANSPORT (LONDON) ACT, 1969

which removes the control of the Transport Tribunal in this respect and enables the Railways Board to fix its own charges in this area as well as elsewhere subject in the case of journeys within the Greater London area to any specially agreed financial objectives or otherwise to general consultation with the Greater London Council. Charges made by London Transport on its rail (and road) services are subject to the approval of the Greater London Council.

So much for the history of railway rates. It is a subject which could and does find a more correct place in a study of the law of inland transport. Nevertheless, the reader should understand the salient features highlighted above in order that there may be a grasp of the meaning and value of recent Acts and the position as it stands today.

9 · Trade Organisations

Introduction

The general term of trade organisation is in this context used as a reference to the many different associations which have grown up over the years as bodies representative of the providers of transport. Associations that act in the interests of the staff that work in transport are not for the purpose of this chapter contained within this classification. Trade unions and the machinery of staff negotiation is dealt with separately in Chapter 12. Another type of organisation is that which represents the users and for the sake of completeness, reference to these bodies will be made in this chapter.

A trade association in its real sense is an organisation that acts in the collective interests of the many independent and self-contained undertakings that function within a particular industry. Such an association might act on behalf of its members by presenting, for example, a united front on representations to Parliament for any change in legislation that might be considered desirable. It might also provide a service that meets a need of all members such as the dissemination of information on legal or technical matters or guidelines on costing and charging and it could produce publicity for the industry with a view to the procurement of a good public image. There is a need for associations of this kind in industries where a large number of small undertakings of the sole proprietor or partnership type predominate and where managements might not include specialists in the various disciplines. The road haulage branch of transport is one that immediately comes to mind. But trade associations and the like are by no means confined to industries whose structure is such. Neither are they confined to national boundaries. Trade associations in the transport field exist in many countries and some of the British associations are considered in this chapter. However, the circulation of information knows no frontiers and the exchange of ideas internationally is both necessary and desirable as the different peoples continue to mix. New technology is being evolved in all modes of transport, spurred on by the ever present need for economy and efficiency. Advancement in one area aids development in another and it is right that international platforms should be available where new methods and new ideas may be discussed and common problems aired. An international industrial association might be a more appropriate description for this type of organisation which has interests on a continental and even on a worldwide basis, administered perhaps through a series of conferences.

In this context, therefore, a trade association is regarded as something rather more than a national body representing the interests of a group of industrialists in a particular line of business, although some such associations certainly are of this type. Collectively they cover not only the interests of the trade but embrace also technical (including safety) and commercial matters in either a regulatory or an advisory capacity. Also included are statutory bodies with group interests set up by Parliament for some specific purpose.

It has been said that staff associations are not for discussion here and it is the users' interests therefore that remain to be introduced. The nationalising of various industries (including transport) which came in the early post-war period brought into being a series of mammoth state-owned undertakings with near monopolies in their respective spheres. In order that these monopolies should not be exploited, Parliament built into these industries (which included for example transport, gas and electric supplies) certain protections for users in the form of consumers' councils. Although not trade organisations by strict interpretation, they are representative bodies and as such it is convenient to consider them in this chapter, even though they are representative of the users rather than the providers of, in this case, transport services. This type of machinery does not exist in all branches of transport but tends to be applied where, as has been said, legislation has restricted competition and in so doing has removed what is in effect a natural spur to the maintenance of proper standards of quality in the services that are provided.

There now follows a review of a selection of the more important associations in Great Britain and of those international organisations in which British operators have an interest. This interest is in some cases technical and in some cases commercial; the function is in some cases regulatory and in some cases advisory. The regulatory function does not imply statutory control of the type discussed in Chapter 8 but means a form of voluntary control to which member operators submit in their common interests. Also included is a mention of certain users' bodies which exist in Great Britain.

British National Organisations

Road Haulage Association
The requisite qualification for membership of the Road Haulage Association is ownership of vehicles engaged in the carriage of goods for other persons or companies for hire or reward. In other words, the members are firms which run lorries as a service to trade and industry. The association assists members in their applications for operators' and vehicle licences and advises them on such matters as rising costs (with help to obtain fair and reasonable rates), new legislation, training facilities, security arrangements, hire purchase and insurance arrangements. It also represents members on the Road Haulage Wages Council, a body which negotiates pay and conditions of the staff in accordance with machinery as is explained in Chapter 12. But it is a two way process. The wide range of knowledge and experience that is to be found among members has to be tapped for the benefit of the industry as a whole. It is the job of the Association to match this experience with an expert staff, skilled in negotiation, law, finance and administration, able to promote the interests of the industry in every way, to interpret them to Parliament, industry and the public and to feed back to members the considerable amount of advice and information that they need.

There are 15 RHA areas and at this level there are sometimes meetings of members specialising in a particular type of traffic. There are 12 functional groups, being agricultural, bulk liquid, car transporters, caravan hauliers, express carriers, heavy haulage, international, livestock, long distance, meat and allied trades, milk carriers and tipping vehicles. Area and functional committees in turn appoint most of the RHA National Executive Council with another member drawn from the affiliated National Association of Furniture Warehousemen and Removers. The National Executive Council, which is the Association's supreme governing body, appoints 8 standing committees with respective responsibilities for commercial, education and training, highways and traffic, labour relations, licensing, public relations, technical and vehicle security matters. This in itself is indicative of the scope and responsibilities of the Association.

Another function of the Association is to issue TIR carnets to its members. These carnets, which have been developed by the International Road Transport Union to facilitate the international transport of goods, will be considered further under the sub-heading of that particular body.

Freight Transport Association
The functions and aims of the Freight Transport Association are very similar to those of the Road Haulage Association. The real difference is that whereas the RHA represents professional road hauliers whose business is to carry goods for others on a hire or reward basis, the FTA represents the interests of own account operators who carry their own goods in their own vehicles. Public hauliers are not eligible to join this association.

As was explained in Chapter 8, own account operators are subject to the new quality licensing regulations in the same way as are the public hauliers and the FTA assists its members in their applications for operators' licences and similarly with vehicle licensing. It has an advisory service on all day to day transport matters, including continental operations, with specific advice available on maintenance systems which has been developed as a specialised consulting service. Other similar facilities are offered in connection with reorganisation of transport departments, selection and appointment of staff, garage and workshop design and vehicle selection. A vehicle inspection service is also available. The Association runs management training courses and a training advisor is appointed whose main terms of reference are to assess the training needs of industrial transport, review the courses that are available to see how far these needs are met in order that they may advise members and to stimulate the provision of training facilities. Another function is to support the case for own account operators and the industry generally in the face of clamour to restrict the operations of heavy vehicles that are made in the overall interests of the environment. Not only are public relations campaigns conducted but research and constructive work is also undertaken. An FTA urban traffic working group is continually examining possible improvements in such matters as urban traffic regulation schemes, night deliveries, off-street loading facilities in urban centres and the provision of adequate lorry parks. Like the RHA the FTA advises members on legal matters and brings the interests of its members and the haulage industry to the notice of Parliament as occasions demand and particularly so in connection with the government's road programme.

The fact that, as a result of the 1968 Transport Act, own account operators are now able to carry other peoples' goods as part of a public transport service, means that some FTA members have now become directly concerned with Road

Haulage Wages Orders (see Chapter 12), although in the absence of an alternative structure, a large number have followed the provisions of the orders anyway. As a result of this legislation, the FTA now has its own representatives on the Road Haulage Wages Council and has established an Industrial Relations Committee which, in addition to its council work, advises members on wage levels, productivity schemes and conditions of employment.

In addition to its interests in own account operation, the FTA does also represent trade and industry in its role as users of all forms of transport, which includes road, rail, ports and to a lesser extent sea and air, for the carriage of freight. A user committee is appointed for this purpose which also concerns itself with various matters of principle including the services that are provided by carriers. Contact is maintained with such bodies as, for example, the National Freight Corporation and British Railways in an effort to ensure among other things that in the event of rationalisation schemes, the standard range of services provided remains adequate to meet users' needs.

As far as operational matters are concerned, the FTA has interests very similar to those of the RHA and whenever practicable, the two associations tend to work in concert. In its other capacity, however, the interests of trade and industry are sometimes different from that of the road haulier and for this reason there is, on occasions, a divergence of views.

Like the RHA, the FTA also issues to its members TIR carnets, the purpose of which is described later in this chapter.

Public Road Transport Association

Following a merger in 1943 between the old Omnibus Owners' Association and the Public Service Transport Association, a new body known as the Public Transport Association was formed. In 1969 it was re-named the Public Road Transport Association. The objects of this association are to watch over, promote and encourage the interests of owners and operators of systems of road passenger transport and also to promote consideration and discussion of all questions affecting directly or indirectly the road passenger transport industry.

The PRTA is the largest road passenger transport association in Great Britain. Membership is open to the British provincial company operators of buses and coaches, the municipal bus and tram undertakings, Passenger Transport Executives, in an extra-ordinary capacity to such bodies as the London Transport Executive and Coras Iompair Eireann and to overseas bus and tram undertakings. All the major British and Irish company bus operators (which includes National Bus Company subsidiaries and many of the independents) and the LTE and CIE are in fact members as are also about half the British municipal operators and the PTEs. There is overseas representation in South and East Africa, Hongkong, Jamaica and Lisbon.

In addition to the operating side, the most important contracting undertakings which supply vehicles, tyres, fuel, oil and any component which goes into the finished bus or coach are also in membership. The PRTA does, therefore, represent the road passenger transport industry in the widest possible sense.

In pursuance of its aim to watch over and promote the interests of its members, the Association acquires and diffuses experimental, statistical and technical knowledge relating to the operation of road passenger transport. It gives to the legislature, public authorities and others, facilities for conferring with and ascertaining the views of owners and operators of road passenger transport systems and it promotes and suggests improvements in the law and administration affecting its members.

Association of Public Passenger Transport Operators
The Association of Public Passenger Transport Operators was until recently known as the Municipal Passenger Transport Association and was formed originally to promote, encourage and facilitate (otherwise than financially) the construction and development of tramways. To keep in line with operational developments, this was in due course amended to cover all forms of public passenger transport and with the general demise of trams in Great Britain the tramway element has now almost disappeared. Membership of the Association consists of all the municipally owned and operated passenger transport undertakings in Great Britain and Northern Ireland (which total 67) together with three of the PTEs and in associate membership are the London Transport Executive, Coras Iompair Eireann and seven other overseas operators.

Like the PRTA to which reference has just been made, the APPTO disseminates information amongst its members, promotes consideration and discussion on all matters affecting public passenger transport and gives to the legislature and others facilities for conferring with and ascertaining the views of its members. In this connection the Association may originate and endeavour to promote improvements in the law relating to any appropriate matter and to support or oppose any proposed alterations with a view to effecting improvements in administration and control. It also aims to confer and co-operate with municipal and other bodies in regard to all matters affecting public passenger transport.

It is apparent that there is some duplication in the facilities that are provided by the APPTO and the PRTA and some undertakings do in fact have dual membership. The formation of a joint organisation would therefore seem to be appropriate. Each Association does, however, service separate labour organisations, viz. the Conference of Omnibus Companies and the Federation of Municipal Passenger Transport Employers, to which reference is made in Chapter 12 and from where it will be seen that the company and municipal groups have their separate machinery for staff negotiation. Any merger considerations would, therefore, have to take account of a need for these distinctions to be maintained.

Passenger Vehicle Operators Association
The Passenger Vehicle Operators Association represents the independent bus and coach operators and the coaching industry as a whole particularly at the international level where PVOA is recognised as the association responsible. The emphasis of this Association is on coaching for as will be seen in Chapter 10, the greater part of the buses in Great Britain is now in public ownership. Although the PVOA as such was formed in 1945, under other names its history can be traced back over more than forty years, in which time it has become accepted by the government, local authorities, the press and the public as the voice of the independent operators. To this sector of the industry, the Association provides services very similar to those that have already been described in respect of the

PRTA and the APPTO. It represents its members interests when new legislation is in the course of preparation, recent examples of particular significance being in connection with the limitations on drivers' hours contained in the 1968 Act, and the law relative to taxation covering both selective employment and value added tax. It also supports its members interests through consultation with local authorities when new orders concerning, say, setting-down points and parking, are proposed. This aspect is of particular importance at seaside resorts where satisfactory arrangements are vital to the popularity of the services and is therefore of considerable interest to members, many of whom operate excursions to the coast. Advice is given on legal, insurance and technical matters and also on continental travel where special control documents are necessary and foreign regulations must be complied with.

A service of particular value to members, bearing in mind the independent character of their organisations and their sometimes rather limited resources, is the administration of a mutual aid scheme. Through this scheme, members have an opportunity to place business with each other and this is likely to be of particular value in cases of emergency or in the event of a breakdown which could, of course, occur many miles from the operator's own base. British coaches abroad can benefit under a similar IRU scheme. One of the primary objects of the Association is to promote unity, friendship and goodwill in the private sector or, in other words in that part of the industry which, by and large consists of many independent and individual parts. The mutual aid scheme fosters this objective by helping to bring the ready assistance and co-operation from fellow members which is needed when hiring vehicles or in an emergency.

British Road Federation

The objectives of the British Road Federation are to promote and protect the interests of all who are concerned with the construction or use of roads, to originate and promote improvements in the law affecting ownership or users of road vehicles and to promote a constructive transport policy in what it considers to be the national interest. Membership of the Federation includes most of the associations representative of the many different trades and industries whose members operate own account road haulage vehicles. Other membership includes the Automobile Association and, incidentally, the RHA and the FTA. BRF receives support from the British Industry Roads Campaign, a body set up by a group of prominent industrialists to focus the views of industry on roads and road transport. One of the prime targets is to endeavour to counter hostility towards roads and motor vehicles and particularly the effects that this can have on political decisions.

The objectives of the Federation are supported by extensive publicity and it produces a wealth of information including statistical data on all matters concerning roads.

Freight Integration Council

To help ensure that the country as a whole has the benefit of a properly co-ordinated freight transport service, Section 6 of the 1968 Act provides for the establishment of a Freight Integration Council to consider and advise the Secretary of State on this matter. This Council concerns itself with the various kinds

of freight services provided by all of the publicly owned undertakings regardless
of whether they are otherwise affected by this Act, which includes the following
bodies:

National Freight Corporation
Railways Board
British Transport Docks Board
British Waterways Board
Scottish Transport Group
BOAC
BEA
British Airports Authority
Post Office

It is not the function of the Council to consider freight transport services or
to deal with individual complaints. Membership includes the chairmen of the
British Railways Board and the National Freight Corporation, up to four who
have wide experience as considered appropriate by the Secretary of State, who
is responsible for their appointment, and two with trade union experience.

National Ports Council
The National Ports Council was brought into being by the Harbours Act, 1964,
under circumstances to be described in Chapter 10. It is an advisory body whose
job among other things is to:

(a)   Formulate and promote the execution of plans for the improvement of
      existing and provision of new harbours in Great Britain (so far as they
      are approved by the Secretary of State).
(b)   Encourage and assist harbour authorities to perform their function in
      the most efficient possible manner.
(c)   Advise the Secretary of State regarding action to secure maximum
      economy and efficiency.

Although one of the powers of the National Ports Council is to submit schemes
for the reorganization of harbours to the Secretary of State, the position of the
Council must be clear. It does not own or operate ports or harbours. It is a
government appointed body to consider and recommend, among other things,
schemes of reorganisation in the port industry and in this connection it has con-
firmed the view that a national plan for the future development of Britain's ports
would best be achieved if based on a limited number of selected major port
authorities generally organised on an estuarial basis. The reorganisation of the
ports and the other steps which the Council is empowered either to take or to
promote are intended to do no more than help remedy the position revealed by
the enquiry of the Rochdale Committee as is referred to in Chapter 10.

The Council also has powers to recommend revisions to and to determine
appeals against ship, passenger and goods dues at harbours.

Chamber of Shipping of the United Kingdom
The Chamber of Shipping of the United Kingdom is the national organisation
representing British shipowners. Formed in 1877, its function is to discuss and
formulate the general policy of the British shipping industry on a variety of technical and commercial matters. The Chamber represents the industry in discussions

with Government and is financed by tolls paid by members, calculated on their registered tonnage. Membership embraces virtually the entire British merchant fleet.

Railways and Coastal Shipping Committee
The geography of Great Britain is such that inland transport is in a strong competitive position with coastal shipping. It has been considered over the years that a large organisation such as British Railways would be able to exploit its position at the expense of shipping interests if some form of control was not imposed and a measure of protection was in fact contained in the Transport Act, 1947. Today, this protection is afforded by Section 150 of the Transport Act, 1968 which introduced the Railways and Coastal Shipping Committee.

The functions of this Committee are to consider and report to the Secretary of State on matters which affect both railway and coastal shipping interests and to deal with any complaint as to charges for the carriage of goods made by British Railways in competition with coastal shipping. Upon receipt of such reports, the Secretary of State may give directions to the Railways Board as he considers appropriate. Membership of the committee consists of both shipping and railway representatives.

International Organisations
International Road Transport Union (IRU)
The economic recovery of Europe that followed World War II resulted in a steady growth of trade with international transport (and road transport in particular) playing an important role in fostering closer relationships between the different countries. It was under these circumstances that an international organisation which brought together the various national associations concerned with road transport became necessary and for this reason, the International Road Transport Union was formed in Geneva in 1948. It was subsequently granted consultative status both by the United Nations Organization and by the Council of Europe. The activities of the Union embrace the privately owned sectors of passenger and goods transport, the latter including both hire and reward and own account operations. Since its formation, membership has extended beyond Europe to include organisations in North and South America, Australia, India and Japan. The affiliated British associations are the RHA, the FTA and the PVOA.

The basic objective of the IRU is to promote the development of international road transport in the interests of carriers and the economy as a whole. It co-ordinates viewpoints, brings together the sometimes divergent conceptions of transport, aims at improving the conditions of its members, rationalising their work and encouraging the adoption of the latest techniques. Groups of experts make their contribution in specialised fields such as combined transport, customs problems, legal problems and road infrastructure.

One of the main concerns of the IRU is the reduction of customs formalities and to this end it has created the TIR (Transport International Routier) carnet which has very much simplified frontier controls. The TIR carnet is an international customs document with the purpose of providing free movement of goods carried in vehicles or containers across frontiers which lie on line of route between the point of origin and the ultimate destination. The possession of a carnet exempts the carrier from customs examination at all frontiers except the first and the last on any particular journey and in normal circumstances, the payment of duty at intermediate customs points is not required. TIR vehicles or containers have the further advantage that, with certain exceptions, they may be cleared at inland centres rather than at the ports where delays are often encountered, a point to which reference was made in Chapter 3. Vehicles used in connection with these arrangements must be of an approved design with their goods carrying area closed and capable of being sealed. In the case of Great Britain, the RHA and the FTA, in their capacities of issuing authorities to British carriers, act as guarantors for carnets issued to their members, who must be on a specially approved list. These associations also issue the necessary vehicle plates.

Although relevant to carnets rather than to trade organisations, it is pertinent to note at this juncture that as far as the European Economic Community is concerned, the TIR carnet procedure is being replaced by a new Community Transit System. This system utilises T forms which both establish the duty status of the goods in the importing country and act as international transit documents.

Other acheivements of IRU include the establishment of an international mutual aid service for passenger operators on the principles as described in connection with the activities of the PVOA and also the formation of an international association to facilitate the transport of perishable foodstuffs known as Transfrigoroute Europe.

International Road Federation (IRF)
The International Road Federation was established in 1948 to encourage the development and improvement of highways and highway transport. In so doing it provides a link between national road associations in 81 countries throughout the world and fosters the organisation of new ones. Its offices are in Washington and Geneva. The British affiliated organisation is the British Road Federation.

The Federation provides consultative and administrative services in highways and highway transport to all interested governments. It also co-operates with all international organisations having comparable objectives and is represented at appropriate international meetings. It is a highway transport consultant to the United Nations and enjoys a similar status with the Organisation of American States, the Council of Europe and other similar bodies. The Federation supports advanced training programmes for highway and traffic engineers, it strives for greater international interchange of data through the collection, publication and distribution of technical, economic, statistical and other educational material and urges the planning and execution of sound programmes for road development.

International Union of Railways (UIC)
Railways have now been in existence for about a century and a half and over this period various bodies were set up for the purpose of dealing with specific international problems. The need arose, however, for an overall organisation which could handle all questions and this was achieved after the cessation of World War I when, through the provisions of the Treaty of Versailles, the International

Union of Railways was formed in 1922 with its headquarters in Paris and with chairmen drawn originally from the French railways. One of its first tasks was to simplify through running between neighbouring countries. Activities virtually ceased during World War II, after which the process of co-ordination was further developed. Various committees are now concerned with planning, commercial questions, movement (operating), rolling stock and motive power, way and works and studies on economic, legal, financial, supplies and staff problems. In addition, certain tasks are entrusted to special groups, particularly in connection with management, cybernetics, standardisation, automatic coupling, the future of traffic, the international coach and the quest for optimum passenger comfort. UIC places an ever growing importance on the dissemination of information to its member railways and also to the public through its Public Relations Centre, Publicity Centre and Railway Film Bureau. The Union groups in membership all the railway systems of Europe (except Albania and the USSR) and others in Africa, North America and Asia. Urban railway undertakings are eligible for associate membership. As far as Great Britain is concerned, British Railways is a member of UIC and London Transport is an associate member.

An achievement of particular interest is the emergence of a system of Trans-Europe-Express (TEE) trains with a high standard of speed and comfort. At the present time there are 29 national and international links between the main cities of Western Europe under the TEE emblem. Certain of these trains, such as the Cisalpin, the Rheingold, the Mistral and the Brabant have acquired a world-wide reputation.

International Union of Public Transport (UITP)
The organisation which is now known as the International Union of Public Transport was founded in Brussels in 1885 as the Union Internationale Permanente de Tramways. Membership consists of transport undertakings, manufacturers and also of individuals responsible for urban, suburban and inter-urban public passenger transport operating motorbuses, tramways, trolleybuses, metropolitan railways, regional railways and other systems and is drawn from 62 countries throughout the world. British membership includes London Transport, the National Bus Company, the Scottish Bus Group, certain of the Passenger Transport Executives and the bus operating municipalities, United Transport Overseas Ltd, the Department of the Environment, the PRTA, APPTO and the Scottish Road Passenger Transport Association and a number of manufacturers to the industry.

The objectives of UITP are to centralise world-wide information and results of experience, to study specific operating and economic problems and to publish information and the results of research. It has been granted consultative status by the United Nations. To deal with certain problems which are of a particularly complex nature and demanding continuous research, a number of International Commissions have been appointed, charged with these studies. Separate commissions have been set up to deal with matters in connection with transport and urban planning, metropolitan railways, regional transport (railways, motorbuses and waterways), study of motorbuses, automation and economic policies on transport.

It will be recalled that the IRU also has interests in road passenger transport.

Plate 32 Tilbury Docks; lighters play an important part in the movement of merchandise by water. One is alongside a cargo boat enabling discharge from either side. This is a valuable aid to the speed and turnround of ships in port but some of the advantages are lost if the lighters or barges cannot proceed beyond the dock area; in Great Britain they cannot penetrate the narrow inland waterways.

Plate 33 One of the large SRN4 hovercraft operated by the Seaspeed Company of British Railways on the cross-Channel service to France. The hovercraft can carry up to 254 passengers and 30 cars and complete the journey from Dover to Boulogne or Calais in about half an hour./*BRB*

Plate 34 BP Tanker Company's 215,000 ton *British Explorer* at BP's Angle Bay Ocean Terminal, Pembrokeshire./*British Petroleum Co Ltd*

Plate 35 BP Tanker Company's 215,000 ton *British Explorer* undergoing trials off Nagasaki, Japan./*BP*

Plate 36 View to show the cellular construction of the *Encounter Bay* which is depicted in a dry dock at Tilbury./*Lloyd's Register of Shipping*

Plate 37 French Railways car ferry *Valençay* on the Newhaven—Dieppe service for which a plan and relevant statistics appear at Figure 5. Note the doors at the stern of the ship through which road vehicles are able to drive on and off./ SNCF

Plate 38 Vehicle ferry across the River Yare at Reedham, Norfolk. This shows the roll-on—roll-off ferry boat in its simplest form and this type of vessel is the forerunner of the now widely used seagoing vessels of the type depicted at Plate 37 and Figure 5.

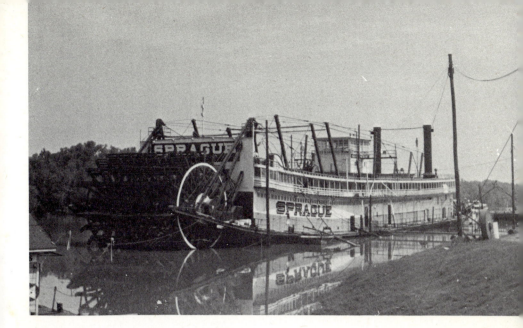

Plate 39 The *Sprague*, a stern wheel paddle steamer on the River Mississippi at Vicksburg, USA. This vessel, which was built in 1902, has towed up to 60 coal boats covering an area of 6½ acres and containing 67,307 tons of cargo. Although no longer in service, this does illustrate the capacity and hence the value of water transport, even on inland waterways, where geographical conditions are right.

Plate 40 Water bus on the Grand Canal, Venice, Italy. These buses provide a frequent service along what is the main traffic artery of this city on water. On the left of the picture can be seen a gondola, or what in Venice is, in effect, a taxi, being propelled by 'animal' power.

Plate 41 Goodyear airship *Europa*. This airship is of the non-rigid type and was constructed at Cardington, Bedfordshire./*Goodyear Tyre and Rubber Company*

Plate 42 The Helicopter Unit of British European Airways undertakes a diversity of tasks in addition to the provision of a regular passenger service between Penzance and the Isles of Scilly. Here, a BEA Sikorsky S61N helicopter is seen delivering a special consignment at Fulham Power Station London./*British European Airways*

Plate 43 The Hawker Siddeley Trident Three aircraft, which is in production for BEA, is the latest high capacity stretched version of the Trident family of airliners. Powered by three Rolls-Royce Spey jet engines, with an additional lightweight booster engine for take-off, this aircraft can carry 152 passengers and their baggage on stages of about 1,600 statute miles. In an all-tourist configuration the Trident Three can carry up to 180 passengers./*Hawker Siddeley*

Plate 44 The mammoth Boeing 747 "Jumbo Jet". An idea of the size of this aircraft can be gauged from the tractor and also from the personnel on the ladder on the side of the hangar./*Boeing Company*

Plate 45 The supersonic passenger aircraft "Concorde" which is a joint product of Aerospatiale France and the British Aircraft Corporation seen undergoing trials prior to entry into passenger service./*British Aircraft Corporation*

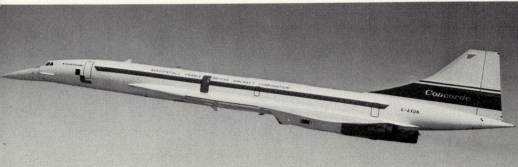

Plate 46 Aerial view of Gatwick Airport, Surrey. Note the terminal buildings and the access facilities. This is one of the few airports that is served by rail as well as by road. Gatwick Airport Station which is on the main London to Brighton line of BR can be seen in the foreground. A covered way links the air terminal with the station platforms and electric trains complete the 28 mile journey to Victoria in the West End of London in about 40 minutes./*British Airports Authority*

Plate 47 A diagrammatic illustration of the projected space shuttle from launch through to separation of the booster from the orbiter, into orbit, re-entry into atmosphere and thence landing on an airfield back on earth. The terms RAO and SRM refer to Rocket Assisted Orbiter and Solid Rocket Motors respectively./*NASA*

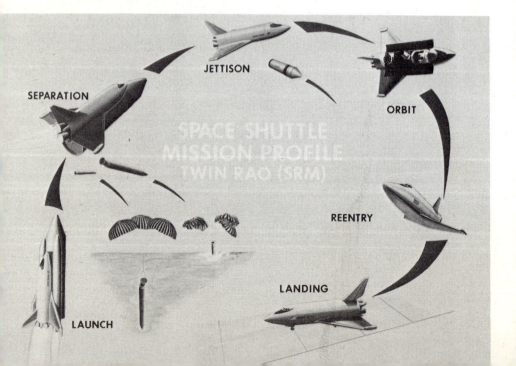

Whilst, however, the IRU groups the main road transport national associations whose affiliates are private enterprises (for example, the PVOA) and caters for the interests of the road transport industry as a whole, including own account and hire and reward road haulage, the UITP caters for only one particular sector, being urban passenger transport with, at least as far as the operating members are concerned, a very strong representation by those undertakings that are publicly owned.

Inter-Governmental Maritime Consultative Organization (IMCO)
The Inter-Governmental Maritime Consultative Organization was established in 1948 as a specialised agency of the United Nations and the only one concerned solely with maritime affairs. Membership embraces 75 states. Its interest lies mainly in ships used on international services and its objectives are to facilitate co-operation among governments on technical matters affecting shipping, with special responsibility for the safety of life at sea and for ensuring that the highest possible standards of safety at sea and of efficient navigation are achieved. This entails providing extensive exchange between nations of information on technical maritime subjects. Also included in the IMCO Convention is an objective to encourage the abolition of discriminatory and restrictive practices affecting ships in international trade and thus to promote the freest possible availability of shipping services to meet the needs of the world.

The functions of IMCO are consultative and advisory. It is a forum where its members can consult and exchange information on maritime matters and make recommendations on any maritime questions. In the co-ordination of work on the maritime aspects of nuclear propulsion, aviation, health, labour, meteorology, oceanography and telecommunications with the activities of the United Nations agencies dealing with those subjects, IMCO's advice is available to those agencies and to any other international bodies concerned. It is also responsible for convening international conferences when necessary and for drafting international maritime conventions or agreements. IMCO is the depositary authority for a number of international maritime conventions, including the International Convention for the Safety of Life at Sea, 1960, the International Convention for the Prevention of Pollution of the Sea by Oil, 1954, as amended in 1962, the Convention on Facilitation of International Maritime Traffic, 1965, the International Convention on Load Lines, 1966, and several conventions dealing with the legal aspects of marine pollution.

Matters which are the subject of consideration include, for example, stability and subdivision of ships, load lines (which are marked on ships' sides to control the safe carrying capacity), fire protection, ship design and equipment, the carriage of dangerous goods and bulk cargoes, sea transport of containers, international code of signals, safety of navigation, life-saving appliances, radiocommunications, the prevention of marine pollution and simplifying documentation and port formalities. IMCO is also dealing with questions of international maritime law.

The work of IMCO often runs parallel to the activities of other agencies in the United Nations family, (including ICAO which is discussed below) in connection with safety at sea and in the air and close contact is maintained with them on projects of mutual concern. There are formal agreements with the United Nations, the International Labour Organisation (which has a particular interest in employ-ment conditions everywhere) with the Food and Agriculture Organisation and with the International Atomic Energy Agency. The latter's work programme covers such subjects of interest to IMCO as the application of atomic energy to ship propulsion and the disposal of radioactive wastes from such ships and the carriage of radioactive cargoes.

In consultative status with IMCO are many non-governmental international organisations representing shipowners, trade unions and other interests, or bodies concerned primarily with shipping matters, especially from the safety aspect. These all play a valuable part in assisting IMCO with its work.

International Chamber of Shipping

Formed originally in 1921 but given its present title in 1948, the International Chamber of Shipping, with headquarters in London, is an association of national organisations representative of, in the main, private shipowners of Europe (mostly the maritime countries), Australia and New Zealand, Japan, India, and North America. Its main objective is to promote the interests of its members in the international field and to exchange views. The activities of ICS embrace not only general policy but also technical, legal and safety matters. It covers, in fact, everything which concerns international shipping except that which appertains to ship's crews and which is in any case the domain of the International Shipping Federation. Efforts are made to preserve the freedom of the seas and to eliminate political inhibitions to individual shipping services or to those of particular nations and representations are made through national governments when appropriate.

The International Chamber of Shipping has been granted consultative status by the United Nations Organization which has enabled it to maintain close con-tact with the Inter-Governmental Maritime Consultative Organization which has just been described and also with other specialised agencies. The International Chamber has, in fact, contributed to much of the work of IMCO.

Baltic Exchange

The Baltic Exchange is, in effect, a selling organisation selling the services of sea-going vessels and particularly the bulk carriers that are available for charter as a whole for specific voyages or for periods of time. Being an international business, vessels of all nationalities are available for charter by merchants of their own or any other country and some thousands of deep-sea tramp ships are thereby con-stantly seeking employment and merchants and shippers all over the world are in continual need of ships to carry their cargoes. This process of mutual search, the right ship finding the right cargo and vice-versa, would be prolonged and difficult without some central organisation where business can be consolidated. This is the function of the shipping section of the Baltic Exchange and it is this activity, with rates fluctuating from day to day according to supply and demand, which constitutes the London freight market — the main freight market not only of Great Britain but of the entire world. Business transacted at the Baltic is not confined to voyages calling at United Kingdom ports. As far as tramp shipping is concerned, there is no business which cannot be worked on the Exchange. The people on the Exchange, whose work involves a process of bargaining requiring diplomacy, skill and experience, are broadly divided between chartering agents representing the users, that is the merchants who charter the ships, and owners' brokers representing the shipowners, each and all of whom may be located anywhere in the world. The Baltic is the nerve centre of the shipping world and the brokers and agents are in constant touch with their clients by cable, telephone, etc, although some merchants and shipowners do actually have their own staff on the exchange.

Although the Baltic is concerned in the main with tramp tonnage, large quantities of bulk cargo are also arranged there for shipment by cargo liners in various trades. Booking items of miscellaneous cargo for liners is the job of the Institute of Shipping and Forwarding Agents and the freight departments of the liner companies.

There are other functions of the Baltic Exchange. The sale and purchase of the ships themselves is a principal activity of some firms on the Baltic who between them are responsible for probably some 50 per cent of the world sale and purchase business. There is also an air chartering section which has developed considerably over the postwar years with a steady improvement of the facilities offered to all who use it. Again the scope is worldwide and more foreign airbrokers and charterers are recognising the leading role of the Baltic Air Market. There are some 100 operators from all parts of the world, both national and independent, represented on the Exchange, a large proportion of whom are members of the International Air Transport Association discussed below. Commodity markets also form a part of the Baltic organisation. These deal with grain imports into the United Kingdom and elsewhere, oil and oilseeds and there is also the London Grain Futures Market, but this aspect lies outside the study of transport.

Lloyd's Register of Shipping

For over two hundred years the Society known as Lloyd's Register of Shipping has been engaged on the classification of ships and throughout those years it has shown the results of its work in a series of register books. Although, however, the description as a classification society is derived from the initial practice of grading ships into classes, for many years now there has been only one standard — symbolised by 100A1 — to which all classed ocean-going ships are required to conform. Centred in London but with branches throughout the world, the Society's main purpose now is the establishment of construction and maintenance standards for ships and the provision of a technical service to help shipowners to maintain those standards. It does, however, also have an industrial services department which carries out a large amount of engineering inspection on land-based industrial installations. Unlike its famous sister organisation, the Corporation of Lloyd's, it does not transact insurance. Both, however, trace their common name and ancestry to Edward Lloyd of the City of London in whose coffee house they had their birthplace in 1760.

At the beginning of the 1970's some 75 million tons or about one third of the world's shipping was classed with Lloyd's Register of Shipping and at the same time, some 26 million tons gross was on order to the Society's class. Although the functions of the Society are now no longer confined to ship classification, it came into being originally because the shipping community took steps to provide for itself a service which it required. To-day it performs basically the same service for, and under the control of, the same community. Direction of the Society's affairs is in the hands of a general committee, composed of underwriters, shipowners, shipbuilders, marine engineers, steelmakers and representatives of various shipping and shipbuilding organisations, all of whom serve voluntarily. Independent of any official control, its authority is, nevertheless, such that classification by Lloyd's Register of Shipping is accepted by all maritime Governments as evidence that statutory requirements in respect of structural strength have been met.

The income of the Society is derived from the fees charged for the services of its surveyors and from subscriptions to the register book, etc. and is devoted exclusively to the operation of the Society for the benefit of its clients throughout the world.

Liner Conferences

Liner Conferences as a sub-heading is somewhat different in character from what has otherwise been considered in this chapter. The term is more descriptive of a system and within that system there are many separate organisations. As, however, it is the purpose of each liner conference to act in the collective interests of its members, it is appropriate to include reference to the system here.

Where several liner companies operate in the same trade, it is common practice for them to form an association known as a conference. Basically, a conference is simply a meeting of all the lines, British and foreign, serving any particular route, for the purpose of evolving a regular pattern of sailings to give the maximum service to shippers and to reach common agreements on rates. According to the importance of the trade, the conference ranges from an informal association to a well-developed organisation with a permanent secretariat. The trading community relies largely on the liner services for its transport needs just as the shipping lines rely on the traders for their support. This mutual support is very necessary if liner operators are to invest in new and better ships and keep those ships on particular services at times when they could be used more profitably elsewhere. To do this the regular lines must have some protection against a pirate ship which might come on the scene in times of prosperity and so earn a high rate or in times of adversity when spare tonnage is available. If the liner companies are to run ships with spare capacity in bad times, keep rates stable when tramp rates soar, carry unattractive cargoes and serve difficult ports, then they require some means of protection from the purely opportunist competitor and also some assurance of continuing support from shippers. Hence the voluntary system of liner conferences has been evolved. There is generally no legal protection from the pirate ship and the conference must, therefore, work on a system of attracting and retaining regular customers.

It is not however only the operators who need some sort of guarantee. The shippers also need to be assured regularity and reliability. They want to be able to sell knowing that the business which results will find transport, not only when that particular trade is good and is attracting plenty of ships but also when it is poor and ships can find better employment in other areas. They also want stability of rates and substantial equality of treatment with their competitors without necessarily being tied to one particular carrier.

For these reasons, conferences have become an essential part of the liner system. To get some assurance of support the conference lines as a whole offer to regular shippers a percentage discount on the tariff rate providing they confine their custom to one or other of the conference lines for a fixed period. This is known as a conference tie, which is in the form of a deferred rebate and except for general rate cutting is the only protection which lines within a conference have against outside ships. Patronage of a conference line is quite voluntary. Shippers are perfectly free to deal with whom they please, but if they do have business with an outside ship without permission from the conference, they will lose their special rebates.

To sum up, the liner conferences provide for:

(a)   Regular, reliable and flexible services.

(b)   Agreed rates observed by all shipping lines within the conference.

(c)   Measures to encourage regular support.

Within a conference, competition is restricted to quality of service. It must nevertheless be remembered that the competitive field remains wide because membership is usually international with a very varied range of ships from which to choose. Also, because of this international character, the analogy which is sometimes drawn with price-fixing by manufacturers in certain trades is not really valid. These price rings are generally within a national market protected by tariffs and/or by the additional transport costs which foreign competitors have to bear. There is of course no such protection for members of an international liner conference. The International Chamber of Commerce (which represents the customers of shipping) has indicated the necessity for reliable and regular services, suitable freight rates and equality of terms to users, in the interests of world trade and commerce. In so doing, it has expressed its support of the system of liner conferences which, being largely free of Government control or regulation, has proved flexible and effective.

International Civil Aviation Organization

The International Civil Aviation Organization is the body charged with the administration of the principles enunciated at the Chicago Conference to which reference was made in Chapter 7. For this purpose the following committees have been established:

(1)   Air Navigation Commission

(2)   Air Transport Committee

(3)   Legal Committee

(4)   Committee on Joint Report of Air Navigation Services

(5)   Finance Committee.

The first two of these committees were established by the Conference but the remaining three have been brought into being subsequently by the council. (The council is made up of 27 member states to carry out the directions of the assembly, the assembly being the ultimate authority at which all member states have the right to be represented.)

In short, ICAO is the international agency of governments which creates world standards for the technical regulations of civil aviation. Its aims and objectives are to develop the principles and techniques of international air navigation and to foster the planning and development of international air transport. As part of its service to navigation it maintains a number of weather ships (which, incidentally, have participated also in search and rescue operations) and in some cases ICAO actually finances the installation of navigational aids. Following an agreement with the Secretary General of the United Nations, ICAO has become a specialised agency in relationship with the United Nations and has thereby joined the United Nations family. It also maintains close liaison with the International Telecommunications Union, the World Meteorological Organization, the World Health Organization, the Universal Postal Union and the International Labour Organization. The International Air Transport Association, reference to which follows, is represented at many of the meetings of the ICAO bodies.

International Air Transport Association
The International Air Transport Association is the world organisation of scheduled airlines. Its members carry the bulk of the world's scheduled international and domestic air traffic under the flags of more than 80 nations. Its major purpose is to ensure that all airline traffic anywhere moves with the greatest possible speed, safety, convenience and efficiency and with the utmost economy.

For the airlines, IATA provides machinery for finding joint solutions to problems beyond the resources of any single operator. It has become the means by which they have knit their individual routes and traffic handling practices into a worldwide public service system despite the difference between languages, currencies, laws and measurements. It is a pool of experience and information and the administrator of many common services and enterprises. It is, therefore, the collective personality of over a hundred airlines and it functions as the international air transport industry's link with governments and the public. It is the world parliament of the airlines and their representative in international organisations.

For governments, IATA furnishes the medium for negotiation of international rates and fares agreements and provides the only practical way of drawing upon the experience and expertise of the airlines. It helps to carry out the fast and economical transport of international air mail and makes certain that the needs of commerce and the safety and convenience of the public are served at all times.

For the general public, IATA ensures high standards of efficient operation everywhere, proper business practices by airlines and their agents, the greatest possible freedom from irksome formalities and the lowest possible fares and rates consistent with sound economy. As a result of such airline co-operation through IATA individual passengers can by payment in a single currency arrange journeys involving many countries and the systems of several scheduled carriers.

IATA was founded in 1945 to meet the problems created by the rapid expansion of civil air services at the close of World War II and in both organisation and activity, IATA is closely associated with ICAO. Membership is open to any operating airline which is licensed to provide scheduled air services by a government eligible for membership in ICAO. IATA's work begins only after governments have promulgated a formal exchange of traffic and other rights (bilateral air transport agreements) and have licensed the airlines selected to perform the service. But from that point on, the activity of IATA spreads through virtually every phase of air transport operations. Creative work is largely carried out by financial, legal, technical, traffic advisory and medical committees. Negotiation of fares and rates and other commercial agreements is carried out through IATA traffic conferences with separate conferences considering passenger and cargo matters and establishing agreements valid for periods of two years.

A function of IATA is to weld its member airlines into a co-ordinated commercial network. In so doing it has produced a series of interline agreements, standardised forms and procedures. Furthermore, all governments in whose countries there are member airlines have delegated to IATA the responsibility for negotiating international agreements on rates and fares subject only to their final approval.

Both IATA and ICAO have the same interest — international civil aviation. As IATA is an association of airlines it is affected by the decisions of ICAO which does, nevertheless, give careful consideration to any recommendations which IATA might make.

Users' Bodies in Great Britain
Transport Users' Consultative Committees
The Transport Users' Consultative Committees were first introduced by the Transport Act, 1947 and were designed to protect users against exploitation by the monopoly undertakings created by that Act. The structure and remit of these committees is not quite the same now as when they were first introduced and to avoid confusion, the following paragraphs are confined to the position as it stands under Section 56 of the 1962 Act, as amended by Section 55 of the 1968 Act, unless otherwise stated.

Transport Users' Consultative Committees are concerned with facilities offered by the Railways Board, the Docks Board, and the National Freight Corporation. Transport Users' Consultative Committees have no power to discuss the services of those undertakings which come within the framework of the National Bus Company or the Passenger Transport Executives.

There is a Central Transport Users' Consultative Committee for England and Wales together with Area Transport Users' Consultative Committees which between them cover the entire country. Both the central and the area committees consist of a chairman and members drawn from persons representative of the users, the chairmen of the area committees being members of the central committee. It is the duty of each committee to consider and report on the quality of the services and facilities provided which:

(a)　have been the subject of representation by the users,

(b)　have been referred for consideration by the Secretary of State for the Environment or by an appropriate board or authority
　　　or

(c)　appears to the committee to be a matter to which consideration ought to be given.

After consideration of any such matter, the area committees report to the central committee and the central committee to the Secretary of State for the

Environment who will in turn consider the recommendation and at his discretion give a direction to the authority concerned.

There is a separate area committee for Scotland which may deliberate on the services of the same undertakings as the other committees together with those of the Scottish Transport Group (except for its road passenger transport interests) but which reports direct to the Secretary of State.

TUCCs have a special responsibility in connection with any withdrawal or major reduction in railway passenger services. The railway authority is required to acquaint the public with any such proposals together with advice that objections may be lodged with the appropriate TUCC. In the event of an objection being received, the proposals may not be proceeded with until the TUCC has considered the matter and reported to the Secretary of State on any hardship that it is thought might arise. The Secretary of State will then review such representations and give directions as he sees fit.

London Transport Passengers Committee
Section 14 of the Transport (London) Act, 1969, provided for the establishment by the Greater London Council of a separate users' consultative body for considering matters affecting the provision of services provided by London Transport.

Post Office Users' National Council
Section 14 of the Post Office Act 1969 provides for the establishment of a Post Office Users' National Council for the British Isles and also for Country Councils for Wales, Scotland and Northern Ireland. It is the duty of these Councils to consider any matter relating to the services provided by the Post Office and to report thereon to the Minister. Country Councils will consider only such matters as relate to their particular areas and will report also to the National Council and the National Council will consult with the appropriate Country Council if it considers matters local to such areas. Section 15 of the 1969 Act requires the Post Office to consult the National Council on any major proposal relating to any of its main services and which would affect the persons for whom they are provided.

Inland Waterways Amenity Advisory Council
The Inland Waterways Amenity Advisory Council was set up in 1968 under Section 110 of the Transport Act 1968.

One of the principal functions of the Council is to advise the British Waterways Board and the Secretary of State on any proposals to add to or to reduce the network of cruising waterways. This would cover a proposal for the restoration of a canal with a view to its eventual addition to the cruising network. They are also to consider and make recommendations to the Board or the Secretary of State about the use or development of the cruising waterways for amenity or recreation, including fishing, and about the provision of services and facilities for those purposes either on the cruising or on the commercial waterways. On these waterways the Council may consider and recommend, at the request of the Board or the Secretary of State, on representations made to them by outside persons or on their own initiative.

It is, therefore, similar in principle to the users' consultative committees already described.

10 · The Structure of the Transport Industry

Introduction

The point was made in Chapter 7 that transport, regardless of the mode, was pioneered largely by private enterprise. Almost every service owes its beginnings, however remotely, to the foresight of individuals or bodies of people prepared to risk capital in the development of some form of transport. The systems have grown in step with the economies of the countries that they serve but for some, and this applies particularly to inland transport, their days of prosperity are over. As standards of living have improved and more and more people are able to run their own private transport, so certain demands for public transport have fallen. In many cases it is the optional rider that has gone, leaving a particularly acute and expensive peak hour problem. Elsewhere, only the very young and the very old now require public transport, which makes it nothing more than a social service. It is certainly not one that can be operated for profit. In other instances, new techniques have rendered former practices and equipment obsolete or have necessitated capital expenditure that small scale enterprise cannot meet. Rural passenger services and railway branch lines, even in built-up areas, are examples of services which are now seldom profitable. Traffic has disappeared from many of the canals, certainly from the British narrow canals, and now the container revolution is endangering the livelihood of the dockers. These circumstances have meant that systems that were built up by private enterprise can now no longer live as commercial concerns. In places they have contracted but their social necessity has prevented complete closure. This has brought forth the need for subsidies, a matter which is a subject of Chapter 12, and governments are often not prepared to inject money into privately owned businesses which are operating for personal gain. It follows that for various reasons, many transport undertakings throughout the world have now passed into public ownership. They have not necessarily been compulsorily acquired but economic and other circumstances are such that the owners have been willing to dispose of their assets in this way. In other instances, political opinion has decreed that essential services, of which transport is deemed to be one, should not be run for profit. There are, therefore, also examples of privately owned transport undertakings being acquired by the state without any option being given to the original owners.

The point being made here is that within the transport industry there is both public and private enterprise and the main forms of ownership within both sectors are considered below. This is followed by a review of the structure of British transport, from which it will be seen that there have been relatively few compulsory acquisitions by the State and none at all in recent years. In other countries, such as in eastern Europe, the position is different.

Taking the private and public sectors of industry collectively, ownership of business units appears in many different forms and the majority of these forms

147

are represented amongst those undertakings which provide public transport. But the differences in types of service and territories served are so great that it is impracticable to generalise on the merits or otherwise of any one form of ownership. A road service into new development could be provided very satisfactorily by small scale enterprise perhaps with only one vehicle, but as the area expands and population increases so the demand grows to a point where the greater resources of a larger undertaking may become necessary. The following paragraphs describe different forms of ownership in approximate ascending order of size although each one provides an equally valuable service to the community in its own particular sphere and within its own natural limitations.

Forms of Ownership

The Sole Proprietor

This form of operator, frequently known as the small man is the sole owner of his vehicles and equipment and he accepts entire responsibility for the running of his business although he could of course employ labour to assist him in his work. His capital assets may have come from personal savings, subject to any hire purchase arrangements on his vehicles or mortgage commitments on his property, which must be redeemed out of income. In addition to his managerial responsibilities, it is not uncommon for the sole proprietor to take an active part in the more manual tasks associated with the working of the business and his staff often consist of his wife or other members of his family, whose remuneration might well be less than a normal rate. His office, if he has one, could be a room in his private house in which he might keep only the most rudimentary system of accounts. It should not however be thought that the one-man business is inefficient. On the contrary, the man who both owns and works his business and lives on the success of his enterprise will invariably make every effort to retain his goodwill and seek new custom. In so doing he will give good service which often more than compensates for any lack of administration.

Because his equipment must be produced from his own private resources, the sole proprietor will seek that branch of transport which requires minimum overheads. It is unlikely that he would wish to lay a railway track or to stand the cost of a modern seagoing vessel or an aircraft. But he could provide his own road vehicle and with that vehicle he could start a business (provided that he also has the necessary licence as discussed in Chapter 8). The road transport industry is therefore the obvious course for this type of ownership. Because of his low overheads and perhaps cheaper labour he will not incur such high costs and for this reason the sole proprietor can often succeed in a rural area where the population and consequently the traffic is sparse and quite insufficient to support the heavier expenses of a larger concern.

But the financial resources of an individual are limited. Expansion of a one-man business is not therefore easy and for this reason the owner-operator seeking a wider field might combine his resources with those of another and thus form a partnership.

The Partnership

A partnership is defined by the Partnership Act, 1890, as the relation which subsists between persons carrying on a business in common with a view to profit.

Two or more persons can by this means pool their resources and together they will be in a stronger position to expand. A partnership is not confined to only two people. It may be two or more, but Section 434 of the Companies Act, 1948, as slightly amended by Section 120 of the Companies Act, 1967, requires that no partnership shall consist of more than 20 persons. If it does, then the business must be registered as a company. The characteristics of a partnership are very similar to those of the business of a sole owner. It can still be hampered by a lack of working capital and the extent of operations is again limited, but the personal touch remains. Administration and financial policy, as with the sole proprietor, might be a little elementary and an annual audit is not obligatory as it is in the case of a limited company. Like the sole owner, partners retain their own personal identities and also like the sole owner, they have an unlimited liability for all the debts of their enterprise — a costly affair if the venture should fail which might even mean selling house and personal belongings. Also the inconvenience of a rearrangement of the legal side is necessary if a partner wishes to withdraw or dies. A need to facilitate expansion and to have some protection against the risks of a partnership brings into consideration the third form of ownership.

The Limited Liability Company
Undertakings within the company form of ownership range from the small to the very large. The dictionary definition of a company is among other things "a body of persons combined for commercial or other purposes". In one sense therefore any organisation except that of a sole proprietor could be regarded as a company, but in this context company has a special meaning. Whilst the literary definition is a general one, the legal interpretation is more precise as an undertaking must comply with the requirements of the Companies Act, 1948, before it can be registered legally as a company. Its name, objects and proposed capital must be set out in what is called a Memorandum of Association. The rules for running it (through the directors and other officials) dealing with profits, payment of dividends, shareholders meetings, and other matters which affect the interests of shareholders and management are laid down in the Articles of Association. Details must be registered with a government official — the Registrar of Companies, before a certificate can be issued to permit the company to start business. Copies of these documents, together with various returns which must be made either annually or when there are changes in capital, directors, or other vital matters, are put into a file which is available for public inspection at the Department of Trade and Industry.

A company is in itself a distinct entity. The members subscribe towards a predetermined capital necessary for floating the business, in return for which they hold shares and receive interest in accordance with the class of shares held and the prosperity of the enterprise. Whatever changes there may be in the ownership of the shares, it is much easier than in the case of the partnership for a participant to withdraw, or for extra shares to be issued if more capital is required.

A limited company gives protection to the shareholders as should the business fail, their liability is limited to the extent of their holdings, hence the term limited. The possible hardship which could be experienced by a sole proprietor or by members of a partnership is thereby avoided. Limited companies may be either private limited companies or public limited companies. The private company is one which does not invite subscription from the general public and shares are often all held by members of the same family. This type of undertaking is able to extend to its members the protection described above and at the same time preserve the character of the family business. But the restriction on the sale or transfer of shares tends to prevent operation on anything more than a medium scale. For further expansion it is often necessary for the company to invite public subscription, when it becomes a public limited company (not to be confused with public ownership as discussed below). There are however certain advantages enjoyed by a private company, among which is that the minimum number of members may be two, whereas in the public company it is seven. Unlike the public company however, which has no upper limit, membership of a private company must not exceed 50, but this nevertheless compares favourably with the 20 maximum of the partnership. Some companies operate under the authority of an individual and particular Act of Parliament. These are known as statutory companies.

The company, in one way or another, as a form of ownership, embraces the largest of the undertakings which operate under private enterprise. A company organisation does not, however, necessarily indicate private ownership.

One outcome of the limited company is that it has divorced ownership from management. Unlike the sole proprietor or the partnership, owners (i.e. shareholders) of a large limited company do not manage its day-to-day affairs. They elect directors who in turn may appoint a general manager or a management team remunerated by salary. It is now but a short step to part public ownership. Purchase by the government of shares in a private concern produces the mixed undertaking (part public and part private ownership) which, although not common in this country, does find considerable favour on the continent and elsewhere abroad. One stage further brings complete public ownership, still in the form of a limited company and without direct state management. If, therefore, transport undertakings are to pass into public ownership, and this is the trend, the company organisation can be retained or introduced as an alternative to the public corporation or department of State described below.

Before leaving private ownership there is one further form which is of interest although not frequently practised. It is—

The Co-operative

The co-operative system is rather extraordinary to British operators. True, there are co-operative societies in Great Britain, chiefly in connection with the retail trade, some of which do certainly own coaches which are used for private hire and tour work. But there is a difference. The drivers of these coaches, like the shop assistants or the milk roundsmen, are usually employees working under a master for a weekly wage the same as they would if they worked for a company or a national board. This is not the case with the system to be described, but it must be stressed that while ownership through companies or their equivalents will be found throughout the world there are but isolated examples in transport of the co-operative system. Israel offers a good example of the co-operative enterprise in which groups of workers band together to cultivate the soil, engage in industry, or provide services. To quote this country by way of illustration, a total of more than 4,000 buses caters for the road passenger transport requirements of Israel and approximately 86 per cent of this number is owned and operated by two co-operatives — Egged, the inter-urban system serving the entire country and Dan, serving the Greater Tel-Aviv area. A candidate for membership of one of these co-operatives must be capable of assuming the responsibilities of a public servant and if otherwise suitable will be accepted for training as a bus driver. After passing a test, he works as a candidate for several years and if he proves himself satisfactory, membership of the co-operative then becomes possible which is acquired by a certain financial investment necessary for the expansion of the concern. The result is that each member holds an equal share in the undertaking, but what is more important, each undertakes the same obligations and enjoys the same rights and remuneration — be he driver, garage hand, or manager — in keeping with the status of equal partnership in the common venture. They all bear equal responsibilities for the maintenance and operation of the public service. Management is in the form of a council freely elected by the members from amongst themselves at the general meeting and those chosen for administrative, control and supervisory duties remain in office for four years or longer as may be determined. Those responsible for the administration of discipline are similarly elected from the members by the members and the code of conduct and award of punishment is very similar to the system described in Chapter 12.

Israel transport is an example of a truly co-operative organisation achieved without any governmental assistance or financial investment other than that of the members. The driver-proprietors decided that the co-operative was most suited to their purpose which was set up on the principles of self-labour, self-financing and self-management. Equality of working conditions and remuneration is guaranteed and members are conscious of fulfilling, ideologically and practically, a task of great public importance. Co-operative transport has, as far as Israel is concerned, given the worker a direct interest in the smooth running of the country's transport system and a sense of his own value within it. He learns to be responsible and efficient, to be a partner and a loyal assistant to his colleagues at work and to identify his personal welfare with that of the community as a whole.

The Public Corporation
Having dealt with the different forms of ownership by private people, both individually and collectively, public ownership is now to be considered.

Between the extremities of the publicly-owned limited company with its loosely defined responsibilities, and direct administration and control by a State department lies the middle course of the public corporation. This type of undertaking is created by special statute which details its rights and responsibilities. Machinery is therefore available to allow privileges and to enforce more stringent conditions than is possible in the case of limited companies, but, on the other hand, there remains a certain freedom of management. The theory of the public corporation is based on the separation of management from ownership as discussed above and the undertaking itself is a separate entity with a degree of independence not found in government departments. It has its own management responsible for the day-to-day running of the business within the terms of its creative Act. According to its constitution, the Government Minister concerned may be answerable to Parliament for policy matters even though local administration would not be subject to his scrutiny. The financial structure of the public corporation is as determined by Parliament. Money may be allocated from public funds or raised wholly or in part by the issue of stock. The latter type can in a sense be seen as a development of the limited company where the entire capital is raised by loans. Like debenture holders, the lenders have no say in the affairs of the undertaking in which their money is invested. They play no part in the election of directors, but their investment is remunerated by interest at a fixed rate in accordance with prescribed terms.

The public corporation is therefore nationally owned, but free to run its business within defined limits as decreed by Parliament, subject only to overall policy control. Legally, it is an independent body as is a limited company. It can sue and be sued and neither its management nor staff can be classified as civil servants. It is a form of ownership introduced in Great Britain at one time or another by each of the two main political parties and the principle has become accepted not only in transport, but also in other branches of industry.

The Municipality

From the middle course of the public corporation we come to direct ownership and management by a government department, in this instance local government, as it is the municipality which is to be considered first.

The powers conferred on local authorities by the 1870 Tramways Act referred to in Chapter 8 were in part responsible for the introduction of municipal ownership into local transport in Great Britain. In the period before World War I, the term municipalisation became fashionable as is the term nationalisation today and many privately-owned tramway undertakings were purchased by local councils. A municipal undertaking is therefore a department of a local authority, and elected members of the Council form a Transport Committee, which determines policy. A manager is appointed to control day to day affairs and the managerial and clerical staff are local government officers.

Municipal transport could, by the very nature of its ownership, be influenced by the colour of local politics, although the general managers who are, of course, professional transport men are available to give guidance and advice.

The State Department

The last form of control to be considered is that of complete ownership and management by National Government with the undertaking functioning as a Department of State.

In this case, overall responsibility, even down to day-to-day running, is vested in a government minister and the employees are civil servants. This type of control, however, tends to produce a policy geared more to the discharge of ministerial responsibility to parliament than to a sufficiently commercialised outlook. It is for this reason that state participation in commercial activities is now effected mainly through statutory bodies such as public corporations which have already been described and which, although under varying degrees of public control, are not part of a government department.

An examination of the merits of different forms of ownership tends to become political and as such is not a part of this study. Professional transport men the world over endeavour to apply the same basic principles, be they in control of services owned by the State, by a public board or corporation set up by Parliament, or by private enterprise. Within the terms of their constitution, they work in the most efficient manner possible to give maximum convenience and service to their customers. The form of ownership is a means to an end, although both the means and the end are sometimes outside the control of the operator. The form of ownership should not influence the science of transport, the principles of which this book attempts to examine.

Review of Forms of Ownership in Great Britain

Having studied the different forms of ownership, it remains to be seen how the theory is applied in practice. A review of the development of transport organisations in Great Britain, which gives living examples of the various structures hitherto described, follows, as the reader should be familiar with the background, some of which is political and some financial, which has produced the position as we know it today.

Road Transport

It is common practice for road operators in Great Britain to specialise in the carriage of either goods or passengers. Although examples to the contrary can be found, the two branches remain very distinct and will be dealt with separately. As far as ownership is concerned, similar circumstances do not arise in other forms of transport and the separate sub-sections for road transport will not be repeated in respect of the other forms.

Road passenger

Remember from Chapter 6 that the passenger is a standard unit — quite different from goods traffic where no two commodities are alike and different materials require different treatment and even different vehicles. But why is such information relevant to forms of ownership? The reason is that this natural difference reflects in the organisation of the management units. The very nature of the passenger industry lends itself to standardisation to a far greater degree than does the goods side which, in many respects, requires specialised treatment. Hence, ownership and control of bus and coach systems, in contrast to road haulage, has fallen quite naturally into larger units. For many years the bulk of the provincial road passenger services in Great Britain was controlled by a relatively small number of sizeable undertakings divided into three groups, namely the British Electric Traction (BET) group,,the Tilling group and the Scottish group. The services of the Scottish group were, as the name suggests, confined to Scotland, whilst the other two covered between them England and Wales excluding London. The services were run by a number of subsidiary operating companies serving areas roughly defined by agreements. Note the *company* form of ownership. (Certain of these undertakings were originally tramway concerns brought into being by specific Acts of Parliament and are therefore statutory companies.) In 1928, the four main line railway companies, as they were then, obtained powers to participate in road passenger transport and their method of exercising this right was to obtain financial interests in the existing company bus network, with the result that they purchased up to 50 per cent of the share capital of many of the bus undertakings, although they did not obtain controlling interests.

The exception to this pattern was in London. The extent of the built-up area of Greater London and the density of the population produced very complex transport requirements. A natural build-up of competitive services in the hands of one or two large companies, various municipalities and a multiplicity of small private concerns, as it was at one time, restricted any form of development which called for large capital expenditure such as for example the further construction of underground railways. It was considered by the government of the day that the transport needs of Greater London could best be met by complete integration. The large undertakings were hard put to give a comprehensive service in face of competition from independents on the more lucrative routes and because of these special circumstances, the London Passenger Transport Act, 1933, brought a monopoly in public transport to a new public board which alone was responsible (apart from the four main line railway companies) for the provision of public passenger transport services locally within a radius of some 25 miles of Central London.

Following the 1933 Act which affected only the London area, the next important piece of legislation as far as ownership is concerned was the Transport Act, 1947. This was introduced by a socialist government whose doctrines did not support private gain from essential services. Branches of transport most affected were railways and road haulage, but as there were also repercussions on road passenger transport, it is necessary to refer here to the now defunct British Transport Commission (already introduced in Chapter 8) even though it has greater significance in other forms of transport. The BTC was set up by the 1947 Act as the responsible authority for internal transport (except air) in Great Britain. It was to be assisted in the discharge of its duties by five executives, being the:

Railway Executive
Docks and Inland Waterways Executive
Road Transport Executive
London Transport Executive
Hotels Executive

The Road Transport Executive was subsequently divided into the Road Haulage Executive and the Road Passenger Executive. The Road Passenger Executive, which is the subject of this section, never had powers of compulsory acquisition, but it was anticipated that area schemes would be prepared somewhat on the lines of the arrangements that were by this time well established in the London area. The Tilling and Scottish groups together with certain other provincial companies voluntarily sold out to the BTC, but in the event, apart from some adjustments to operating areas, the identities of most of the individual companies were retained. In the London area, the London Passenger Transport Board became an Executive of the Commission, but apart from these changes the 1947 Act did, after all, have comparatively little effect on road passenger transport. The Transport Act, 1953, was concerned in the main with railways and road haulage and the Transport Act, 1962, as far as this chapter is concerned, dissolved the Commission and brought into being a Holding Company which assumed responsibility for those sections of the BTC which did not form part of one of four new Boards. The bus companies of the Tilling and Scottish groups therefore became subsidiaries of the new publicly-owned Transport Holding Company, but although the financial structure was different, to all outward appearances the industry remained unchanged. The London Transport Executive became the London Transport Board with again no visible change. However, like the Holding Company, the Board became financially self supporting instead of being tied in with other sections of the former BTC, a feature further discussed in Chapter 13.

In 1967, the Government, in its White Paper "Public Transport and Traffic", indicated its intention of introducing further legislation which, among other things, could have increased the extent of public ownership in road transport. There was, therefore, the threat of compulsory acquisition and the BET group voluntarily sold out to the Transport Holding Company early in 1968, for which the Transport Holding Company Act, 1968, gave statutory sanction to the THC for the necessary increase in borrowing powers. The latest development lies in the Transport Act, 1968. As a result of this Act, the road passenger transport interests of the THC in England and Wales were transferred to a newly formed National Bus Company and those in Scotland to a Scottish Transport Group, although the operating companies have so far generally retained their identities.

A feature of the 1968 Act which requires special mention in this context is the formation of passenger transport areas. In such areas (and so far there are five) Passenger Transport Authorities and Passenger Transport Executives have been set up with rights and duties as were described in Chapter 8. What is important here is that the assets of the municipal bus and ferry undertakings which formerly ran within the designated areas have been transferred to the new Executives, who are the professional bodies responsible, among other things, for day to day operation, subject to overall policy direction by the new Authorities. The Authorities consist of representatives of local councils whose spheres of influence fall within the passenger transport areas. The Passenger Transport Executives are, therefore, rather a unique form of ownership, but, in a sense, one that is destined to be short lived as the Local Government Act 1972 provides for, inter alia, the dissolution of the PTAs as they are at present constituted. Their functions will, in 1974, be taken over by new Metropolitan counties (of which there will be six), still with the PTEs as the professional bodies. Their structure will then be similar to that of the London Transport Executive which is discussed below, and the form of ownership, if not control, will be more truly municipal, albeit on a county rather than on a county borough or borough basis.

In addition to the major provincial companies under the National Bus Company and the Scottish Transport Group there are still bus and coach services in the hands of privately owned concerns, i.e. sole proprietors, partnerships and companies which are collectively known as the independents. There are also, of course, the services of 67 municipalities which continue to operate buses.

A further development lies in the Transport (London) Act, 1969 which

transferred to a local authority (the Greater London Council), responsibility for
what was a nationalised enterprise. A new London Transport Executive was set
up in which was invested the main assets of the former London Transport Board
and which now bears responsibility for the operation of the former Board's railway and most of its bus system subject to general policies laid down by the
Greater London Council. Bus services on the outer fringe of the former LTB
area were transferred to a new company within the National Bus Company
framework.

Road passenger transport in Great Britain does therefore produce examples
of most forms of ownership hitherto described. Small independent concerns
owned by sole proprietors, partnerships, the family businesses of the private
companies, large scale public and statutory companies and municipalities all have
their place.

Political interference has also been considerable on the goods side, the repercussions of which on the forms of ownership follow.

Road haulage
The more specialised nature of road haulage has already been explained. Standardisation was not therefore a natural development and until Parliament inter-
vened with the passing of the Transport Act, 1947, there were comparatively few
large scale road haulage undertakings in Great Britain. However, with the political
pendulum swinging to the left, the publicly owned Road Transport Executive
(subsequently the Road Haulage Executive) of the British Transport Commission
became solely responsible for the conveyance of traffic for journeys in excess of
approximately 25 miles. The rights and privileges of the Road Haulage Executive
under the terms of the 1947 Act, which are now only of historic interest will not
be detailed here, but for this text the important feature is that a nationwide
integrated system of road haulage known as British Road Services and not subject
to the licensing laws as were in existence at that time was brought into being.
There was thus a sweeping change in the ownership of road haulage from the
small units under private enterprise to a large scale public monopoly. However,
this position was not to last as by virtue of the Transport Act, 1953, a Conservative government restored the rights of the private operator by withdrawing the
monopoly of British Road Services and enforcing the sale of a large part of its
vehicle fleet back into private hands. At the same time, what was left of British
Road Services became subject to the licensing laws. In the event some difficulty
was experienced in the disposal of the British Road Services' fleet and the
position today shows the industry divided between public and private ownership,
competing on equal terms, with the BRS network somewhat larger than was
intended.

Another feature of the 1953 Act was the disbandment of all of the Executives
of the British Transport Commission except the London Transport Executive.
The constituent parts of British Road Services became limited companies under
BTC ownership and under the 1962 Act these companies passed to the Transport
Holding Company, but as on the passenger side, repercussions were financial and
to all outward appearances there was little change.

The current position under the Transport Act, 1968, is that the securities of the road haulage undertakings which were part of the Transport Holding Company organisation were transferred to a new National Freight Corporation which included, among others, British Road Services and Pickfords. Also transferred to the National Freight Corporation, the responsibilities of which are detailed in Chapter 8, were the road collection and delivery vehicles of British Railways. There is, therefore, a sharp distinction between the state-owned road haulage organisations envisaged in the 1947 and 1968 Acts although they were both introduced by socialist governments. It was intended under the 1947 Act to bring into public ownership and control all medium and long distance traffic, including, of course, railway traffic. Freight integration under the 1968 Act is confined to those activities which were already within the public sector but it abolished separate road and rail managements for road transport. The National Freight Corporation is the parent of subsidiary operating companies, and brings together under one umbrella the former THC interests in freight companies, the BR sundries business, now known as National Carriers Limited, and the Freightliner Company.

At this juncture attention may be given to the Post Office, which provides two major public utilities — posts and telecommunications. The postal section of the Post Office, i.e. the business of carrying and delivering letters and parcels, brings it into the field of transport in its own right, even though for the major hauls it utilises the services of other public carriers, particularly rail. As, however, the Post Office owns a sizeable fleet of road vehicles, it is reasonable to discuss the postal services under the road haulage sub-heading.

Until recently, the Post Office was the classic example in the transport industry of a State Department, where the Postmaster General was a Minister of the Crown and the postal workers were civil servants. However, as the total annual value of the transactions handled approached £8,000 millions, it was felt that the structure and methods of a Department of State were not entirely suited for running and undertaking of that magnitude. Trading operations on this scale must be managed on commercial lines and successive Governments sought to adapt the status and structure of the Post Office to meet this requirement. This began with changes in organisation which followed the Bridgeman Report in 1932 and since 1955 the Post Office has been responsible for balancing its own income and expenditure and has been explicitly encouraged to conduct its business as a commercial enterprise. The Post Office Act, 1969 carried this process to its logical conclusion and transferred the Post Office (except the Post Office Savings Department which remains part of the Civil Service as the National Savings Department) from a State Department to a public corporation and its staff, therefore, can no longer be classified as civil servants.

The financial duties of the Post Office are discussed in Chapter 13.

Railways

In common with other forms of transport, the railway system of Great Britain grew up from a large number of small units. Statutory companies with necessary powers to construct railways were formed for the purpose of promoting particular lines and railway history is one of pioneering, development and amalgamation under private enterprise leading eventually to public ownership.

Before the 1914—18 war, Great Britain was covered by a network of some 27 main line railway companies and nearly 100 smaller concerns. The principal reasons for the passing of the Railways Act, 1921 are contained elsewhere, it being sufficient to note here that large scale amalgamation resulted in nationwide coverage, with only minor exceptions, by four large undertakings. The important point on the subject of ownership is that, except for the London Underground which passed to a public board in 1933 and disregarding wartime control, the railway industry remained in private ownership up until the passing of the Transport Act, 1947, when the four main line companies passed to the publicly owned British Transport Commission administered through the Railway Executive. The disbandment of the Executives under the 1953 Act brought the railways under the direct control of the BTC until the passing of the 1962 Act when the Commission itself was dissolved, but public ownership remained under the Railways Board. The effects on British Railways of the 1953, 1962 and 1968 Acts are fundamentally commercial and financial and are dealt with in greater detail in Chapters 8 and 13 respectively. Responsibility for the railways of London Transport passed to the Greater London Council (i.e., from state to municipal ownership) under the Transport (London) Act, 1969 in the same way as did the bulk of the Board's road passenger services as has already been mentioned.

In Great Britain only very few minor railways remain privately owned.

Shipping

British shipping is basically international in character and both the Irish and continental short sea routes and the world-wide services are shared with foreign lines. Although, in Great Britain, there is more private ownership in the shipping industry than in any other form of transport, there is, nevertheless, a substantial element of state participation on the short sea routes. Over the years, the former main line railway companies built up a network of steam packet services linked to their railway systems and these came under public ownership as a result of the Transport Act, 1947. The present position is that most of the former railway shipping interests are now vested in the British Railways Board and those of the Caledonian Steam Packet Company and David MacBrayne in the Scottish Transport Group in accordance with the provisions of the Transport Act, 1968.

Hovercraft

Reference has been made in Chapter 4 to the development of sea-going hovercraft. Regular services are now provided by public enterprise in the form of British Railways from Dover to Calais and Boulogne and by private enterprise (Hoverlloyd) between Ramsgate and Calais. Other local services with smaller hovercraft, particularly between the mainland and the Isle of Wight are run by both British Railways and private operators.

Inland waterways

Ownership of the inland waterways of Great Britain has followed a pattern very similar to that of the railways. Flourishing as they were over half a century before the introduction of their more speedy competitor, canals were privately developed by numerous companies formed for that particular purpose. Like the railways, the history of canal ownership has its record of absorption and amalgamation before many of the waterways finally passed into public ownership in

1948 as a result of the 1947 Transport Act. The advent of the railway had a serious effect on canal undertakings and their near annihilation was in some ways accelerated by railway policy. But reasons for this decline cannot be attributed entirely to the railways. The canal undertakings themselves failed to obtain any degree of standardisation, which made it difficult to cater for through traffic. For speed, there was of course no comparison and it was inevitable that traffic was to be lost. Many canal proprietors were therefore glad to sell out to the railways and a number of waterways did in fact become railway owned. Among those which remained independent, amalgamation came in 1929 when certain companies in the Midlands merged to form the Grand Union Canal Company, which linked, under one administration, the Regents Canal in London with Birmingham and incorporated a branch from near Daventry to the River Trent.

With the formation of the British Transport Commission in 1948, former railway-owned canals were divorced from railway management and, together with a number of non-railway undertakings, were placed under the control of the Docks and Inland Waterways Executive, subsequently to become a division of the BTC when the Executives were abolished by the 1953 Act. Finally, the 1962 Act was responsible for the formation of the British Waterways Board whose arteries embrace a number of the few commercially navigable routes (be they natural or canalised rivers or purely artificial canals) in Great Britain and including on the one hand the active routes such as the Aire and Calder Navigation, the Gloucester and Sharpness Canal, the Lee Navigation, etc, and on the other the narrow canals along which traffic has dwindled. Associated with these waterways are nearly 100 reservoirs, various docks and warehouses and a certain amount of estate property. As a canal carrier the Board has only a minority interest in the goods which pass on the waterways but it has, nevertheless, a fleet of carrying craft together with road delivery vehicles and some hire-pleasure craft. The Board is primarily the provider of a way which is used on payment of tolls by privately owned canal carrying undertakings.

There are also British inland waterways which are not vested in the Board, among them being the Thames and other rivers, the Norfolk Broads, the Manchester Ship Canal together with the Bridgewater Canal, the Rochdale Canal, the Exeter Canal and others.

Ports
Ports lend themselves to standardised methods of operation perhaps less than any other part of transport. The layout of the harbour, the geography of the hinterland, tidal conditions, types of commodities (whether bulk or general cargoes), are all factors which must have individual consideration and methods of working must be adapted to suit local circumstances. Similarly, there are various types of controlling authorities.

In Great Britain today there are four main forms of port authority:
(a)   A publicly owned board (the British Transport Docks Board) set up by the Transport Act, 1962, comprising in the main the former railway-owned docks inherited by the BTC. The British Waterways Board and the Railways Board also own certain minor ports.
(b)   Independent statutory trusts such as the Port of London Authority and

the Mersey Docks and Harbour Board (a similar form of ownership to (a) above).

(c)   Municipal ownership as at Bristol.

(d)   Statutory companies which own and operate ports either for general merchandise or for some specialised and private purposes such as those of the major oil companies through which pass the oil imports from ocean going tankers.

Many of the 300 odd ports in Great Britain were established before the advent of mechanical road haulage, when the effective hinterland of each port was much smaller than it is today. As is emphasised in Chapter 3 every port must have a prosperous hinterland, but as inland transport facilities have increased, so it has become possible to tap wider areas. It follows, therefore, that these geographical regions now tend to overlap. For this reason the number and distribution of ports is no longer related satisfactorily either to their own or to the country's economy and in 1961 the Government appointed a committee under Lord Rochdale to make a comprehensive survey of the ports.

The Rochdale Committee recommended unified control of ports in major estuaries, considering that this would lead to better use of existing port capacity and facilities, more rational planning of future development, more realistic charging schemes and a stronger financial position, increased scope for staff training, etc. In the event, the Harbours Act, 1964 which followed did not bring about any changes in ownership. What it did do, however, was to establish the National Ports Council for the purpose of advising the Secretary of State on port matters as was described in Chapter 9.

Airlines

From the oldest form of transport — movement by water — we pass to the youngest, the commercial air services. The first regular British international air service began only in 1919 when a small aeroplane belonging to a company called Aircraft Transport and Travel Ltd, flew from Hounslow Heath near London to Paris. Other companies opened air services soon afterwards and in 1924 four of these early airlines amalgamated to form one company called Imperial Airways Ltd, which inherited 1,760 miles of air routes across the English Channel and an assorted collection of 18 aircraft, in many cases adapted and developed from World War I planes. Imperial Airways, under private enterprise but with State assistance, together with Dominions and Colonial operators, pioneered routes to the Far East, Australia and South Africa, and by 1939, the Company and its associates were flying over about 27,000 miles of routes. In 1935, another company, British Airways Ltd, was formed to merge some existing concerns and operated a number of services between the United Kingdom and Europe and at this time the railways were also developing air services.

The British Overseas Airways Act, 1939, established the British Overseas Airways Corporation as a Government-owned airline and in 1940 it took over formally Imperial Airways and British Airways — operationally the merger took place in 1939. During the war, BOAC played a very important part in keeping open the vital lines of air communication and it rendered valuable assistance to the British fighting services in various theatres of war. One of its most successful wartime achievements was the pioneering of the North Atlantic Return Ferry Service which was the first to operate regularly all-the-year round in both directions across that ocean. After the war, the Civil Aviation Act, 1946, created two further airways corporations in addition to BOAC: British European Airways and British South American Airways were formed to operate to Europe together with the domestic services within the United Kingdom and to South America respectively. Later, the Airways Corporations Act, 1949 merged BSAAC with BOAC leaving the two public corporations — BOAC and BEA. The Air Corporations Act, 1949, consolidated the enactments relating to the constitution and functions of the British Overseas Airways, British European Airways and British South American Airways Corporations. A further Act, the Air Corporations Act, 1967, consolidated with certain exceptions the provisions of the 1949 and subsequent Air Corporations Acts. Air transport was not, however, entirely in the hands of the public corporations. The Civil Aviation (Licensing) Act, 1960, to which reference was made in Chapter 8 permitted the then Air Transport Licensing Board to grant air service licences at its discretion to applicant airlines regardless of whether they were publicly or privately owned and private enterprise did as a result play at least a minority role in the provision of scheduled air services.

Reference is made elsewhere in this book to the remarkable growth of air transport in a relatively short space of time and as far as Great Britain is concerned, with most services being international, the industry makes a substantial contribution to the balance of payments through its earnings of foreign currency. A continued contribution by British airlines to the nation's economy must depend on their continued growth and prosperity and it was against this background that in 1967 the Government of the day appointed a Committee of Inquiry into Civil Air Transport under the chairmanship of Sir Ronald Edwards to inquire into the economic and financial situation and prospects of the British civil air transport industry and into the methods of regulating competition and of licensing that was then employed. The committee was also required to consider with due attention to other forms of transport what changes might be desirable to enable the industry to make its full contribution to the development of the economy and to the service and safety of the travelling public. The subsequent Civil Aviation Act, 1971, affected both the statutory control and the structure of the industry, the former of which has already been discussed in Chapter 8.

As far as the structure of the industry is concerned, the 1971 Act introduced the British Airways Board with powers to provide air transport on both a scheduled and charter basis and other aerial work in any part of the world and to control the activities of BOAC and BEA. As such, the Airways Board is in a position to ensure that the two airlines' fleets and routes are planned and marketed to secure the best overall advantage and to achieve economy through amalgamation. It must be clear that the Board does not merely constitute an additional layer of decision making. It is in complete control of the two national airlines and plans to merge them by 1974 have, in fact, been announced, when they will become one large airline known as British Airways. But British air transport is not entirely within public ownership. It will be recalled from

Chapter 8 that the Civil Aviation Authority (which was also created by the 1971 Act) is required to give opportunities to at least one British airline that is not controlled by the British Airways Board to provide air services. In other words, Government policy is that there should be at least a second force airline which would be in the private sector and the Secretary of State has issued guidance to the Civil Aviation Authority to the effect that British Caledonian Airways should be the principal independent scheduled operator. As a result, both the British Airways Board airlines (BOAC and BEA) and British Caledonian are being given opportunities to develop. Other independent airlines may also be granted licences. The position to-day, therefore, is a blend of public and private enterprise in the air transport industry. Whilst the bulk of the air services is in the hands of the public corporations, the private operator in the form of a second force airline is being allowed to develop and other independent airlines do also provide scheduled services.

Airports

Prewar responsibility for providing aerodromes within the United Kingdom rested in the main with local authorities, the only ones owned by the state being at Croydon, Heston and Lympne. The municipal airports were not subsidised although it was agreed in 1938 that grants should be made from the Exchequer towards provision of full night lighting equipment at certain main aerodromes.

The expansion of civil air transport in the early 1950s necessitated the transfer of aerodromes from military to civil use, compulsory acquisition of land for new airports and substantial expenditure from public funds. For these reasons, State participation in ownership in the immediate post-war period was appropriate. There was no early prospect of making aerodromes pay and any alternative ownership would have been heavily dependent on grants from the Exchequer with little freedom of management. Central control and financing were, therefore, essential to avoid dislocation and delay in providing aerodrome facilities at this crucial time in the development of air transport and by 1964 the State owned and operated through the then Board of Trade, 21 civil aerodromes against 26 municipal and 45 private aerodromes licensed for public transport or flying training. Those owned by the State at that time ranged from the large international airports at Heathrow, Gatwick and Prestwick to small aerodromes in the Scottish highlands and islands. Some of the municipal airports such as those at Manchester, Southend and Birmingham handled more traffic than many of the state aerodromes and those privately owned differed widely in size and activity.

Although however central control was essential for the establishment of a co-ordinated network of aerodromes, the time came when it was no longer necessary for day-to-day management. There is now less need for assistance from the government or for direct ministerial responsibility and supervision from the centre over day-to-day matters in what has become a business enterprise. For this reason there has been a policy of decentralisation.

The former Government aerodromes have now passed into local authority or private hands or have been taken over by public authorities in the form of the British Airports Authority and the Civil Aviation Authority. The British Airports

Authority was brought into being by the Airports Authority Act, 1965, to take over the ownership and management of airports at Heathrow, Gatwick, Stansted and Prestwick, and it has since assumed control (in 1971) of Edinburgh Airport. The authority has the statutory duty to provide adequate facilities at its aerodromes except that it may not provide navigation services unless specifically authorised. The 1965 Act states that the Authority shall not provide any navigation service except with Government consent.

This partial transfer to the British Airports Authority left only the aerodromes in the north of Scotland that were directly owned and operated by a State department. It was not until 1972 that this form of direct State participation finally ceased when, in accordance with the provisions of the Civil Aviation Act, 1971, the Civil Aviation Authority referred to in Chapter 8 assumed control of the former Department of Trade and Industry airports at Aberdeen, Benbecula, Inverness, Islay (Port Ellen), Kirkwall, Stornoway, Sumburgh, Tiree and Wick.

Navigation Services
Air
As was stated in Chapter 8, the Civil Aviation Authority is also responsible for the operation of air navigation services and the Secretary of State for Trade and Industry has issued a directive to the Authority vide the Civil Aviation Authority (Air Navigation Services) Directions 1972 that it will join with the Secretary of State for Defence in exercising this function through a joint organisation to be known as the National Air Traffic Services (NATS).

The services provided through NATS are available to all classes of civil and military aircraft within the United Kingdom national airspace and elsewhere if in pursuance of international arrangements. Proper provision is required to be made to meet the needs of all users to allow optimum utilisation of aircraft consistent with safety and cost. Approach and aerodrome control services may also be provided. As far as civil airports are concerned, such facilities are provided at the aerodromes of the British Airports Authority and exceptional arrangements also govern the provision of technical services at the municipal airports at Manchester, Liverpool, Birmingham, Glasgow and Glamorgan where NATS has now provided these services as part of the terms on which it was originally agreed that the local authorities should manage the airports. The cost of these services is, however, borne by the local authority concerned. Otherwise, the aerodrome technical services, that is to say, the aids necessary for the approach, landing and take-off of aircraft are normally provided by the aerodrome owner with standards of safety maintained through a requirement for annual licensing, which is another function of the Civil Aviation Authority.

Sea
The general lighthouse authority (that is, the provider of warning and identification lights, etc., for ships at sea) for England and Wales, the Channel Islands and Gibraltar is the Corporation of Trinity House. Lighthouses in Scotland and the Isle of Man are the responsibility of the Commissioners of Northern Lighthouses and those in Northern Ireland and the Irish Republic of the Commissioners of Irish Lights. Trinity House is also the largest pilotage authority but most pilotage authorities are separately constituted bodies at ports around the

United Kingdom. In some cases a harbour authority or local authority is the pilotage authority. It is of interest in this context that although the Department of Trade and Industry administers the Coastguard Service which calls upon lifeboats for sea rescue purposes, the Royal National Lifeboat Institution is supported entirely by voluntary contributions and depends for its operation on voluntary workers.

Conclusion

To summarise, it has been seen that both public and private ownership is represented in all forms of transport in Great Britain. Municipalities have had interests in transport for many years with tramway acquisitions dating back to the 19th century and one of the earlier public boards was formed, it will be remembered, in 1933, when private and municipal road and rail passenger transport in London was vested in the London Passenger Transport Board. The 1933 Act introduced what was then a rather new form of ownership within British transport. The 1947 Act transferred to the erstwhile BTC, railway and canal undertakings, which included the four main line companies and the LPTB together with various joint committees, plus 18 independent canal undertakings. No undertakings of any other form of transport were expressly nominated in the Act for takeover, but general powers of acquisition were given. However, in taking over the railway and canal companies the Commission became automatically the owner of a number of other (ex-railway) canals, docks, buses, etc.

Although the BTC has long since been disbanded, except for certain very minor lines, the whole of the railway system remains under public ownership together with the major part of the nation's buses and coaches, some road haulage vehicles and docks, most of the canals and the railway shipping services. The air services are part publicly and part privately owned. British transport is therefore something of a compromise between public and private ownership.

11 · Administration

Introduction

We now pass from the structure to the administration of the transport industry. It has been seen that transport is a service activity concerned with moving people and merchandise from place to place. It is a vital service. Modern civilisation was built up as a result of it and life as we know it could not go on without it. Although transport facilities were introduced in the first place by private endeavour for personal gain, they have in many cases become a part of our national heritage and even though the ventures may now have lost their profitability, social needs could preclude such services being withdrawn. Their provision cannot, therefore, rely only on the economic forces of supply and demand.

Transport involves people and where there are people there must be proper standards of safety even though such measures entail spending money which brings no additional return. Whilst it is not suggested that if left to their own discretions, responsible operators would allow their services to be run dangerously, as was said in Chapter 8, burdened as they are with financial responsibilities, their interpretation of the essentials might not be quite what an independent third party might deem to be necessary. Transport has many users but there are also many providers. It is a matter for consideration whether there should be uncontrolled competition or enforced co-ordination and in Great Britain there are examples of both. On ways that are shared, traffic must be regulated to avoid chaos, if not danger. The industry is labour intensive and there must be harmony between employers and employed if the wheels are to turn smoothly. Satisfactory labour relations are, therefore, essential. All these topics are dealt with at length in other chapters. The point here is that transport by any means, public or private, passenger or goods, must observe certain standards and there must be proper stewardship. Essential services must, in the national interest, be subjected to some form of policy control. Subsidy and public ownership might become desirable. Satisfactory safety standards must be determined. Control from outside might be desirable to achieve proper co-ordination of facilities and provision must be made for the establishment of conciliatory machinery if adequate labour relations are to be maintained.

The Function of Government

It is a function of government through parliament to pass laws regulating the life of the community in the interests of the people. Transport must work within a legal framework and it is the responsibility of parliament to at least establish that framework. The supporting government administration must then process the will of parliament to convert it into a working reality. In other words, it must establish a system which both enables and ensures that the requirements are observed.

The Function of Management

Management has a duty to the legislature, to its governing body whomsoever that may be, to its customers and to its staff. The purpose of business is invariably to remunerate capital and management is required to conduct its affairs accordingly and in keeping with the policies as laid down by its board of directors. A transport undertaking must provide satisfactory services for its customers at reasonable charges and its staff must be given adequate reward with acceptable working conditions. All this must be done within the legal framework applicable to the industry. If it is a statutory undertaking, its terms of reference may well have been decreed by parliament and if that statutory undertaking is a nationally or locally publicly owned corporation it is likely that its board of management will have been appointed by and will be responsible to the appropriate government minister or to local civic dignitaries. Whilst, therefore, the transport industry as a whole is required to conform to general statutory requirements, in the case of some undertakings, those requirements may be more specific.

Organisation

It has now been established that government must prepare and administer its legal framework. Management must accept that legal framework and also take directions from its governing body on policy matters. To discharge its responsibilities and achieve its objective (which, in this case, is a safe arrival) management must, at the same time, give directions to its staff through proper channels of command. Whatever the administration, be it a part of central or local government, or public or private enterprise, objectives must be achieved and to do this there must be a suitable arrangement of the various functions to ensure a satisfactory conduct of business. In other words, there must be a proper organisation. The effects of government deliberations are studied elsewhere. The purpose of this chapter is to examine the administrative methods that are adopted by government for initiating and enforcing its requirements and by managements for running their businesses whilst observing those requirements.

Government Structure

The head of the Government of the United Kingdom is the Prime Minister whose authority is derived from his ability to command a majority in Parliament and from his power to submit his own choice of ministers to the Sovereign. He presides over the Cabinet, which is composed of a number of ministers, the functions of which include the determination of policy for submission to parliament and the continuous co-ordination and delimitation of the authority of government departments. It is the departments that are the main instruments for giving effect to government policy when parliament has passed the necessary legislation. In so doing they may work through local authorities and government-sponsored organisations, examples of which have already been met. Most departments are headed by a minister who is answerable to parliament and who, in some cases, may be known as Secretary of State.

The specific way in which functions are distributed among departments is varied from time to time but the main factor taken into account is that of major purpose. This has led to the grouping together within a single department of all activities relating to a particular set of objectives. In recent years there has been a growing trend towards the unification of similar policy functions into a smaller number of large departments. The functional principle is not, however, always applied as there are examples of administration on an area basis. This method of administration is adopted for Scotland and Wales where the Scottish Office and Welsh Office have a range of functions which within England would fall to several different departments.

The broad division of departmental responsibility for the main fields of government activity is as follows:

Function	*Main Departments Responsible*
Central Departments	Treasury
	Civil Service Department
	Cabinet Office
Law and Order	Home Office
	Lord Chancellor's Department
	Law Officers' Department
Overseas and Defence	Ministry of Defence
	Foreign and Commonwealth Office
Fiscal, Economic and Industrial	Ministry of Agriculture, Fisheries and Food
	Department of Employment
	Ministry of Posts and Telecommunications
	Department of Trade and Industry
	Board of Inland Revenue
	Department of Customs and Excise
Physical	Department of the Environment
Social	Department of Education and Science
	Department of Health and Social Security
Scotland	Department of Agriculture and Fisheries for Scotland
Scottish Office	Scottish Development Department
	Scottish Education Department
	Scottish Home and Health Department
Wales	Welsh Office

The three departments which have direct responsibilities for transport in one way or another are the Department of the Environment, the Department of Trade and Industry and the ministry of Posts and Telecommunications.

The Department of the Environment
The Department of the Environment has been set up, under a secretary of state, to assume responsibility in England for the range of functions affecting the physical environment in which people live and work, which were formerly divided between the Ministry of Housing and Local Government, the Ministry of Public Building and Works, and the Ministry of Transport. The secretary of state for the Environment is assisted by three ministers, being the minister for Housing and Construction, the minister for Transport Industries and the minister for Local Government and Development. The Department of the Environment is

also concerned with the co-ordination of work on the prevention of environmental pollution, with special responsibility for clean air and anti-noise functions, and research into roads, building, hydraulics, water pollution, fire prevention and uses of timber. It is also responsible for the administration of the Ordnance Survey which is in charge of the survey and mapping of Great Britain. Of the three ministers mentioned that assist the secretary of state, the latter two have transport connections. The Minister for Transport Industries is responsible for ports, general policy on the nationalised transport industries; roads, railways, inland waterways, and the channel tunnel; road haulage; buses; the international aspects of inland transport; road and vehicle safety; and driver and vehicle licensing, whilst the Minister for Local Government and Development is responsible among other things for regional, land use and transport planning.

It is of some significance that transport should be placed among the collective responsibilities of the Department of the Environment. It underlines and gives official acknowledgement to the fact that transport is closely interrelated with the other physical factors that together make up the total situation. It is comparable with building programmes, with land use and with planning. It is a part of the life of the people — a part of the environment.

The Department of Trade and Industry

The Department of Trade and Industry, under a secretary of state, combines most of the functions that were previously exercised by the Board of Trade and the Ministry of Technology. As far as transport is concerned, the department is responsible for shipping and marine matters and for civil aviation policy. It is also concerned with pipelines and with the efficient supply and distribution of fuel and power.

The Ministry of Posts and Telecommunications

The Minister of Posts and Telecommunications is responsible to parliament for the Post Office. The ministry does also have control over the licensing of radio frequencies, which is of some relevance to those parts of transport that use radio for control purposes.

Other Departments

Whilst the three departments mentioned are those that are directly responsible for transport matters, other government departments have an indirect bearing on the transport industry. Of particular note is the Department of Employment with its interests in wages and terms and conditions of employment, conciliation, arbitration and investigation of industrial disputes, industrial training and staff welfare matters.

The Structure of Transport Undertakings

It has been seen that as a general principle, the Government of the United Kingdom splits its administration on a functional basis. In other words, a number of different departments each conducts its particular business within the same area. There are, however, exceptions in that administration is in certain cases designed on an area or geographical basis and the authority or department for that area embraces many different functions. This distinction is fundamental to the subject of organisational structure, the theory of which must now be examined.

As has already been noted, organisation means simply the arrangement of the various branches of administration in order to ensure the satisfactory conduct of the business. Like forms of ownership, therefore, it is a means to an end and not an end in itself. A successful organisation must so utilise the resources of the undertaking to produce maximum efficiency and economy. Different levels of responsibility must be clearly defined and understood by all concerned. There must be sufficient flexibility to permit prompt decisions with adequate machinery to ensure that they are properly carried out. Some pre-determined form of organisation is therefore essential. There must always be control, but as the number of people whose work one man can efficiently control is limited, delegation of authority becomes necessary and duties have to be defined. A chain of responsibility must be laid down which permits top management to delegate certain of its functions to one or more persons and so on down the line to the man charged with least responsibility.

The functions of a manufacturing concern fall into three groups. The raw material must be bought, it must be processed and the finished product sold. Each one of these functions is a necessary attribute to successful business and the failure of any one would lead to collapse. In transport this theory does not change; the fact that the ultimate product is intangible makes no difference. Raw materials (vehicles, vessels or aircraft, together with other capital equipment) must be bought and, like machinery bought for manufacturing purposes, they must be maintained. Once the carrying units become available they must be used — in other words, the capacity must be skilfully utilised to provide (or "manufacture") a public transport service. At the same time, the service must be sold. The haulier must have customers, the bus undertakings must have passengers, and in selling this service, just as other manufactured products are sold, the price must be determined.

In transport these three groups may be broadly identified as:

Buy — Engineering
Make — Operating
Sell — Commercial

which between them conduct the day-to-day running of the system. As in any other business, there must also be managerial control over financial and legal matters and general administration, which could all come under the jurisdiction of a secretary, or if the undertaking is a large one, each function could become a separate section. These various activities must be *organised*, or as the dictionary states, put into proper working order and an organisation chart for a small or medium sized undertaking would, in its simplest form appear thus:

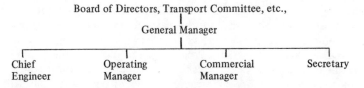

Board of Directors, Transport Committee, etc.,

General Manager

Chief Engineer   Operating Manager   Commercial Manager   Secretary

For clarity, the operating and commercial departments are shown separately, but these two functions are frequently combined under a traffic manager, in which case, the three chief officers reporting to the general manager would be the chief engineer, the traffic manager and the secretary. These terms are commonplace in road and rail transport. In sea and air transport, different phraseology is sometimes used. For example the terms operating and commercial might be referred to instead as movement and sales, but the functions of each and the principles involved are nevertheless the same.

It is not sufficient in this process of determining organisation merely to enumerate the inherent parts. These parts must work together in a manner most suitable for the particular circumstances and the individual organisational structure of any undertaking stems from one or other of two systems, namely the departmental or divisional chains of command.

The diagram above shows a skeleton of what might be developed into a departmental or functional organisation and is typical of the system adopted by the average bus undertaking. The chart at Fig 8 shows the organisation of the Eastern National Omnibus Company, an NBC subsidiary with a staff of some 2,100 operating 591 vehicles and whose bus services cover Essex, being an area of approximately 1,530 square miles. Responsible officers – a secretary, a traffic manager and a chief engineer – are in charge of each of the three departments, all of whom report to the general manager and control their respective staff. Note in this instance that the Traffic Manager is in charge of Operating and Commercial functions.

There are however distinct dangers in departmentalism when applied to very large scale enterprise. Large departments tend to act for the benefit of themselves rather than for the interests of the undertaking as a whole and of which they are but a part and much time is wasted in committee where departmental representatives battle in support of their sectional interests and where the result can be a bad compromise instead of a personal decision. There is therefore an added responsibility for top management to see that this does not happen. Because official contact between departments is usually most easily accomplished through departmental heads, top management requires a sizeable supporting headquarters staff and day-to-day matters are likely to travel up to and across a top-heavy administration and down again after a decision has been taken by officials remote from the scene of operation. But this must not be taken as criticism of the system as such. Although an organisation of this nature is not ideal for very large scale business which is competitive and where quick on-the-spot decisions are necessary to meet particular local circumstances, it is quite satisfactory where the size of the undertaking permits centralised management to keep sufficiently close to the ground, or even in large units whose activities are sufficiently stereotyped and/or disciplined to make local discretion less necessary. But in a dynamic industry where the challenge of competition and the ever-changing pattern of demand must be met, the man on the spot should have executive power. In a very large undertaking, through no fault of its own top management is liable to become indistinct, remote and almost unknown to staff at ground floor level and it is the line or divisional system which can and does meet this difficulty.

Think again of the embryonic structure drawn on page 169. Four departmental heads (and we have seen that the number is elastic) were responsible for their respective functions right down the line. Consider now the position as it would

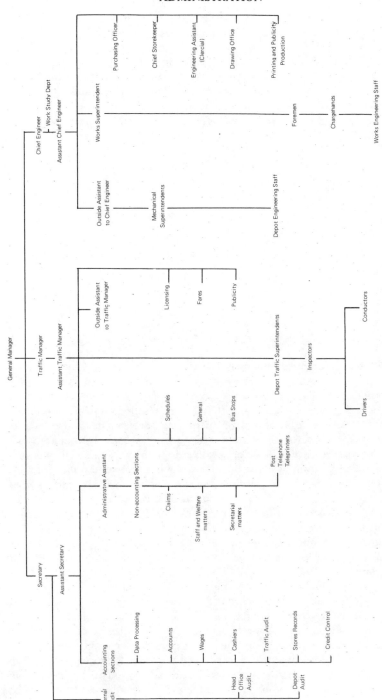

Fig 8. The organisation of the Eastern National Omnibus Co. Ltd. [*Information supplied by and reproduced by permission of Eastern National Omnibus Co. Ltd.*]

be if these departmental chiefs, responsible as they are for specific matters over the entire system, were replaced by local managers reporting direct to the general manager on *all* matters within specified areas. True, certain aspects of management must cover the organisation as a whole, for example the undertaking must speak publicly with one voice, it is desirable that there should be a common pay scale with uniform conditions of service throughout, financial and legal matters etc. will embrace the entire system, but provision can be made for this. The skeleton chart pictured above for our hypothetical transport system would now appear thus:

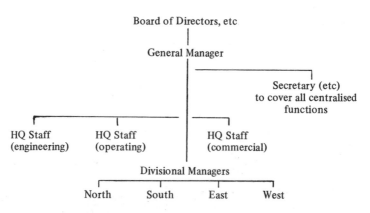

This chart, which represents the divisional system in its simplest form, assumes that the operating area is split into four divisions, north, south, east and west. Such divisions could be geographical regions or districts or perhaps lines if there are two or more main trunk routes within the organisation. The important point is that the divisional, regional, line or district managers, whatever they may be called, are responsible for all matters local to their sphere of influence which would otherwise be in the charge of separate departments and are subject only to policy directives from headquarters. One man is therefore responsible for obtaining the traffic, moving it and providing the motive power. A reduced headquarters staff is responsible for policy and general co-ordination together with those functions which must be reserved for the centre and are in this instance, for simplicity grouped under the secretary, although in practice there would be several different sections with the heads of each reporting to the general manager. The feature of the divisional system is that it brings management level right in on the ground floor and gives to the local managers much of the responsibility which otherwise would be held by headquarters departments.

These then are the broad principles of the two basic systems which form the nucleus of the many variations in the organisational structures of industry today. There are no rules and the ultimate pattern is no more than a development of the thinking described above, modified to meet particular requirements of the service for which it is intended. Some undertakings find the departmental or functional system very suitable. Others require an adaptation of the divisional or line theory and a blend of both is very common. The significance of the Scottish

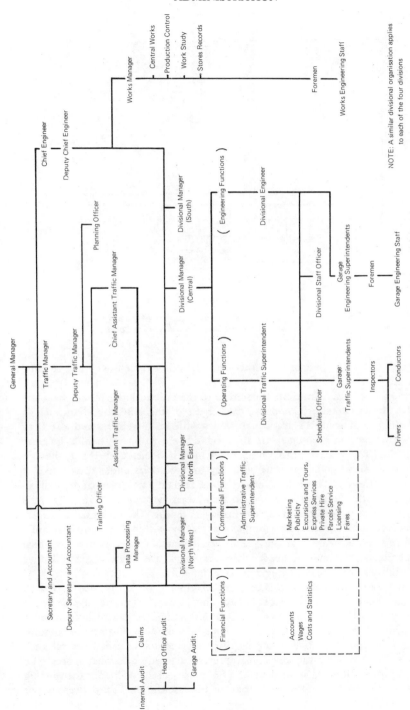

Fig 9. The Organisation of the Birmingham and Midland Motor Omnibus Co. Ltd. [*Information supplied by and reproduced by permission of Birmingham and Midland Motor Omnibus Co. Ltd.*]

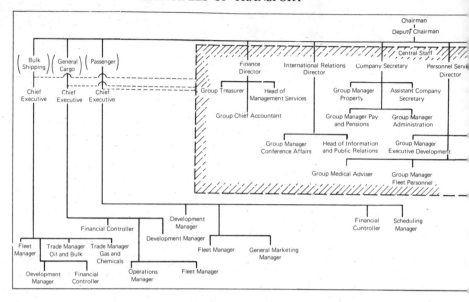

Fig 10. Organisation of the P & O Group. [*Information supplied by and reproduced by permission of the Peninsular and Oriental Steam Navigation Company*

and Welsh Offices as part of the structure of HM Government will now be more apparent.

To turn once again from the theoretical to the practical, the Birmingham and Midland Motor Omnibus Company, the largest of the NBC subsidiaries which serves an area of some 12,000 square miles with 1,575 vehicles and a staff of about 6,000 has, on account of its size, found the divisional system to be more appropriate. The chart of this Company, which is depicted at Fig 9, shows a relatively small headquarters staff with day to day affairs under the control of four local managers. There does, nevertheless, remain an element of departmentalism as it is the functional heads who are ultimately responsible to the general manager and to whom the divisional managers report. The divisional managers do, however, have substantially complete authority within their respective areas of influence. This means that they have overall control locally on matters which are separate departments at head office and they have, therefore, a collective responsibility to each of the three departmental chiefs.

To quote another example, this time in the shipping world, the chart at Fig 10 shows the organisation of the P & O Group, which again exemplifies the divisional system, but on a larger scale. The P & O Group is, in effect, an amalgamation of various and at one time independent shipping interests. For purposes of administration, it is split into five operating divisions and six so called central staff divisions. The five operating divisions represent the truly divisional or area type of organisation, all being headed by chief executives responsible for the running of their respective businesses. Note that in this case the chief executives are not

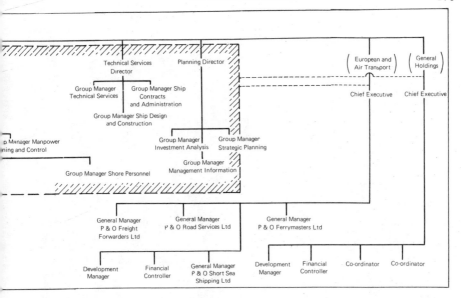

responsible to various functional chiefs at headquarters (as in the case of BMMO) but direct to the chairman. The nucleus of the Group, which is the central staff contained within the six central divisions is, in effect, the headquarters administration organised on a departmental basis. The various group managers within the central staff have functional responsibilities on common matters which extend throughout the group.

This delegation of authority to divisions is yet again exemplified by another variation, that adopted by British European Airways, a division of the British Airways Group under the control of the British Airways Board as was described in Chapter 10. In this case, a one time departmental organisation has given way to a system based on task responsibility and financial accountability.

The chart at Fig 11 shows the broad organisation of BEA from which, it will be seen, consists of ten divisions supported by seven group staff departments. Divisions are treated as individual profit centres in that their performances are measured in terms of the return on investment made in them and management sets specific financial targets for which they are held accountable. A separate profit and loss account is maintained for each unit and internal transactions between one profit centre and another involving the provision of products or services are accounted for by divisional charges agreed by negotiation. Subject to any constraints imposed by management, heads of profit-centered units may execute the work involved in meeting their responsibilities by:

(a)   Setting up their own organisation;
(b)   Entering into a contractual relationship with another unit of the BEA organisation; or
(c)   Going to an outside contractor (say, another airline).

The central staff departments are not profit-centered as such although they

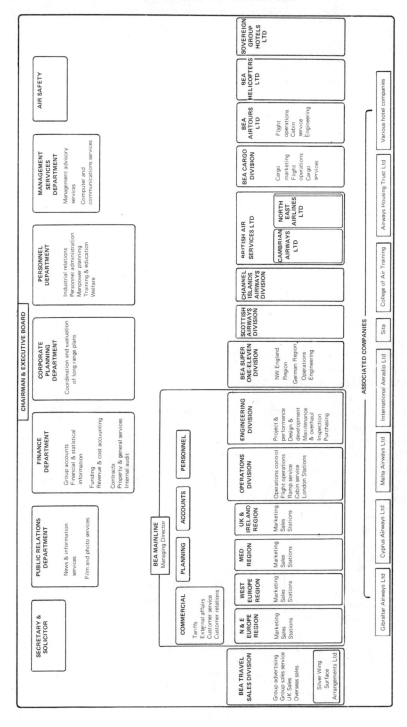

Fig 11. Organisation of British European Airways. [*Information supplied by and reproduced by permission of British Airways Board*]

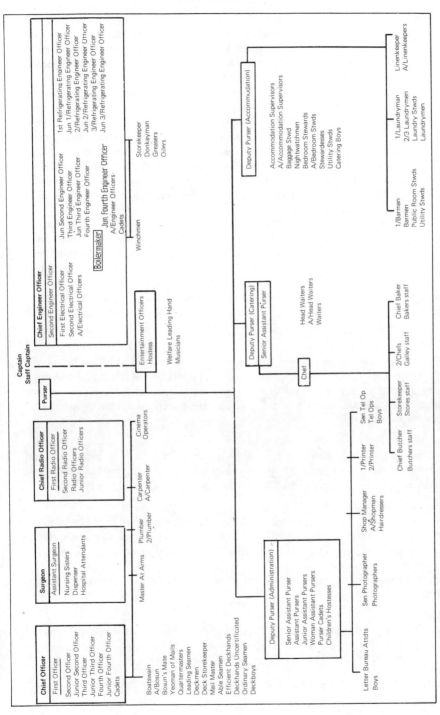

Fig 12. Organisation of a ship's crew. *[Reproduced by permission of P & O Passenger Division]*

are still required to account for their expenditure. It has already been seen that control of certain functions from the centre is more appropriate and there is no exception in the case of BEA. Nevertheless, the use of the services provided by the central departments is charged to the user divisions (or other departments) when the cost can be realistically established.

Of interest in this study of organisation and the delegation of authority is that which involves the crew of an ocean going liner. The organisation of a large shipping combine, that of the P & O Group, has already been examined, but large passenger ships carry a crew of anything up to, say, 1,000, which is many more than the entire payroll of some road transport operators. It is necessary, therefore, to have a form of staff organisation within the ship itself with the Captain or, what is really a better term, the Master, responsible to the type of organisation that has already been described (and which in the P & O example would be the Passenger Division).

Remember, there are basically three main sections within an organisation, namely the engineering, operating and commercial departments. Similar principles can be traced even when applied to the manning of an ocean-going liner which is in effect an organisation within an organisation. The staff, or rather the crew, on board ship again fall into three main groups, being the engine room department, the deck department and the purser's department — a direct reflection of engineering, operating and commercial functions respectively about which we are now familiar. The responsibilities of each section are briefly as under:

Deck

Responsible for navigation and for the safety of the ship and all on board; for the carriage of cargo, for the maintenance and operation of life saving and cargo gear, for the maintenance and cleanliness of the hull, superstructure, the outside of the ship and the cargo holds. In fact, all the functions normally covered by the term seamanship.

Engineer

Responsible for the main engines, auxiliary machinery such as generators and steering motors, electric lighting, air conditioning, the refrigerating plant and hotel equipment. In other words, everything mechanical.

Purser

Responsible for the hotel services on board. A large passenger liner is very much the same as a big hotel ashore, as restaurant, cabin and public room services, bars, entertainments, laundries and many other facilities must be provided for passengers.

There are in addition two other smaller departments which provide essential services:

Radio

Responsible for the ship's communications. (This department is manned only by officers.)

Medical

Responsible for the health of the passengers and crew and for complying with the medical formalities required by port health authorities. This department staffs the ship's surgery and hospital.

A chart prepared by the P & O Passenger Division showing the organisation of the crew of a passenger liner appears at Fig 12.

12 · Staff Matters

Introduction

Although Britain has been a pioneer in the introduction of protective legislation for the safety, health and welfare of employees, the determination by statute of minimum wages and conditions was in principle confined for many years to those industries where the organisation of employers and workers was inadequate to negotiate and enforce collective agreements. Otherwise there were until recently relatively few legal restrictions on the right of an employer to engage staff on any terms that he might think fit or to dismiss him. This is not now the case as current legislation provides for considerable safeguards for employees in these respects. For example, the Terms and Conditions of Employment Act, 1959, as amended by the Industrial Relations Act, 1971 makes provision for an employer to be forced to observe terms and conditions as established by collective agreement in his industry. As was recorded in Chapter 11, the Department of Employment is the principal instrument of the Government's labour policies in Great Britain.

When new employees enter the service of the larger undertakings they are advised regarding the conditions related to their service. These conditions will have been determined through the appropriate negotiating machinery as is to be described and agreed by both employer and representatives of the employed. Constant reference to employers and employees has led to a common conception of two sides in industry — the management side and the workers' side. This is unfortunate as according to the dictionary a side is one of two sets of opponents or its cause. If the staff are to prosper then the business of which they are a part must also prosper. Not only is there a common cause but a successful enterprise must have the loyalty of its staff whether they have high responsibility or whether they have no responsibility at all. There cannot be two sides as such within any one organisation and bargaining for improved pay and conditions should not be allowed to foster this concept and so jeopardise good relationships.

Employers' Associations

Many employers in Great Britain are members of employers' associations. Such organisations are generally arranged on an industry basis, the main ones having a regional structure with the local bodies combined into national federations. In the case of the larger associations, some form of indirect representation of members is necessary and the elected representatives including probably a small working group meet to make policy decisions, to appoint committees and to ratify their work. One of the major functions of these employers organisations is to establish wage structures, conditions of employment and proper staff relations. The machinery is thereby provided for many different employers to negotiate collectively with the trade unions in the way that will be discussed later in this chapter.

The central body of British employers is the Confederation of British Industry, which deals with all matters (not only labour relations) affecting the interests of organised employers and represents them nationally to the Government and to the public and also internationally, for instance, in the International Labour Organisation.

Trade Unions

In most industries, and transport is certainly no exception, workers are organised into trade unions which have as their objective the improvement of the wages and conditions of their members. The unions have grown up gradually over many years, beginning with skilled craftsmen but spreading to the unskilled and more recently to the clerical and supervisory staff. Because of their slow and independent growths, traditions and attitudes vary and some such associations which now negotiate salary scales were originally formed more for preserving and improving professional standards. Some unions such as the craft unions recruit only from those employed in a particular occupation whilst others are prepared to accept members on an industrial basis regardless of their occupation within that industry. For example, the Associated Society of Locomotive Engineers and Firemen is a craft union which caters for railway footplate personnel but the National Union of Railwaymen accepts into membership all grades, with the result that some train drivers are ASLEF members whilst others belong to the NUR.

In Great Britain, the national centre of the trade union movement is the Trades Union Congress. The objects of the TUC are to promote the interests of its affiliated organisations, being the trade unions, and to improve the economic and social conditions of the workers. The congress meets annually and a general council of the TUC is responsible for carrying out congress decisions throughout the year.

Industrial Relations

The structure of labour relations in Great Britain has been established very largely on a voluntary basis whereby associations of employers and employees negotiate, through the media of joint bodies such as the National Joint Industrial Councils representative of complete industries, terms and conditions of employment for the staff concerned. Whilst in the past the policy has been to produce at least model agreements applicable to an industry as a whole but adjusted in detail to meet local circumstances, more emphasis is now tending to be placed on formal agreements at local company level. In this case, instead of national councils with wide representation, there are works councils and committees in individual workplaces. The scope of these local bodies varies. Some negotiate and some also now discuss a wide range of topics. The principle of local collective bargaining has in the main been found to be very satisfactory although provision for independent arbitration is sometimes made. Standing arrangements also exist for consultation at national level between the Government, the CBI, the TUC and the nationalised industries through the National Joint Advisory Council under the chairmanship of the Secretary of State, set up to advise the government on matters in which employers and workers have a common interest.

Although the establishment of national or local joint councils is now wide-spread, there are, nevertheless, certain industries where the characteristics are such that machinery for collective negotiation on a voluntary basis is, or was, difficult or impossible to organise. If this is not the case now, it was at one time, and it was for this reason that in some industries statutory wage regulating bodies known as Wages Councils were formed. Within the transport industry, road haulage offers a good example of wages council procedure, which will be discussed in the appropriate sub-section later in this chapter.

As will be seen from subsequent paragraphs, in the public sector of industry, the main corporations have a statutory duty to establish satisfactory arrangements for collective bargaining and also for joint consultation, which is yet to be considered. The main difference between the public and private sectors of industry is that the corporations are often not members of employers' associations and in some cases they are the main or even the sole employers. In these circumstances, representative associations are not appropriate and there is direct negotiation between managements and trade unions.

The Industrial Relations Act, 1971 provides a new legal framework for industrial relations in the United Kingdom. The main provisions of this Act include the right of an individual to join or not to join a trade union; increased protection against unfair dismissal; the presumption that written collective agreements are legally binding unless otherwise specified; the granting of new and existing privileges, including the right to recognition by employers, to those trade unions and employers' associations whose rules and conduct meet the standards laid down by legislation; the setting-up of a new system of industrial relations courts to hear complaints about and adjudicate on unfair industrial practices, and be empowered to award compensation and to make restraining orders; the enlarging of the functions of and giving statutory status to the Commission on Industrial Relations, a body set up originally to examine matters concerning the conduct of industrial relations as might be referred to it by the Secretary of State; and the creation of new emergency powers which enable the Government to impose a 60-day cooling-off period or to order a secret ballot of workers in disputes where strike action threatens the national economy.

In short, although changes have been brought about by the 1971 Act, the voluntary principle of labour relations has been retained. The system still rests on the organisation of employers and employed into associations and trade unions. At the same time, new provisions are designed to ensure fairness and equality to all sectors of the community and also to prevent any one body from exploiting the strength it may have attained through weight of numbers to the detriment of other people.

Application to the Transport Industry
The foregoing has outlined in general terms the structure and legislative background of labour relations in Great Britain as applicable to all industry whilst the subsections which follow expand on the position relative to the various modes of British transport. As these specific provisions usually supplement the general legislation it is necessary that one should be read in conjunction with the other if a complete grasp of the situation is to be obtained.

Road passenger transport

It is laid down in Section 152 of the Road Traffic Act, 1960 (amended by Section 35 of the Transport Act, 1968), that wages and conditions enjoyed by bus and coach workers will not be less favourable than those which would be observed under a contract which complied with the requirements of the Fair Wages Resolution of the House of Commons. An allegation of non-compliance of this section can, if necessary, be passed to the Secretary of State for Employment for consideration by the Industrial Court and if it is found that a breach has been committed the appropriate Traffic Commissioner (referred to in Chapter 8) may revoke the public service vehicle licence (which is a necessary requisite for the operation of a public service vehicle as is also defined in Chapter 8). A further statutory requirement is contained in Section 137 of the Transport Act, 1968, which requires two of the Boards and also the Authorities to seek consultation with any appropriate organisation with a view to the establishment of adequate machinery (unless of course machinery already exists) for settlement by negotiation of terms and conditions of employment. As far as this paragraph is concerned, therefore, Section 137 applies to the provincial companies under the National Bus Company and the Scottish Transport Group, to the Passenger Transport Executives and, vide Section 13 of the Transport (London) Act, 1969 to London Transport.

That is the legislative background to wages and conditions in road passenger transport. However, it has in any case been the practice over the years to settle these matters by negotiation, for which purpose there are three joint councils. As explained in Chapter 10, disregarding the small independent firms, control of the bus industry in Great Britain outside London and the other Passenger Transport areas is in the hands of provincial companies and municipalities. There is separate but very similar machinery for each, joint councils being formed representative of employer and employed as under:

Provincial companies (National Bus Company and Scottish Transport Group)
The National Council for the Omnibus Industry.
For all wages grades.

Municipalities
The National Joint Industrial Council for the Road Passenger Transport Industry.
For wages grades other than craftsmen.
The National Joint Council for Craftsmen employed in Municipal Passenger Transport Undertakings.
For craftsmen.

Each council consists of equal representation of management and men drawn from the Conference of Omnibus Companies and the Federation of Municipal Passenger Transport Employers in the case of the company and municipal undertakings respectively on the one hand and the appropriate trade unions on the other, which freely negotiate and produce model agreements on wages and conditions for drivers and conductors of buses, coaches and trams and garage and skilled maintenance workers as indicated.

In the case of London Transport and the other Passenger Transport Executives being single administrative units a special council representative of a group is not appropriate. They, therefore negotiate direct with the trade unions.

Road haulage

In contrast to the passenger side, the road haulage industry in Great Britain, with the exception of the National Freight Corporation has consisted in the main of a large number of small competitive units. Under this type of ownership it was difficult for organised labour to obtain any form of stabilisation of wages or conditions which, in some instances, were not ideal. Hence the Road Haulage Wages Act, 1938, set up machinery for the determination and enforcement of rates of pay and conditions of service for workers employed in connection with vehicles operating under A and B licences. This Act also contained in Section 4 a Fair Wages Clause similar to that applicable to road passenger transport employees but in the interests of workers of C licence vehicles. (It must here be explained that A and B licenees were, in effect, a means of administering a system of quantity control which was introduced by the Road and Rail Traffic Act, 1933. A licences were issued for public haulage and B licences, which were strictly limited, were for both public and own account work. C licences were for own account operators. This method of licensing has been completely superseded by the Transport Act, 1968 and the current position is as explained in Chapter 8). The Road Haulage Central Wages Board was established together with a number of area boards whose duty it was to submit to the then Minister of Labour proposals for fixing the remuneration of workers of A and B licensed vehicles. The Minister was given power to make orders giving effect to such proposals. The principle was thereby established of employers being under a statutory obligation to observe agreed rates of pay and service conditions. This principle remains, but the detail has changed. The central and area wages boards no longer exist, but the Wages Councils Act, 1948, converted the Central Wages Board to a wages council operating in relation to workers of the same description as were covered by the Board. Other Wages Councils Acts were passed in the period 1945 to 1948 which were consolidated into the Wages Councils Act, 1959. The Road Haulage Wages Council consists of equal representatives of employers and employed plus three independent persons, one of whom is chairman. It is now Section 11 of the 1959 Act which empowers the now Secretary of State for Employment to make orders enforcing proposals submitted by the Wages Council.

It was not intended that this legislation should be applied in cases where there is already adequate negotiating machinery and the railway companies were expressly excluded from the provisions of the 1938 Act. Today, Section 82 of the Transport Act, 1962, as modified by Schedule 16-6 of the Transport Act, 1968, excludes employees of the Boards and Authorities, which, as far as this section is concerned covers, for example, the National Freight Corporation. Wages and conditions of road haulage workers employed by these undertakings (which includes British Road Services) are negotiated direct with the appropriate trade unions and Section 137 of the 1968 Act (as explained in the paragraph relating to road passenger transport) does, in this instance, have relevance. Similarly, Clause 11 of Schedule 1 of the Post Office Act, 1969 requires the Post Office to negotiate and establish conditions of service for postal workers who are also excluded from wages council machinery.

Railways

As, with very minor exceptions, the entire railway system of Great Britain outside the London area is under the control of a single authority, the Railways Board negotiates direct with the trade unions in respect of its railway workers. London Transport similarly negotiates direct with the unions as it does in respect of its road staff. The legislative background now lies in Section 137 of the 1968 Act (as explained in the paragraph relating to road passenger transport) although adequate negotiating machinery had already been established by virtue of the requirements of the Railways Act, 1921, and the London Passenger Transport Act, 1933.

Sea

The basic rates of pay and conditions of service of officers and men of the British Mercantile Marine are determined by the National Maritime Board. The Board is divided into six separate panels for masters, navigating officers, engineer officers, radio officers, sailors and firemen and catering staff, and on each panel there is equal representation of employers and employed with joint chairmen. The British Shipping Federation appoints the shipowners' representatives to the Board and the Marine Wireless Employers' Negotiations Committee is also represented. Employees representatives are drawn from elected seagoing masters and from various associations and trade unions representing both officers and men.

Against a background of industrial unrest, the emergency conditions of World War I made some form of joint negotiating machinery imperative. The result was the formation in 1917 of the original National Maritime Board, the employers being represented by the Shipping Federation with societies and unions representing the employees. There was a Government-appointed chairman and secretary. It was not intended that this machinery should have been other than a temporary wartime expedient. In 1920, therefore, as a result of consultation between Government departments, the Shipping Federation, the Employers' Association of the Port of Liverpool (subsequently merged to form the British Shipping Federation) and the seafarers' representatives, the National Maritime Board in a new constitution as described in the opening paragraph of this section was formed. It differed essentially from the previous board in that all connection with any Government department was severed and entire responsibility for making and carrying out agreements was placed on the shipowners' and seafarers' organisations themselves. It is of interest that during the 1939–45 war when a large section of British tonnage was again under Government control, the Government did not ask for representation on the board, which is a tribute to the success of the scheme.

With regard to the legal background, the Merchant Shipping Act, 1970, which relates to the employment of seamen and covers such matters as engagement and discharge, payment of wages, safety, health and welfare matters, the administration of discipline, manning, etc., requires employers to honour their agreements. Section 7 of this Act stipulates that, subject to certain provisos, the wages due to seamen under a crew agreement relating to a ship shall be paid to them at the time they leave that ship on being discharged.

Docks

The negotiating body for dock workers is the National Joint Council for the Port Transport Industry, which consists of representatives of the National Association of Port Employers and the appropriate trade unions. The Council's principal responsibilities are: (a) the settlement of national terms and conditions of employment; (b) the functioning of the industry's conciliation machinery; (c) the expression of collective views on matters affecting the industry; and (d) the nomination of eight members of the National Dock Labour Board. The last named, (item d), calls for some further explanation.

Throughout the early history of the docks, the supply of labour was invariably greater than demand, hence the vast majority of the men secured only irregular or casual employment. Conditions such as this offered no security for the docker and were a continual source of discontent. Certain improvements were effected in 1941, including the introduction of a guaranteed weekly wage, which acknowledged the essential nature of the work of the docker in wartime and after the end of hostilities, the Dock Workers (Regulation of Employment) Act, 1946 prolonged these arrangements and allowed time for a single consolidated plan to be formulated by the National Joint Council. In the event, despite protracted negotiations between employers and employed, agreement was not reached, there being a divergence of views on the question of joint management. The Dock Workers (Regulation of Employment) Order incorporating the Dock Workers (Regulation of Employment) Scheme was therefore made by the Minister of Labour and National Service in 1947 by virtue of the powers conferred on him by the 1946 Act, which departed from the employers' recommendations on this controversial issue.

The National Dock Labour Board was set up to be responsible for the administration of the scheme and provision was made for local Dock Labour Boards in each port area. Although the original scheme has been subjected to subsequent changes the Board still remains as originally composed. The National Board consists of four members representing dock employers, four members representing dock workers and a chairman and vice-chairman independently appointed by the Secretary of State for Employment. The National Board delegates many of its functions to local boards which are similarly constituted. The administration of the scheme therefore depends on joint control with both employers and employed accepting equal responsibility for recruitment, discharge and discipline of the dock labour force. It must of course be understood that these Boards have no responsibility for the actual workings of the docks themselves, or for staff negotiations which are conducted through the machinery outlined above.

Notwithstanding the substantial improvements in conditions achieved since the 1930s, the casual element still caused dissension in the docks. The Rochdale Committee referred to in Chapter 10 reported in 1962 and recommended among other things the establishment of a National Ports Authority and a system of independent port trusts with estuarial responsibilities over port authority functions. This would have reduced the number of employers, but, as was noted, the 1964 Harbours Act which followed did not tackle the labour problem and decasualisation became the subject of a more detailed consideration by the Devlin Committee which reported in 1965. This report supported, inter alia, the view of the Rochdale Committee in that it recommended a reduction in the number of employers. The subsequent Docks and Harbours Act, 1966, gave statutory sanction to certain of the proposals contained in the Devlin Report. Port employers became subject to licence, the licensing authorities being the appropriate port authority and provision was made for welfare amenities.

As an immediate outcome of the Devlin Report, the National Joint Council, in accepting its findings, set up a National Modernisation Committee to discuss issues associated with decasualisation and a new wage structure. After a further report from Devlin and that of the National Modernisation Committee, the then Minister issued in 1967, by virtue of the powers conferred on him by the 1946 Act, the Dock Workers (Regulation of Employment) (Amendment) Order, 1967, which gave to dockers a permanent employer.

The National Dock Labour Board is now the statutory authority which administers the 1967 Dock Labour Scheme, the objects of which are to ensure greater regularity of employment for dock workers and to secure that an adequate labour force is available for the efficient performance of dock work. Among other functions, the Board maintains a register of dock workers and employers, organises training and is responsible through its local boards for certain disciplinary procedure in the industry. At the inception of the 1967 Scheme, all registered men, with the exception of those designated as temporarily unattached were allocated as permanent workers to registered employers duly licensed in accordance with the 1966 Act. Under agreements of the National Joint Council, registered dock workers became subject to guaranteed minimum wages and other benefits. The cost of operating the scheme is met by payments made by registered employers to the National Dock Labour Board based on stipulated percentages of gross earnings.

Arising from a continuing declining trend in employment, in the case of the ports due largely to modernisation and hence mechanisation, redundancy problems have arisen and in 1969, new provisions designed to facilitate a run-down in manpower were introduced in a National Voluntary Severance Scheme. The administration of this scheme on behalf of the National Joint Council for the Port Transport Industry is another responsibility of the National Dock Labour Board.

Inland waterways

Joint negotiating machinery for manual workers employed on inland waterways was introduced following nationalisation in 1948 when, by agreement, the National Joint Council for the Inland Waterway Industry was established. This council was composed of representatives from the British Waterways Board, private canal operators and carriers and the appropriate trade union and comprehensive agreements covering wages, hours and working conditions were evolved. However, the private carriers subsequently withdrew from this arrangement and set up their own joint negotiating body. The Council has, therefore, been reconstituted as the National Joint Council for British Waterways Wages Grades. Section 72 of the 1962 Act now forms the legislative background in so far as the British Waterways Board is concerned.

Air

The machinery of joint negotiation in civil air transport dates from 1946, when the nationalised airways corporations, by agreement with the trade unions concerned and in compliance with the obligations laid upon them by the Civil Aviation Act, 1946, set up the National Joint Council for Civil Air Transport. This statutory requirement is now contained in Section 23 of the consolidating Air Corporations Act, 1967. The constitution of the council is so framed to allow also for the inclusion of independent and private enterprises providing air transport services.

The council has established machinery for the regulation of terms and conditions of employment, etc. and chairmanship alternates annually between the employers and employees. As employees covered by the National Joint Council vary widely in occupation, the constitution provides for separate sectional joint panels for various groups according to the nature of their work; for example, there are panels covering engineering and maintenance; supervisory engineering and technical; clerical; ground service workers; pilot officers; engineer officers; and air cabin crew.

The British Overseas Airways Corporation, British European Airways, certain of their subsidiary companies and a number of independent operators including British Caledonian Airways are today represented on the National Joint Council. Whilst, however, the two publicly-owned corporations are, as already noted, under a statutory requirement to formulate an acceptable scheme, membership by the independents is quite voluntary. It is significant however, that private enterprise air undertakings are required by Section 15 of the Civil Aviation Act, 1949, to observe terms and conditions which are not less favourable than those observed by the corporations except where regulated by another enactment or where such terms and conditions have been otherwise agreed between the parties.

Joint Consultation

The foregoing has described the machinery set up for negotiating rates of pay and conditions of service. The result of these negotiations is a formal agreement between employers and employed. But there are other factors which can affect the daily working life far beyond what is provided for in these formal agreements. Traffic demands change and so do, therefore, the duties of the staff. New methods of working are introduced, workplaces are moved and establishments are closed whilst new ones are opened. The different duties that evolve in terms of time, place or method would still observe the agreed conditions but the repercussions on the individual could be considerable. With the perpetual passing of time, management must make changes in the interests of both its customers and the organisation which it represents. At the same time, if it is to retain the co-operation of its staff, and this is essential if its business is to function smoothly, it must confer with them in advance when such projects are being formulated. This is the essence of consultation. If there is a lack of proper understanding, actions of a prudent management sometimes appear unpalatable to the staff and this can foster a spirit of resistance which will destroy harmony so necessary for the smooth functioning of all transport. Joint consultation anticipates and attempts to forestall this resistance. It is a process of management taking the workers into its confidence at an appropriate stage to discuss problems and reasons for current policy. By so doing, those in command can at the same time take benefit from the experience of men who are actually doing the job. Consultation is therefore a two-way process, necessary not only on major national issues but also on day-to-day local matters and is applied at all levels of management. If joint consultation is to achieve its purpose, the participants must be sincere. The relationship should be more spiritual than formal as it is the informal approach which is more likely to succeed. Care must be taken regarding timing. Although an early approach might in some ways be desirable, it would be unwise to disclose plans in the embryonic stage which might never materialise and so cause unnecessary alarm. On the other hand, the release of information at a time when proposals are virtually a *fait accompli* would destroy the consultative spirit.

To sum up, the system provides for consultation between management and employees about matters of common concern and which are outside the scope of the negotiating machinery, although the distinction between the two is very fine.

Subjects discussed could be, for example:
(a)   Changes or improvements in methods of working, including the encouragement of suggestions;
(b)   The safety, health and welfare of employees;
(c)   Systems of training, education, codes of discipline, etc.

Without any hard and fast rules, for good staff relationship there must be goodwill on the part of both management and men to sit down and frankly discuss mutual problems. In joint consultation, the word "joint" is very operative; all concerned must play their part. It must at the same time be understood that joint consultation is not joint management. Joint discussion is one thing, but decision remains the responsibility of management alone.

Discipline and Staff Records

Discipline is described in the dictionary as that kind of training which produces self-control, orderliness, obedience and capacity for co-operation, all of which are very necessary in our communal way of life. Whatever we do, discipline must consciously or unconsciously play a part. When waiting for a bus we form a queue, having written a letter we address the envelope and affix a stamp in the accepted manner, if we drive a vehicle we obey the Highway Code, and the person who does not is a nuisance and a danger to the community. We are all subject to some form of discipline and those engaged in transport are certainly no exception. The very nature of the work requires men to undertake duties away from immediate supervision and an adequate code of discipline is vital. This can be administered through standing orders or collectively if there are sufficient in number, through a rule book, the contents of which every member of the staff must be familiar. These rules are in effect instructions to staff on their method of working and embrace such matters as punctuality, absence, timekeeping, general conduct, methods of working, etc. It is neither necessary nor practicable to explain in detail here the rules applicable to the many grades of transport personnel, it being sufficient to know of their existence as an instruction to staff. But they have a secondary purpose. The rules form a basis for the administration of discipline as they are a means of bringing forward an offender who has failed to comply with their requirements. It is the usual custom for an employee charged by his immediate supervisor for acting contrary to the provisions of standing (or special) orders to be brought before a senior official who considers the case and awards punishment appropriate to the gravity of the offence. Such punishment could vary from a warning to dismissal. Provision may be made for a right of appeal and to representation by a trade union in the case of serious offences. It is probable that management will maintain a comprehensive record of each member of its staff which will contain in addition to service history, a record of offences subjected to the disciplinary procedure. Recourse to this record should not of course be made for the purpose of determining guilt, but such background knowledge is necessary after a charge has been proved and sentence is to be passed.

The rulebook and disciplinary system are sometimes confused with conditions of service. True, they are closely associated, but the distinction must be clear. Conditions of service cover matters which form the basis of a contract between employer and employed such as the number of hours to be worked per week, annual holiday entitlement, guaranteed payments, sick pay, etc. freely negotiated between management and men by the various joint councils as described in the preceding paragraphs. A requirement to observe the provisions of the rulebook is a part of the conditions of service, but the compilation of the rule book is the responsibility of management although an approach to staff on matters affecting its composition could of course be made through the joint consultative machinery.

Yet another branch of staff administration which is closely allied to but distinct from conditions of service is staff welfare.

Staff Welfare

Welfare may be described as a state of wellbeing and any steps taken by management which serve to relieve the employee of worry and strain, safeguard his health, cultivate his interests or make his working life generally more congenial can be classified under this heading. Conditions of service are one thing, but, in Great Britain, which is, in many respects, already a "welfare state", such conditions rarely provide for certain extra but desirable amenities and it is for the good employer to recognise this need. Even so, shipping is rather different. When at sea, a man remains "on his employer's premises" even during his off-duty hours. His workplace is his home for the duration of the voyage and for this reason, welfare is for seafarers much more a part of service conditions, Whilst welfare is the responsibility of management, there is no reason why the provision of such facilities should not be discussed with the staff through consultative machinery. In fact, Section 72 of the 1962 Act calls for the establishment of suitable machinery for this purpose as far as the Boards and the Authorities are concerned.

Examples of matters which come within the sphere of staff welfare are:

Canteens
Provision of canteens at strategic points open at times convenient to staff,

particularly to those engaged on shift work. The overhead expenses of the canteen could be borne by the management to allow meals to be served at more favourable prices.

Medical service
Provision of adequate first-aid posts and rest rooms. Visiting staff who are sick and facilities for convalescence.

Sport
Financial aid to sports clubs. Provision of sports grounds and management support of social activities and recreation.

House magazine
A domestic publication written by the staff for the staff to stimulate interest in the undertaking.

Heating, lighting, ventilation, washing and toilet facilities
Although minimum standards may be defined there is sometimes scope for a little more lavish provision.

Personal problems section
To cover a wide range of subjects affecting the domestic life of the employee on which he requires advice or help.

Benevolent funds and friendly societies
Support to societies designed to assist staff in times of financial distress and give relief during times of sickness, particularly to those staff whose conditions of service do not make provision for sick pay.

Education
Payment of fees and for textbooks and grant of necessary time to permit staff to follow a background course of further education.

A good worker must be a contented worker and it is the function of the welfare officer to make reasonable provision for such amenities and services as may be desirable according to the nature of the duties upon which the staff are engaged. Indeed, in times of full employment, welfare facilities help recruitment.

The separate functions of staff administration, which include negotiation on pay and conditions, discipline, records, joint consultation and welfare must be understood, although it is quite usual for each of these functions to be under the overall jurisdiction of a staff or personnel manager. This is, in fact, the case in the examples of organisational structures contained in Chapter 11.

13 · Finance

Introduction

Transport, like any other industry, cannot live without adequate financial backing. There must be capital in the first instance to purchase assets with which to provide the service. There must also be revenue from the sale of that service to meet running expenses and interest payable on borrowed capital, leaving sufficient profit to remunerate shareholders.

Accountancy is a specialised subject. Nevertheless, finance cannot be divorced from transport and even in a study of the basic principles, the need for at least some knowledge of the fundamental principles of transport accounts is necessary. Without a reference to the subject, this book would be incomplete and the following is a brief review of how money is obtained, earned, and accounted for.

Capital

The obtaining of capital

The manner in which capital is raised is influenced by the form of ownership, a subject discussed in Chapter 10. Capital can be obtained in four ways:

(a)   by the owners supplying their own capital from personal savings, as in the case of a one-man business or partnership,

(b)   by asking privately or publicly for investment in the business by the issue of stocks and shares, as in the case of private and public companies,

(c)   by borrowing privately or publicly,

(d)   by ploughing back profits.

Most transport undertakings are brought into being by some special authority. generally by registration in accordance with the provisions of the Companies Act, 1948, also discussed in Chapter 10, or alternatively created by some special Act. In either case they will be authorised to issue capital stock up to a prescribed amount. Large undertakings usually operated by statutory bodies, municipalities or the State, are often wholly financed by loans from the public, or from the State itself, the public loans being guaranteed by the Exchequer.

Shares and Stocks

A company's capital may be made up of one or more classes of shares.

Preference shares

Preference shares, as the name indicates, come before other capital and receive a ceiling dividend. If the company goes into liquidation the holders receive repayment before other shareholders. Most preference issues are what are called cumulative, which means that if there are not enough profits in any year to pay the dividend, it is carried forward until there is sufficient to give the shareholders their due. Some preference shares are redeemable at stated prices either annually on a specified date or dates, or in certain circumstances. With the rare exception of some which participate in surplus profits, preference shareholders, in return for the extra security, never get more than their ceiling dividend.

Ordinary shares

Ordinary shares are the risk capital of the company and are last in line for dividends and any return of the money invested if the company goes into liquidation. If things go well ordinary shareholders benefit by way of good dividends and appreciation in the market value of their shares. On the other hand if a bad patch is struck, they stand the brunt of the loss as dividends will fall or may not even be paid at all and the share price drops. Factors such as these account for the much greater movement in the prices of ordinary shares. These are often referred to as the equity of a company.

Preference shares generally have what is known as a par, or face value of £1. The par value of ordinary shares may however be as little as 5p. The choice often depends on the desire to keep the market price to easily manageable units; but many companies stick to the £1 figure which was almost universal up to some 30 years ago.

Stock

When shares are fully paid up (the company might not require shareholders to subscribe the full value of the shares at the outset), they can be consolidated into stock. Shares are only dealt with individually in units according to their value at par, but stock can be sold in any quantity unless regulations are made to the contrary. It is a question of so many or so much. One would speak of so many shares but so much stock.

Debentures

Debenture stocks are in the nature of a loan to the company. Rather like a mortgage, they are usually secured on all or some of the assets, receive a fixed rate of interest and are usually repayable at fixed dates or in annual amounts. Interest is payable whether profits are made or not. If the undertaking gets into difficulties and fails to pay this interest, the debenture holders can sell it up or take over management. Apart from this, however, capital raised by loans does not give the lender any say in the affairs of the business.

The Stock Exchange

The London Stock Exchange is part of the financial machine that is called "The City" — the City of London — perhaps the greatest monetary centre in the world. Besides the London Stock Exchange, there are others in many cities and provincial towns and they are all simply markets for the stocks and shares of companies and of government.

Like so many of the most famous British institutions, the Stock Exchange developed slowly, in response to the needs of the changing business world. In the seventeenth century, the Government and many trading enterprises, being unable to raise sufficient money from their own sources, invited the public to put up the money it needed. The Government and the companies which were formed, issued stocks and shares which were bought and sold. Those who held government stocks received each year a fixed rate of interest. Those with shares in a company received a share in the annual profits (if any). People began to make a living by bringing together buyers and sellers of stocks and shares and thus a market — a stock exchange — was formed.

A person wishing to buy issued stocks and shares must do so through an accredited stockbroker who is a member of the Stock Exchange and has a right to buy and sell shares. At the London Stock Exchange the stockbroker must purchase the securities through an accredited jobber who is also a member of the Stock Exchange. The jobbers are like wholesalers and they deal with brokers and never directly with the public.

The Stock Exchange is governed by a council which regulates procedures and secures the maximum protection to members and public alike. For example, before the shares of any enterprise can be dealt with on the Stock Exchange, permission must be obtained from the council. So, when a company is being started and desires to issue shares which can be freely bought and sold, the company must obtain this permission, which is granted only if it fulfils certain strict conditions and publishes full and true particulars. When permission is granted, it means that the shares of the company are quoted on the Stock Exchange and dealings in them can take place in the open market.

Capital assets
To the shareholder, capital used for the purchase of shares is an investment and to the company, it represents assets purchased for working the business. But to the accountant capital means money owned by shareholders, etc.

Assets are those possessions which assist in earning revenue or have a realisable value. They fall into two parts — fixed and current (or floating) assets. Capital which is invested in durable items such as land, buildings, machinery, vehicles, etc., represents fixed capital as it is held for the purpose of earning revenue. Capital remaining after the fixed assets have been purchased and which is used to meet day-to-day running costs such as fuel, wages, etc, is called floating or working capital. These circulating assets (fuel, stores, cash, etc) are expendable. They are used once and are replaced. The distinction between a fixed and a floating asset depends on whether it is to be kept for a period of time within the business or whether it is held for the purpose of consumption or sale. To a vehicle manufacturer, therefore, a bus (which he has built for sale) is a floating asset, but to the operator after purchase, it is a fixed asset.

Revenue

Revenue is earned through the sale of articles or service produced and is used for the following purposes:
- (a)   To meet the direct operating costs (i.e., fuel and wages of the operating staff).
- (b)   To meet administrative and other indirect expenses.
- (c)   To replace fixed assets as they become time expired.
- (d)   To meet interest on loans.
- (e)   To make adequate provision for the future.
- (f)   To remunerate shareholders.

Revenue is necessary to keep the business in being and its first purpose is to constantly replenish the circulating assets and to remunerate labour. If the requirement at (a) is not met, the undertaking would come quickly to a standstill. Similarly, revenue must be available at (b) to cover the immediate costs of administration and overheads such as vehicle overhaul. Over a longer period, fixed assets must be replaced at (c) and interest on borrowed capital must be paid at (d), otherwise the business would again have to close down. The duration of a loan is generally fixed, in which case, provision must be made out of revenue to meet redemption at the due date. This can be done by the creation of a sinking fund whereby sums set aside each year will at compound interest produce the required total at the end of the period. This wiping out of a debt is known as amortisation. Where a business is successful or well-established, however, redemption is possible by the issue of a new loan to replace the old. Investors are in such cases usually willing for their money to be transferred into the new loan.

It is a facet of business life that some years may be good and others bad. As a safeguard against contingencies, therefore, it is prudent to set aside a reserve fund as indicated at (e). Such reserves could be ploughed back into the business to avoid further borrowing at a higher rate of interest, or be invested elsewhere until such time as required, thereby producing an additional source of income.

Depreciation and Obsolescence

Depreciation

At the outset, the value of the capital equals the value of the assets, but with general use and the passage of time, assets usually lose some of their value and are replaced through appropriations set aside out of revenue. This is known as depreciation for which there are several methods of calculating, but the two most frequently adopted are:

(a) The straight line method

This term is applied to the provision by equal yearly instalments of the total provision required over the estimated life and is perhaps the most common of the various methods adopted for allowing for depreciation.

(b) The reducing instalment method

The reducing instalment method provides for the asset to be written down each year by deduction of a fixed percentage of the remaining balance.

To illustrate the point, the following tables show the amount of depreciation set aside under the straight line and the reducing instalment methods for machinery bought for £100 and estimated to have a scrap value of £5 after 10 years:

	Straight Line	Reducing Instalment
	£	£
1st year	10% – 9.50	25% of £100 – 25.00
2nd year	10% – 9.50	25% of 75 – 19.00
3rd year	10% – 9.50	25% of 56 – 14.00
4th year	10% – 9.50	25% of 42 – 11.00
5th year	10% – 9.50	25% of 31 – 8.00
6th year	10% – 9.50	25% of 23 – 6.00
7th year	10% – 9.50	25% of 17 – 4.00
8th year	10% – 9.50	25% of 13 – 3.00
9th year	10% – 9.50	25% of 10 – 3.00
10th year	10% – 9.50	25% of 7 – 2.00
	£95.00	£95.00

It will be seen that under the straight line method, depreciation is charged at £9.50 each year, but under the reducing instalment method, it ranges from £25 in the first year to £2 in the tenth year.

The idea of any system of depreciation is to measure as accurately as possible the loss in value of the assets and to build up a fund for their renewal at the end of their useful life. Depreciation is based on original cost and no provision is made for any increased cost of replacement or for loss in value due to obsolescence. This replacement of assets is known as keeping capital intact.

Obsolescence

Obsolescence is the artificial shortening of the life of an asset through technical development or change in public taste. This is of particular importance in air transport where, as is noted elsewhere, technical development is very rapid. Where this can be predicted assets can be depreciated over a life dictated by obsolescence factors. Alternatively, an obsolescence fund may be established from which the balance, after allowing for depreciation and sale of the asset at the highest possible price, is taken. In other cases it is prudent to establish a general reserve from which occasional and unexpected demands can be met. The risk of obsolescence is influenced by the length of life of the asset in question.

Accounting Methods

Attention was drawn in Chapter 10 to the separation of ownership from management. For management purposes the owners (i.e. the shareholders) elect a board of directors who, in producing to the shareholders an account of their stewardship, include a revenue account and a balance sheet to show the financial position of the undertaking. Books of account must be opened and maintained to record business done and it is essential that such books are kept accurately and up-to-date in order that the position can be easily ascertained at regular intervals as well as at the end of the financial year.

The usual system of keeping books of account is called double entry bookkeeping, so called because each entry is shown twice, on the debit side of one account and on the credit side of another. There are two principles to which double entry may be applied — to single accounts or to double accounts. The single account system is that used for normal commercial business whereby assets are depreciated annually and capital remains at a fixed figure. Under the double account system, the capital and revenue accounts are separated and assets are never written down since in this instance it is considered that because of proper maintenance, they never wear out. Replacements are added to capital. This method was adopted by the former railway companies and it is still used occasionally. It was, however, abandoned by the British Transport Commission and it is not proposed to elaborate here on the double account principle.

The single account system

The single account system is known as such because the balance sheet, which is the final summary of all accounts, is produced as a single statement. In the double account system, the balance sheet is in two parts because of a permanent distinction between capital subscriptions and the assets purchased therewith and the rest of the liabilities and assets of the undertaking.

In accordance with the rules of double entry book-keeping mentioned above, each transaction involves the giving up in one ledger account (credit) and the receiving by another ledger account (debit). In this way the totals of the accounts are always in balance.

The types of ledger accounts are:

(1)   Personal accounts which record the sums owing to or by the business.

(2)   Real accounts which record the possessions of the undertaking − e.g., assets.

(3)   Nominal accounts which relate to gains (receipts) and losses (expenses). Debit balances can be defined as representing possessions or losses and credit balances liabilities or gains. The distinction between possessions and liabilities and losses and gains is all important in preparing final accounts, as gains and losses (from the nominal accounts) are entered in the profit and loss account and possessions and liabilities (from the personal and real accounts) are included in the balance sheet.

The profit and loss or revenue account
The profit and loss (or revenue) account is a summary of the items of revenue receipts and revenue expenditure (as opposed to items of capital receipts and capital expenditure which appear in the balance sheet). Referring back to the paragraph on revenue, the difference between the total revenue and the direct costs at (a) on page 194 represents the gross profit. The net profit, which is ultimately passed to the balance sheet, is the gross profit less the other working expenses at (b), (c) and (d).

The balance sheet
We have seen that the balance sheet is a summary of the accounts remaining open in the books after the nominal accounts have been closed and carried to the profit and loss account. One purpose of the balance sheet is to afford the shareholder, who has placed his capital in the concern and the creditor, who does business with it, an opportunity of estimating from time to time its financial stability. The amount of working capital may be weighed against the possibility of depreciation in the value of stock or the degree of possible bad debts, for if these were of a greater amount than the working capital it would not be possible for the undertaking to meet its current liabilities. It should also be possible to see the trade debtors and creditors for comparison with the amount of sales and purchases and to ascertain the amount of credit allowed and received both of which have their bearing upon the amount of working capital that is required.

In all but the simplest cases the balances must be contained in a compressed summary, but must exhibit enough detail to enable a correct judgement to be formed. Only those balances of similar accounting significance should therefore be grouped together. Fixed assets for example should be separated from floating assets.

The practice in Great Britain of placing liabilities on the left-hand side and the assets on the right-hand side is not universal, but as the modern balance sheet is not a ledger account but merely a summarised extract from the ledger, the difference is not important as long as it is recognised. In short, the balance sheet must show clearly the capital, what reserves have been built up, any external debts and the nature and value of possessions.

Internal check and audit

To remain on a proper financial footing, not only must the books of account be properly kept, there must also be adequate safeguards against error and fraud. This is achieved by two methods known as internal check and audit.

Internal check calls for the arrangement of duties of staff so that whoever receives or pays money does not also deal with the book entries concerning them. In this way, a cashier who pays out and receives money neither prepares wages and records nor renders accounts. Any figures out of balance are thereby disclosed and fraud becomes possible only by collusion between two or more persons, which is more likely to be detected.

Audit is both internal and external. Internal audit involves the checking of items and accounts by staff other than those directly concerned with the job in question. In large undertakings special staff do no other work than this checking. In addition it is a statutory requirement that accounts are audited annually by outside qualified accountants whose report is usually appended to the balance sheet for issue to members of the company. In the case of public companies, copies are sent to the Registrar of Public Companies and some statutory bodies are also required to send copies to other government departments. The investors and the public are thereby protected to the maximum possible extent.

The Application of Sound Financial Principles

Most financial principles consist merely of applied commonsense. Some have already been mentioned, such as keeping capital intact. It is in this sphere of sound principles that the more modern branch of cost accounting has its greatest effect as management often needs to know the financial effect of proposed changes. It also enables a series of productive operations to be costed independently to pinpoint losses and facilitate remedial action but cost accountancy is something beyond this study. Ordinary accountancy portrays the financial position over fixed periods; cost accountancy produces an enlargement of a small piece at any one time or over a period for easy examination.

Another technique developed to help maintain stability is budgetary control. In this, the financial year is divided into convenient periods, e.g. four weekly or monthly, and on the basis of past experience and allowing for changing circumstances, an estimate is prepared of the anticipated revenue and expenditure for each period. Actual figures are subsequently compared with the budgeted estimate which enables financial results to be critically examined at frequent intervals. This process can influence the conduct of business in an endeavour to achieve the ultimate anticipated profit.

Basically, good accounting principles are good business principles. They ensure that business is carried on economically and efficiently, that the assets of the firm are maintained in good condition and that provision is made for their replacement when the need arises.

Assistance from Public Funds

The contribution made by transport to the economic and social life of a nation was discussed in Chapter 1. An adequate system of communication is a vital factor in the life of the community and its provision is something that cannot necessarily rely on purely commercial considerations. It is well known that over recent years the private car has abstracted traffic from bus and train. This has brought financial difficulties to many operators who still need to cater for the residue, which is mostly peak commuter traffic and the needs of the young and the old. This situation applies particularly to urban transport and it is in these areas that physical problems are also arising by the presence of ever increasing numbers of private vehicles on what is, inevitably, limited highway accommodation. Predictions are that by the turn of the century if not earlier, road capacities and parking facilities in towns will be quite inadequate to cater for the unrestrained needs of the private car. Full provision would be exorbitant in cost and detrimental to the environment and circumstances such as this indicate a justification to develop a system of public passenger transport even if the services cannot be viable in their own right. The problem of passenger transport in urban areas is becoming world-wide and is one that is being tackled by different governments in different ways. Grants may be made from either national or local sources or both. They may be in the form of revenue grants to cover specific deficits, capital grants to assist expenditure on vehicles and the infrastructure or general block grants to cover contingencies or to meet or compensate for special circumstances. The question of subsidy is often allied to form of ownership as there tends to be a political disinclination to support a system which is being run for private gain. Acquisition by some form of public authority is then often a pre-requisite to assistance in this way.

The most car-orientated nation in terms of vehicles per head of population is the United States of America. Although when compared with British standards, there is, by and large, still plenty of room to move around, in some twenty urban conglomerations of the U.S.A. which have populations in excess of a million, some real traffic and parking problems are arising. One result of this is that United States legislation has initiated a programme of federal (i.e. central government) grants to assist in providing capital for the development of public transport. Only public agencies are eligible for such grants, with the result that there has been a swing away from private enterprise in North American transit. The federal grants may extend to two-thirds of that part of the cost which cannot reasonably be financed from revenue and local matching funds must be available to make up the balance. The provision of such matching funds is subject to local politics and may be raised in a variety of ways. In Boston, Massachusetts, for example, the requirement has been met in part by the issue of bonds and in part by imposing a State tax on cigarettes. Similarly on the continent of Europe, there is a widespread acceptance that local public transport cannot be self-financing with the result that what are in the main municipal undertakings receive substantial subvention payments mostly from local, but in some cases supported by national, government.

It is not, however, only the local services that governments have seen fit to subsidise. Main line railways are regarded by many as a valuable national asset and to quote again from the United States, there are now examples of long distance passenger services being resuscitated at public expense. In the north-east of the United States where there is a heavy concentration of population, the demand for road and air transport is expected to rise rapidly in the next ten years. Environmental considerations militate against an unrestricted development of highways and airports, much of which might not be necessary if the extra traffic could travel by rail and this in itself is an incentive to try and keep the trains running. Passenger services have long been a drag on the privately owned North American railways and financial responsibility for this part of the business has now been shed to a publicly owned National Passenger Railroad Corporation, known locally as Amtrak. Federal grants and an increase in the government guaranteed borrowing ceiling have been extended to Amtrak, which has taken over a selection of inter-city passenger services of some twenty different railway companies who now operate them on an agency basis.

In those countries which are a part of the European Economic Community, a regulation has been adopted which lists the circumstances under which state aid for rail, road and inland waterway transport may be permitted within the terms of the Rome Treaty. State aids will now be authorised if:

(a)   they are granted to railways as compensation for additional financial burdens which, as part of their operations, they bear in comparison with their competitors.

(b)   they help those transport undertakings that have to bear infrastructure costs that are not similarly borne by their competitors.

(c)   they are for research and the initial development of more economic transport systems and technologies.

(d)   they are granted as a temporary measure in order to eliminate as part of a reorganisation plan, excess capacity which is causing serious structural problems.

(e)   they compensate rail, road or inland waterway transport undertakings for any losses incurred as a result of obligations imposed on them such as the application of low tariffs or the maintenance of uneconomic services.

At the same time, member states are required to adopt a uniform method of accounting for expenditure on transport infrastructure in order to harmonise the conditions of competition within the transport sector.

The point was made in Chapter 1 that in sea and air transport, some governments see fit to maintain services regardless of their commercial viability. A sizeable merchant fleet with vessels capable of relatively fast speeds and easily convertible for military use is a valuable asset in time of war and some nations maintain tonnage for defence purposes. The shipping lines of those countries have, of course, a considerable advantage over their competitors whose vessels are not subsidised in this way. Again, in the field of civil aviation, it is a part of national pride to possess an airline flying in the name of the country and showing the flag across the world. Prestige reasons alone are enough to prompt some governments to meet substantial deficits that might be incurred by their own airline and to thereby avoid their need to rely on the services of foreign powers.

The position in Great Britain is in the main covered in a following sub-section of this chapter which deals with the financial arrangements that apply within the public sector of British transport. The 1968 Transport Act, however, not only sets the financial patterns of the public authorities, it also makes provision for assistance to be given for specified purposes to transport undertakings generally, and regardless of whether they are publicly or privately owned. To that extent, the Act is perhaps unusual, although in practice, of the eligible recipients, those in the private sector are very much in the minority. Sections 32, 33 and 34 of the 1968 Act provide respectively for government grants to be made available to bus operators to assist them in their purchase of new vehicles, for grants towards the duty charged on fuel used by buses working as stage carriages and for assistance to be given by county councils at their discretion towards the cost of running rural bus services and ferries. Similarly, Sections 56 and 57 of the same Act provide respectively for grants to be made at the discretion of central or local government to any person for the purpose of the provision, improvement or development of public passenger transport excluding airfields and harbours or jetties unless used by ferries and for government grants for research and development in connection with the provision or improvement of transport services by land or inland waterway or of harbour facilities.

Also of interest in this context is the Highlands and Islands Shipping Services Act, 1960, which enables the Secretary of State to give financial assistance to those undertakings concerned with the provision of sea transport services in the Highlands and Islands area of Scotland.

Cost Benefit Studies

It will now be clear that commercial viability is not the only reason that is used to justify the retention of a transport service. Social benefits might be sufficient to attract a public subsidy but there can be more to it than that. Even though public transport may not be a financial success in its own right, its retention and development could still be to the advantage of the country as a whole in view of other benefits that it might bestow. The purpose of a cost benefit study is to provide a framework within which it is possible to conduct a systematic evaluation of these wider economic and social costs and benefits*. In so doing, external factors enter into the considerations which are never found in the accounts of the transport undertakings themselves, but which do have their effects on the nation at large. Reference has already been made to the private car and its impact on the environment. The resultant costs which arise through traffic congestion are a typical example of what are known as externalities. A cost-benefit study, therefore, involves the evaluation of these various externalities to bring them into a consistent relationship with the commercial costs and benefits which are, of course, the normal revenue and expenditure cash flows. In other words, a cost-benefit analysis is an attempt to balance the total costs to the community of a particular project, as, for example, a public transport system or service, against the total benefits to the community. In this way, the net advantages, if any, can be judged. Those with total responsibility such as national government or a planning authority are then in a better position to make rational decisions which are to the maximum advantage of the people generally, even though public

* First report from the Select Committee on Nationalised Industries Session 1967–8 Ministerial Control of the Nationalised Industries. Volume III, Appendix 8.

expenditure might be involved. Decisions of this kind could not and would not be taken by those with only sectional interests and responsibilities.

In the world of transport, the railway, with its high capital cost but often high return, if not to itself, to the community and to the environment, is an appropriate subject for cost-benefit analysis. A railway administration that is charged with the responsibility of running its system as a purely commercial venture will look only at its own profit and loss account when considering which lines it should retain and develop. From the railway viewpoint, domestic costs and revenue will decide whether a line should be kept open and, if so, a proposal for, say, electrification, proceeded with. The important consideration here is just those extra costs and revenue that would be attributable to the change of traction as opposed to any alternative modernisation scheme; it being only those costs and benefits that are directly attributable to the particular project to be undertaken that would be taken into consideration. The same principle applies to a cost-benefit study except that instead of railway interests, it is the community interests that are evaluated. Considerations that are brought into a cost-benefit calculation are again nothing more and nothing less than those elements which are directly related to that particular project and benefits which would not otherwise be realised. The construction of an underground railway, for example, might well relieve highway congestion and consequent expenditure in another way. There could be repercussions on other existing public transport networks, it could influence traffic patterns and flows by encouraging more people to travel along certain corridors and indeed into the centres of particular towns and land and rateable values in the vicinity of stations are likely to rise. Few of these items will have any direct impact on railway accounts but they all have very considerable community interests. The same thing applies in reverse if a line is considered for closure. The railway might lose a service and with it an operating deficit but the loss to the area if it could be quantified could be very real. If a conurbation is to develop there must be proper communication. There are alternative ways of providing those communications, of which the railway is one, but a new motorway, for example, might be a practical alternative. A cost-benefit study must consider all reasonable alternatives in which the declared objectives might be achieved, which includes both capital investment and regulation such as road pricing or parking restraint. A general economic assessment of the relative advantages and disadvantages of the possible options is a pre-requisite to a detailed analysis of one particular solution. Again, however, only those factors must be considered which would not take place but for the implementation of the project in question. Reference is made in the next chapter to a possible space shuttle and the advantages to mankind that could follow from the exploitation of the potentials of outer space. Inevitably, such a project is expensive and again a government decision whether or not to participate would need to be preceeded by a cost-benefit analysis. If, as would seem to be the case in this instance, the scheme is to be developed by another power in any event then, as far as other participants are concerned (and the United Kingdom is an example), only those benefits that would accrue solely as a result of direct financial and hence management participation are for consideration. Benefits that would come anyway by the system being operated by other countries would be disregarded.

A cost-benefit exercise is dependent upon predictions and it requires a price to be set on the various options that emerge to deal with anticipated situations. Evaluation, particularly of the externalities is, however, a problem and one which distinguishes it from other financial approaches. To quote from previous examples, it is known that there is road congestion and that it involves cost to the users when, for instance, vehicles, drivers and their loads are kept idle and hence unproductive in traffic blocks. It is also known that a nation would benefit to some so far undetermined extent by participation in the space shuttle project. But cost-benefit analysis requires a monetary value to be attached to all costs and benefits including those which have no market price and which cannot easily be quantified. It is clear that the resultant figures will not be precise but the principle is there. As far as transport is concerned, it takes it out of its isolation to become instead a part of the social environment, where it rightly belongs.

Financial Provisions Relating to the British Publicly Owned Undertakings
Road, Rail and Inland Waterways
General

In Great Britain, successive governments have sought various remedies to the problem of how to maintain essential transport services that are no longer viable in their own right. The Transport Act, 1947 brought the railways among other branches of transport into public ownership, and created the now defunct British Transport Commission financed by loan capital with a redemption requirement over a period of 90 years. To tide over initial difficulties resulting from railway modernisation the Commission was granted certain borrowing powers but the extent of the net capital liabilities of the BTC (and this was attributable to deficits on the railway side of the undertaking) reached such proportions that in the end it became clear that the losses could not be recovered. Further legislation, therefore, came in the form of the Transport Act, 1962 which split the constituent parts of the British Transport Commission into four new boards and a holding company. These individual units became separately accountable for their own financial performances, each being required to conduct its business so as to ensure that its revenue was sufficient to meet all charges properly chargeable to revenue, taking one year with another, except that the Railways Board and the British Waterways Board were relieved of this obligation for the first five years of their existence. They began life with capital debts and in the case of the railways, part of their former deficit was written off and part placed to a suspense account. However, for the reasons already described, coupled with incessantly rising costs, the fortunes of public transport generally and the railways in particular continued to deteriorate. The government of the day resolved that it was unrealistic that transport undertakings providing essential services should have to reconcile two incompatible objectives, i.e. to provide a service and to pay their way, which it was in any case becoming increasingly difficult to do and it was considered that the problems could not be overcome in exclusively commercial terms. The resultant Transport Act, 1968, contained provisions which affected the finances of road, rail and inland waterway transport.

The 1968 Act as it affects ownership and the formation of new public authorities has already been covered in Chapter 10. Each of the Boards and new authorities, i.e. the National Freight Corporation, the National Bus Company and the Scottish Transport Group, again have commencing capital debts and the assets of the municipal bus and ferry services within designated areas became vested in the appropriate Passenger Transport Executives. Basically, the principle of the 1962 Act that each of the Boards and the Holding Company should remain solvent has been retained and is applicable equally to the new authorities, including the PTEs. The requirement has, however, been made more realistic as financial assistance can now be given where considered necessary and desirable. The following is a summary of the more important provisions.

Road

As already mentioned, the 1968 Act gives general powers to the Secretary of State to make grants subject to conditions as may be considered fit towards capital expenditure incurred in the provision, improvement or development of public passenger transport in Great Britain. As far as road transport is concerned, therefore, this could cover the construction of new bus stations or garages and interchange facilities with other forms of transport. All bus operators become eligible for possible grants towards the purchase of new vehicles and assistance is given to partially offset the cost of fuel duty. The difficulty of maintaining rural bus services is being met by considerations through local authorities for possible grants. One of the novel features of the 1968 Act is the creation of passenger transport areas with their respective Authorities and Executives as was explained in Chapter 10. Policy matters are determined by the Passenger Transport Authorities (and this can apply not only to buses but also to local rail passenger services and ferries). Policy includes the extent and quality of the services and the level of fares that may be charged and the Authorities have power to meet any deficits that may thereby be incurred by calling for a precept on the local rates.

Special reference to the Post Office is made below.

Rail

The suspended debt and part of the original capital debt of British Railways is extinguished and assistance becomes available at the discretion of the Secretary of State in the form of revenue grants to meet deficits incurred by individual passenger services (other than those of the main inter-city network) and which would be closed but for social reasons. As stated above, for local passenger services which run within passenger transport areas, subject to certain provisos it is the PTAs that maintain financial responsibility and not the Secretary of State, although even then, the authority may be assisted from central funds. Government grants have also become available towards expenditure on surplus track and signalling equipment pending elimination and insofar as local passenger transport is concerned to cover such items as major improvements or extensions of railway track, signalling systems and stations, re-equipment with new type rolling stock and the development of underground and other specialised railways.

Inland Waterways

The legal framework for the waterways outlined in Chapter 8 which classified canals into three groups and facilitated closures has relieved the British Waterways

Board of some of its maintenance burdens. Additionally, local authorities are empowered to assist in maintaining or improving inland waterways for amenity or recreational purposes. Assistance may be given under the general powers for passenger transport and by PTAs for the provision, improvement or continuance of any passenger ferry service. The Secretary of State for the Environment pays a substantial grant in aid to the British Waterways Board in respect of its recreational and amenity functions on inland waterways. This has been increasing steadily in recent years. The new Regional Water Authorities, which are planned for 1974, are also likely to have a duty to make the best possible amenity and recreational use of the inland waterways owned or managed by them.

The Post Office
The Post Office Act 1969 reorganised the Post Office into a public corporation and with it an obligation to pay its way, with sufficient margin between income and expenditure to make suitable allocations to reserves. Targest are set by the Minister of Posts and Telecommunications after taking into account the continuance of certain facilities which cannot be made financially viable such as the inland telegraph service and other services which the Post Office is required to perform.

Docks and Harbours
The requirement of the Transport Act, 1962 that the British Transport Docks Board should pay its way has been brought forward into the Transport Act, 1968, with an increase in the Board's borrowing powers. Mention has already been made that the Secretary of State is empowered vide Section 57 of the 1968 Act to make grants for research or development in connection with transport services, which includes harbour facilities.

Air Transport
As was explained in Chapter 10, the three publicly owned authorities within British air transport are the Civil Aviation Authority which, apart from its regulatory role, owns and operates certain airports in Scotland and also provides navigational services, the British Airways Board which controls the two air corporations, and the British Airports Authority. The former two bodies were created by the Civil Aviation Act, 1971, and it is this Act which stipulates their financial arrangements.

In accordance with a pattern that has already been followed elsewhere, the Civil Aviation Authority began life with a debt to the Secretary of State in respect of the property and rights that were transferred to it and it is required to conduct its affairs so as to ensure that its revenue covers costs. Its financial policy has been the subject of guidance from the Secretary of State who has decreed that the whole of its costs must be recovered as soon as possible. Also required is a return on capital reasonable in relation to the nature of its activities, recoverable from those, including government departments, that use its services. Until the Authority breaks even, the government has agreed to pay grant-in-aid sufficient to meet the expected deficits on revenue account, but the aim is to dispense with such aid by 1977/8. It is appreciated, however, that particular problems exist in the Scottish highlands and islands where air services and hence the supporting facilities, although unremunerative, are essential to the regions economic and social development. For this reason it is appreciated that the Authority will be unable to make any significant progress towards the recovery of its costs in respect of this particular part of its activities. The Authority is nevertheless required to examine with the airlines concerned the economics and organisation of air services and aerodromes in this area and to make recommendations to the Secretary of State accordingly.

As far as the British Airways Board is concerned, there are transitional and ultimate provisions. Initially, capital amounts outstanding on loans previously made to BOAC and BEA vide the Air Corporations Act, 1967, are deemed, vide the 1971 Act, to have been made by the Secretary of State to the Board on the original terms. Additionally, the Secretary of State may pay to the Board such sums and under such conditions as is seen fit. This arrangement is expected to apply until 1977. After that date, the Board will still be empowered to borrow money, either in the form of a government loan or by the issue of stock, but by this time, the by now familiar proviso will apply that it will be required to so conduct its affairs as to secure that the revenue of the group is not less than sufficient for meeting costs.

With regard to the remaining nationally owned airports, the Airports Authority Act, 1965, established the British Airports Authority which again began life with a capital debt. This Authority is also required to so conduct its business as to ensure that, taking one year with another, its revenue covers expenditure, including proper provision for depreciation and allocation to reserves. It also has to meet a target return of 14 per cent on its net assets. In the three years period up to 1971/2 it returned an overall rate of 13.54 per cent and has, since its inception in 1965, wiped out the cumulative losses of its airports and translated them into substantial profits.

Conclusion

A very great part of British transport is organised into some form of national or local public ownership with each separate undertaking or group charged with the responsibility to maintain its own accounts and generally to manage its affairs on a proper commercial basis and thereby earn sufficient to cover expenditure taking one year with another. The nationalised systems with their outstanding capital debts are subject to overall policy control by the Secretary of State to whom they are required to submit annually their report and accounts. It is recognised, however, that many of the services provided, although not financially viable, have a distinct social or economic value in other ways. Whilst, therefore, it would not be in the interests of the nation as a whole to allow some of these essential public services to wither and die, it is not sensible to thrust their continued maintenance on to managements which have a parallel duty to show a proper return on the capital invested. It was considered, therefore, that there was a need to give some sort of financial assistance from national or local funds as appropriate and it is this opinion that lies behind much of the legislation to which reference has been made.

It is significant that it is usually the passenger side of the business that qualifies for subsidy. Freight transport can be more easily tailored to operate on a commercial basis. There are not the pre-scheduled services for freight as there are for passengers, with their attendant capacities that if not sold at the time they are provided, are lost for ever. With goods transport it is not as much individual pre-scheduled services that are on tap for everybody to use when they see fit so to do but a system that can be adjusted to meet individual needs on the occasions when they are required.

For a sizeable part of passenger transport there has now been a swing from profitable enterprise to subsidised service. Given that those services do meet a social need and that hardship would arise if they were withdrawn, it is right that operators should not be obliged to run them at a financial loss to themselves. Even so, considerable public spirit has been shown in this direction and loss making services have been maintained by means of cross-subsidisation with those that are more remunerative. There must, however, be a limit to this arrangement and there has long been a clamour for some sort of recompense to meet this social liability. As far back as 1959, a committee of enquiry which was set up under the chairmanship of Professor D.T. Jack to study rural bus services pronounced as one of its main recommendations that there should be a measure of financial aid. However, the subsequent 1962 Act did little to ameliorate the position. In fact, as has already been noted, it required the public boards and authorities to pay their way. Under the circumstances, British Railways, under the chairmanship of Dr. (now Lord) Beeching undertook in 1963 a major pruning exercise which eliminated many of the heaviest loss-making rail services. These consisted in the main of cross-country and branch line local stopping trains serving rural areas.

The 1968 Act established machinery which enables financial assistance to be afforded to operators at the discretion of national or local authorities. But for the operator, in easing one problem, there is always the danger that it may create another. To a truly commercial concern and subject to its statutory limitations and to its responsibilities to its shareholders, its passengers and its staff as has already been described, management is free to run its business in the way that it sees fit. If a transport undertaking is to be subsidised by a third party, then that other body will inevitably and with justification expect some say in what should be provided, where and at what times. Management might then no longer be master of its own house in the hitherto accepted sense. But the problems do not end there. With British Railways, for example, where freight and inter-city passenger services are run as a commercial venture alongside grant-aided passenger trains which are maintained at the discretion of the Secretary of State and, if within a passenger transport area, of the appropriate Passenger Transport Authority, all using the same track, the same stations and the same equipment, difficult questions of administration and priority are bound to arise.

In short, financial aid is necessary, if unremunerative, but essential services are to be maintained. To the operator, however, it can never be the ideal solution, for the reasons that have been stated. Support in this way is a means of survival but at the expense of independence. Unless, therefore, it is subsidy without strings (to which taxpayers and ratepayers can rightly object) it is something that operators might prefer to avoid if possible.

14 · The Future

Introduction

Looking into the future is never easy and subsequent events do tend to have the awkward habit of disproving the most intelligent forecasts. Whilst, however, a little crystal gazing cannot always be avoided in a study of this kind, the task of anticipating what is to come can be made easier by examining the immediate past and from that past, endeavouring to detect a trend which is likely to continue in the years ahead.

Throughout the pages of this book some attempt has been made to produce a potted version of transport as it is to-day with references to various technological developments that have been achieved over recent years. The result is, in effect, a still photograph within what is otherwise a perpetually moving evolutionary film. The one thing that is certain is that time will not stop. Life must go on and there will always be change. Hitherto accepted practices must give way to new ideas. Improved methods will be introduced as the older ways are abandoned and man will continue to progress into time unknown, perhaps until the earth becomes finally engulfed in a ball of man-made fire, if that is to be the ultimate destiny of a generation yet to come.

A mention of things to come is apt to produce visions of rockets probing outer space driven by nuclear power and probably engaged on some aggressive mission. In this study of transport it is important not to confuse science fiction, which is suitably coloured for leisure reading, with the more rational predictions of future developments, even though much of what was at one time regarded as fiction is now gradually being transformed into fact. Certainly, space travel is becoming a reality and its development will inevitably have a profound effect on the life of man here on earth. As such, the subject must be given proper attention. At the same time, it must be remembered that whilst the development of air and now space travel has been rapid and spectacular, we are still likely to have need for our buses, our trains and our ships for many years yet and they also will become subject to new techniques in design and operation. The changing face of to-morrow's transport will stem from the problems that are with us to-day. A study of these problems in conjunction with the present day evolutionary process will, therefore, provide the most satisfactory basis for predicting the sort of transport system that will be with us at, say, the turn of the century. We know that the world's population is steadily increasing and that in some places this is producing another problem of space. Not, in this case, through the sheer magnitude of it but by the lack of it. We also know that in most areas, society is becoming more affluent, which means that among other things, an ever increasing number of people are able to afford their own private transport, at least on land. The combination of these factors is resulting in patches of acute traffic congestion, the world's resources of the basic raw materials for fuel and power being used at an alarmingly fast rate with an ultimate promise of complete exhaustion, heavy pollution of the atmosphere by the different types of power units and higher and higher wages which are making the labour content of total costs exorbitantly high.

It is circumstances of this kind and the problems that they bring that hold the clues from which one can predict a likely pattern of events in the future. The latent potentials that lie beyond the surface of the earth are certainly a stimulant to the development of space travel. Turning to rather more everyday matters, the increasing degrees of traffic congestion suggest a return to public transport in the larger centres of population and particularly to rail rapid transit, probably underground. With rapid transit as, indeed, with all other forms of transport, an increasing degree of automation can be expected to meet what would otherwise involve heavy labour costs. For the longer distance services, other economies are likely in the form of larger carrying units and, to combat the time factor (a commodity which is always in an incredibly short supply), ever increasing speeds. Bigger and faster seems to be the order of the day.

A quick glance at the evolution of transport shows that this really is the process that has been going on for a long time, in fact ever since man first began to ride in mechanically propelled vehicles and vessels. The trains have become faster and we are now thinking in terms of over 150 mph, technically it is possible to dispense with drivers and new methods of propulsion are being tested. Buses have grown in size from a one time thirty or forty seats to an average of nearer eighty and one man is now doing the work that was formerly undertaken by two. The economy of the bus in terms of road space (in about four times the road space it can carry twenty times as many people) lends support to its future anticipated role in congested areas. No motorist or, for that matter, no pedestrian, will need to be reminded that road haulage vehicles have become larger and faster with their attendant disadvantages to other road users and to the environment generally, not only in towns where their presence is essential for collection and delivery purposes but also on the trunk highways where there is a case to consider a transfer of more freight to rail. (In passing, remember from Chapter 8 that provision for something on these lines was contained in the 1968 Act but remained unimplemented until a change of government expressed disinterest in such a policy. This does not mean, however, that thoughts on these lines might not be revived if the administration once again changed its colour). Seagoing vessels have progressed in size to the stage of the very large crude carriers of around 500,000 tons but a similar trend cannot be detected in passenger vessels as the incessant quest for speed has taken the one time seagoing passengers into the air where development has been rapid in the extreme compared with other modes. Reference has been made elsewhere in this book to the jumbo jet with nearly 500 seats and the Concorde with its speed of twice that of sound. Once again, however, the effect on the environment of these developments could be very serious and this was the reason which influenced the selection of the site at Foulness (now known as Maplin) for the construction of London's third airport. It was considered that this was the site where the environmental impact would be the least severe. Even on the water, seagoing hovercraft have cut to a third the time taken to cross the Channel. Already they are moving 30 cars with their passengers and larger craft can be expected.

So much for the highlights of the evolutionary process as it is seen in the 1970's. All these developments have been mentioned in previous chapters. There now follows a brief review of those areas of research which are likely to have the greatest impact on the provision of transport services in the forseeable future.

Space Travel

It has been said that space has a potential which, if made accessible for human endeavour, could bring tremendous benefits to mankind. Already, over half of all trans-Atlantic telephone calls are handled by Intelsat, a communications satellite, television pictures are being transmitted long distances in this way and a single weather satellite can plot temperatures over every part of the earth twice a day. This process could be developed and improved. Further satellite applications would enable man to survey and thereby maximise the use of the earth's resources, improve manufacturing processes and maybe even harness the sun's rays and thereby produce a source of pollution free energy. However, whilst the last mentioned possibility, if it is ever realised, might solve the fuel and pollution problems that were considered in Chapter 5, the study of satellite applications as such is not a part of the principles of transport. What is important is that this development cannot materialise without a satisfactory means of conveying ordinary men and women and their equipment between earth and their work-places in the sky. The passengers that would have occasion to use such a service would, as far as the carrier is concerned, be no different from any other normal airline passenger who travels to-day. They certainly would not be trained astronauts and neither would they wear special clothing. Their skills would lie in the various tasks that they would perform on the satellite and not with the means of getting there.

Following the success of the Apollo moon-landing programme, the National Aeronautics and Space Administration (NASA) of the U.S.A. is now embarking, with the backing of the United States Government and with or without European participation, on a six year plan to develop a space shuttle. Proposals are that it will consist of several parts, including boosters and an orbiter. For launching purposes they will be joined in piggyback fashion and will take off like a rocket. At high altitude they will separate and the orbiter will proceed under its own power into orbit, to whatever destinations may be required, then return to earth where it will land like a conventional aircraft. It is likely that it will be powered by high pressure oxygen-hydrogen engines and with its delta wing will look very much like an ordinary aeroplane. Like the orbiter, two solid rocket boosters will be recoverable but a large tank carrying the oxygen and hydrogen will not be recoverable. Even so the cost of space travel compared with the expendable rockets that have been used so far will be reduced. A diagrammatic illustration of the space shuttle mission appears at Plate No. 47.

There is no intention nor is there any need even to attempt to explain the technicalities of a project such as this. As far as this book and this chapter is concerned, its relevance lies in the fact that here is an indication of a new transport service which will, if it succeeds, open up new horizons in every sense of the word. It is an indication of what can be expected in the future. The project does, however, also exemplify the principles enunciated in Chapter 1. The demand for a transport service between the earth and its satellites is a derived demand. The real demand is for the satellites themselves and the benefits that they will bestow. But they cannot function satisfactorily unless they are made easily accessible for both passengers and freight. This will be the function of the space shuttle.

Air Transport

Turning to the demands for air transport that are local to our own planet, there is little doubt that the needs or desires of the people to move around will only increase. As man has become more affluent and his horizons have widened, the greater is the area that he wishes to cover both for business and recreational purposes. The constraints of the social system are such that although he will travel more, it must be accomplished in a shorter space of time; too short, in fact, to permit a passage by sea. This can only mean pressure for yet more air transport. The demand, therefore, is not only likely to remain but to increase and speed and capacity will be the essential ingredients of the future generations of aircraft. The demand might become particularly heavy in the case of the United Kingdom which, although a part of the European Economic Community, is physically separated by water from other member states with the result that connections by surface transport are not easy. Demands on the shorter continental routes could become very great indeed.

Airports constructed in the way that was described in Chapter 3 with their long runways necessary for the conventional type of jet aircraft have so far generally contained the traffic that has needed to use them. Although, however, this has to date been the case at most of the major air terminals, the time is rapidly approaching when there will be virtually no room for further expansion. The construction of additional airports is not an ideal solution as apart from environmental problems, siting difficulties and the inevitable distances from the objectives that they purport to serve, airlines suffer a loss of flexibility with services tied to particular terminals and through passengers are unable to interchange freely between different routes.

A possible solution lies in an economic aircraft suitable for shorthaul work that is independent of the main runways used by the inter-continental services and which is socially acceptable. Such an aircraft would have the merit of increasing the efficiency of the airport and air traffic complex by increasing its throughput and would eliminate any economic penalties to longer haul aircraft caused by congestion. It is also the case that although the operation of an airport at the present time causes a worsening of the environment through noise and visual intrusion, to take away the noise by building an airport in a sparsely populated place is really no solution. The ideal, as seen by the British Aircraft Corporation, for example, lies in some form of development which preserves the existing airports and eliminates the intrusion of the aircraft to the surrounding community. Most notably, this means reducing noise levels, but also to be considered is the visual effect of aircraft on take-off or on long shallow approaches. Furthermore, solutions to these problems must not introduce new ones such as air pollution.

In recognition of this problem, the British Aircraft Corporation, in conjunction with other European aircraft manufacturers, is working towards an aircraft that is capable of using major airports without adding to runway occupancy problems, with steep take-off, approach and landing profiles, minimal noise effects and with high combustion efficiency power plants. This or, in other words, the QTOL (Quiet Take-Off and Landing) is seen by BAC as a solution that must be found to permit the unfettered development of short haul air transport.

Perhaps then, the QTOL aircraft will have a future role in maximising airport capacities and so facilitate a further concentration of services. But remember the point that Great Britain is an island and hence air transport has a natural advantage for international journeys which it does not necessarily enjoy on the larger land masses or, for that matter, for domestic journeys here.

Surface Transport

Where there are no physical barriers to surface transport and changes of mode are not involved, the railway can be a serious contender for all classes of traffic, both passenger and freight, and this is certainly the case for internal journeys within Great Britain and on the continent of Europe. Has, therefore, the main line railway a future potential for the medium distance traffic of up to, say, several hundred miles? To many railway managements the answer seems to be yes. British Railways, for example, is developing an advanced passenger train (APT) for this category of travel.

As in the case of air, the attractions are seen as speed and comfort and the principle surrounding APT is the achievement of faster speeds on existing track and with the existing signalling equipment and without, therefore, any expensive (and often impracticable) re-alignments to reduce the severity of curves. Tilting of the body up to 9 degrees on curves will allow higher speeds without passenger discomfort and with each APT powered by gas turbines or electricity, speeds of 160 mph or more will become possible. For non-electrified lines, the gas turbine is being developed for railway traction purposes not only in Great Britain but also in Canada, France and elsewhere in view of its high power/weight ratio compared with diesel. For the electric version of APT, at the speeds envisaged, power will be supplied through the overhead catenary system but beyond these speeds there is doubt whether current collection by this means will be satisfactory. In this case, there could be a return to the third rail which would, of course, have considerable repercussions on present day practices. Nevertheless, when looking into the future, the possibility cannot be ruled out.

From the foregoing it is clear that British Railways plans further exploitation of the inter-city market. But if a railway is to be profitable within the terms of its domestic revenue account, it must be heavily used in view of the considerable capital expenditure that is involved. Remember, however, from the previous chapter the valuable social benefits that a railway system can bestow and looked at in this way, its real value to the nation certainly cannot be ascertained from any set of accounts that railway management might produce. The advantages of a rail service could be very great even when revenue does not cover costs, although it is true that the benefits cannot easily be quantified. For this reason, support for railways by taxpayers becomes a controversial issue. Political decisions are the hardest to anticipate, not least because those with interests and/or responsibilities in this respect are sometimes able to sway public opinion, not by their depth of knowledge, but by their eloquence of speech. Until such time as public transport, and the railway in particular, becomes generally accepted as a part of the environment and all of its costs and all of its benefits are properly identified instead of being regarded as a self-contained commercial enterprise, then the future density of the railway network must continue to be in doubt. Nevertheless, apart from the heavily used trunk routes which in themselves could remain remunerative, there are now signs that more reliance is to be placed not only on public transport generally but the railway in particular for mass transit in urban areas. It was said in Chapter 2 that if car ownership continues to increase at its present rate, then the time must come when, in those places that are already heavily congested, neither the money nor the space will be available to construct roads adequate for the demands that will be placed upon them. If restraints on private cars are imposed, then a very high standard of public transport must be provided if commercial activity within town centres is to be maintained. This could well take the form of fully automated underground railways like, for example, the recently opened line of the Bay Area Rapid Transit District (BART) which serves the San Francisco and Oakland areas of California, USA. On this line which is, in effect, a new suburban railway, electronic control systems monitor and adjust train speeds, govern stops and starts, open and close doors and maintain safe spacing between trains.

Whilst developments that are currently under way might well set the pattern for the future, it is always possible that new technology might produce equally acceptable if not better alternatives. It is particularly apparent in North America with its high ratio of car ownership to population that private transport alone cannot continue to provide the required mobility in urban areas while preserving an acceptable environment. Although the conventional forms of public transport are likely to have renewed emphasis, new techniques could enable further breakthroughs to be made in this field. Research undertaken by the Department of Transportation and Communications of the Government of Ontario, Canada, for example, suggests that tracked hovertrains and the linear induction motor and magnetic levitation have possibilities. The hovercraft was considered in Chapter 4 in its role as a carrier across water. It was noted at the time that it is an amphibious animal and a series of air cushion vehicles linked to form a train, following a specially constructed way is, therefore, a possible alternative to the conventional steel wheel on steel rail. A tracked hovertrain supported by a frictionless cushion of air which is trapped between hoverpads on the vehicle sides and the concrete guideway could give a smooth ride at speeds of 250 mph or more. Another possibility is the linear induction motor, which offers the unique advantage of propulsion without wheels, depending upon the attractive force between two magnetic fields. These two fields are flat and the magnetic force causes one field to move laterally along the second without any physical contact between the two motor parts, one of which is attached to the bottom of the vehicle while the other is fixed to the guideway. Magnetic levitation may also be used with either the attractive or repulsive force of magnets providing vehicle suspension. Speeds of up to about 300 mph could be possible.

The road protagonists might be tempted to say that these few thoughts on the future, at least insofar as surface transport is concerned, have been coloured by the potentials of the railway whereas, in practice, the railway is a dying industry. It is certainly true that in Great Britain train miles have fallen by nearly 30 per cent between 1962 and 1970 whilst the number of road vehicles has risen by nearly 30 per cent over the same period. However, this very distinct trend with its demands on road space and the inevitable congestion is a reason in itself for suggesting that this way of life cannot continue. But there is another factor that may materially alter the pattern of events in the years to come. This concerns the future availability of oil.

The first successful oil well was drilled rather more than 110 years ago and the oil industry has, since that time, produced something approaching thirty thousand million tons. The forecast, however, is that to meet current demands, as much as this will have to be produced in only the next ten years and the question that immediately comes to mind is whether the natural resources will be adequate to support such a figure. To this, the industry would no doubt reply in the affirmative, but if oil is to remain the major source of energy, then, with a progression on this scale, doubts are bound to arise in some quarters as to its continued availability by, say, the turn of the century. Again it can be argued that natural resources will still be adequate for man's requirements as they will be at that time, but in a generalisation such as this, adequacy and the extent of need remain undefined. Whilst there may be doubts about the physical resources, there is a similar uncertainty about the long term demand which can only be determined by reference to such other factors as future population densities, standards of living, efficiency of machines and the development of alternative fuels, the quantification of which is heavily dependent upon a range of assumptions. To-day, when oil is recovered from underground reservoir rock, more remains than is actually extracted but the yield could be increased at a cost. Similarly, there are substantial reserves of oil in tar sands and shales which could be processed to obtain crude oil, as also can coal, but again, the resultant product would be more costly than conventional crude. Under these circumstances, although oil might remain available in the forseeable future, its price would rise. This in itself could regulate demand, by which time an alternative in the form of electricity produced from nuclear power could have become established and followed perhaps by production even from solar power. In this case, oil supplies might be adequate for a reduced demand. If, however, production of electricity from nuclear power is perfected later rather than sooner, then, with the energy demands of transport being, as they are, in heavy competition with those of industry and domestic purposes, priorities would have to be established. In either case, there could well be a greater dependence on electricity produced from coal if not for nuclear power and liquid fuel for transport purposes would become restricted. Unless by this time the battery vehicle had been perfected, a swing to electricity could mean little else than a redevelopment of railways, tramways and trolleybuses.

It is not intended even to try to predict what the future might hold in terms of world supplies and demand for oil. Whilst the industry itself might predict with good reason adequate supplies for the rest of the century and beyond, from other quarters there are suggestions of a shortage and a need for alternatives. It was said in Chapter 1 that political action is sometimes necessary to counter the natural force of economic laws which come in times of shortages and in a condition such as this, should it ever arise, government might see fit to direct stocks of liquid fuel to those places where it was most necessary.

It is not the purpose of this chapter to suggest that such a situation is either imminent or that it will arise at all. What is being said is that in view of the other associated but unquantified factors, the possibility or the threat of it cannot be ruled out. A sudden warning of dwindling stocks of oil, justified or otherwise, could spark off political action literally overnight. This could mean the resuscitation of railways and tramways, with electrification not only on the main lines but also on the once abandoned branches, freight transferred from road to rail wherever possible regardless of economics and the construction of light railways duly encouraged by infrastructure grants, etc.

In a subject such as this it is only too easy to digress from fact to fancy but it is hoped that enough has been said to give food for thought on the infinite variety of possibilities that lie before us.

Index

(Note: If consecutive pages have relevance, only the first page number is shown)

217

ACTS OF PARLIAMENT TO WHICH REFERENCE IS MADE